Canadian Travellers in Europe

Canadian Travellers in Europe, 1851-1900

Eva-Marie Kröller

University of British Columbia Press
Vancouver
1987

CANADIAN TRAVELLERS IN EUROPE, 1851-1900
© The University of British Columbia Press 1987

This book has been published with the help of a grant from The Canadian Federation for the Humanities, using funds provided by the Social Sciences and Humanities Research Council of Canada.

CANADIAN CATALOGUING IN PUBLICATION DATA

Kröller, Eva-Marie.
  Canadian travellers in Europe, 1851-1900

  Bibliography: p.
  Includes index.
  ISBN 0-7748-0272-3
  1. Canadian prose literature - 19th century - History and criticism.
2. Europe - Description and travel - 1800 - 1918. 3. Travel in literature.
I. Title.
PS8183.K76 1987   C818'.4   C87- 091109-0
PR9192.4.K76 1987

International Standard Book Number 0-7748-0272-3
Printed in Canada

For Marie Luise Moseler

Contents

Illustrations

Acknowledgements

Many Canadian librarians and archivists have helped me compile the material for this book. Most of all, the librarians of the University of British Columbia offered efficient and friendly services: Anne Yandle, Joan Selby and George Brandak of Special Collections, Joseph Jones of the Humanities Division, and Alice McNair and Tanya Gorn of Interlibrary Loan. In the Rare Books Room of the National Library, I was assisted by Liana van der Bellen and Linda Hoad, at the Public Archives of Canada, by Patricia Kennedy of the Archives Branch, Raymond Vézina, Marc Lebel, Gilbert Gignac, and Jeanne L'Espérance of the Picture Division, and Joy Houston of the National Photography Collection. As director of the Centre de recherche en civilisation canadienne-française at the University of Ottawa, Pierre Savard gave me access to the collections of his centre and provided invaluable historical and bibliographical guidance; as a colleague, he supplied inspiration and understanding from start to finish. Thomas P. Rooney, librarian of the Ottawa Room of the Ottawa Public Library, was a knowledgeable guide. At the Archives du Séminaire de Québec and the Musée de Québec, Fathers Louis-Joseph Lépine and Laurent Tailleur and Marie-Monique Turgeon provided assistance. At the Canadian Academic Centre in Rome, Roberto Perin, Gabriele Scardellato, Susan Ianucci, and Carlo Chiarenza offered hospitality and advice and responded to enquiries as did Giovanna Capone, Carla Fratta and Liano Petroni at the University of Bologna and Luigi Bruti-Liberati and Nicoletta Serio at the University of Milan.

Libraries, archives, museums, societies, and individuals across Canada and the United States responded to enquiries: the British Columbia Provincial Archives, the Italian Cultural Institute in Vancouver, the Provincial Archives and Legislative Library of Manitoba, the Elizabeth Dafoe Library at the University of Manitoba, the Brockville Public Library, the History Department of the Woodstock Public Library and Art Gallery, the Royal Society of Canada, the Copyright and Industrial Branch of Consumer and Corporate Affairs Canada, the National Gallery of Canada, the National Museum of Science and Technology, the Ottawa City Archives, Beechwood Cemetery in Ottawa, the University of Toronto Library, the Ontario Ministry of Government Services, the Art Gallery of Ontario and The Grange, Eaton's Archives, the Hudson's Bay Company, the Montreal Museum of Fine Arts, the Notman Photographic Archives at the McCord Museum in Montreal, the Archives nationales du Québec, the Société de Généalogie de Québec, the Public Archives of Prince Edward Island, the Robertson Library at the University of Prince Edward Island, the Harriet Irving Library at the University of New Brunswick, the Public Archives of Nova Scotia, the Dalhousie University Library, the Peabody Museum in Salem, Massachusetts, and the Steamship Historical Society of America at the University of Baltimore Library.

Ted Ferguson sent me his radio-play on Kit Coleman; Heward Stikeman responded to enquiries about a James Wilson Morrice painting in his possession. Raymond Gingras provided me with biographical information about his ancestor, the Abbé Nérée Gingras, and Joan Hart and Margot, Viscountess Hardinge, descendants of Sir Sandford Fleming, kindly permitted me to quote from Gertrude Fleming's diary. Very special thanks go to Sandra Gwyn, who helped me find members of the Fleming family.

Many colleagues and friends generously gave of their time and knowledge, especially Réjean Beaudoin, Margaret Blom, Thomas Blom, Richard Cavell, Jocelyn Foster, Heather Frankson, Michael Goldberg, Wolfgang Klooss, Ross Labrie, Tony Lavin, Dianne Newell, Grove Powell, Angelo Principe, Lil Rodman, Ian Ross, Mary van Rijn, and James Winter. When it came to identifying Henry Wentworth Monk's Pre-Raphaelite connections, I benefitted from William E. Fredeman's expertise. Richard Bevis not only inspired me with his own work on travel in the Mideast, but also attentively read the entire manuscript. Much helpful criticism came from the senior editor of the University of British Columbia Press, Jane Fredeman.

Jody Harper and Doreen Todhunter typed the manuscript, and Mrs. Todhunter, besides offering valuable editorial advice, also shared her knowledge of Loyalist history with me.

Portions of chapter 7 previously appeared in *Canadian Literature* and in *Paris et le phénomene des capitales littéraires*, ed. Pierre Brunel (Paris:

Presses de l'Université de Paris-Sorbonne, 1986).

Financial support was provided in 1981-82 by a SSHRCC post-doctoral fellowship and, in 1982-83 and 1983-84, by UBC research grants.

1

Introduction

The idea for this book first came to me in 1981 when I was looking for a study or anthology of nineteenth-century Canadian travellers' responses to Europe, books equivalent to Philip Rahv's *Discovery of Europe: The Story of American Experience in the Old World* (1947) or Frank McShane's *The American in Europe* (1965), but there was no such work. Since then, two collections have appeared: *Views from the North: An Anthology of Travel Writing* (1984), edited by Karen Mulhallen, contains poems, stories, essays, and photographs by Canadian writers and artists including Robert Kroetsch, Daphne Marlatt, Roy Kiyooka, Gwendolyn MacEwen, Michael Ondaatje, P. K. Page, and others, while Kildare Dobbs's *Away from Home: Canadian Writers in Exotic Places* (1985) assembles excerpts from travelogues, fictional and factual, ranging from sea captain Sir Edward Belcher and journalist Sara Jeannette Duncan as representatives of the Victorian Age to contemporaries like Charles Ritchie, A. M. Klein, George Woodcock, and Bharati Mukherjee. Neither, however, provides a scholarly introduction to the history of travel and travel-writing in Canada. Motivated perhaps by a post-colonial desire to discredit as much as possible Canada's cultural connections with Europe, the *Literary History of Canada* (1967 and 1976), the *Oxford Companion to Canadian Literature* (1967 and 1983), and the *Canadian Encyclopedia* (1985) all largely ignore English-Canadian responses to Europe (or any other country for that matter) under the heading "exploration and travel," an omission which led reviewer George Galt to suspect that "there is no strong sense that life away from home is interesting or important enough to our self-definition to merit much space,''[1] the more so since related entries in the *Encyclopedia* on external relations or agency work in the Third World are also regrettably brief. Although here too a well-edited anthology is still missing, French-Canadian scholars, operating possibly out of a spirit of greater cultural self-confidence, have covered the terrain rather more extensively. John Hare's bibliography *Les Canadiens-français aux quatre coins du monde* (1965) and historian Pierre Savard's many articles on the subject, including an entry (co-authored with R. Ouellet) in the *Canadian Encyclopedia* and essays on the classics of travelogue literature in the *Dictionnaire des oeuvres littéraires du Québec* (1978),[2] all pay tribute to the considerable contribution these texts make to an understanding of Canada's cultural history.

And yet Europe inspired *both* French and English-Canadians. Essays on British, French, Italian, and German art, architecture, city-design, and topical political and social events filled the periodical press. Like their British and American counterparts, Canadians closely followed the Italian fight for freedom, pondered the role of the Vatican in an increasingly secular world, and avidly read the sensational news about the Siege of Paris. Authors used European settings as backdrops for historical and suspense novels and for fictionalized travelogues, not only because these settings offered escapist entertainment, but also because they had a direct or indirect bearing on Canada's own growing culture. The poet Octave Crémazie, for instance, who travelled to Europe in 1851, 1853, and 1855 to acquire new stock for his bookstore on Rue de la Fabrique in Quebec, responded to numerous current events in his poetry, celebrating France's involvement in the Crimean War (''La Guerre d'Orient,'' 1855 and ''Sur les Ruines de Sébastopol,'' 1856) and deploring Pope Pius IX's losing battle against Vittorio Emmanuele's troops (''Guerre d'Italie,'' 1860 and ''Castelfidardo,'' 1861), besides describing in his poem ''Les Mille-Iles'' (1860) a romantic imaginary journey into southern lands, passing through ''la fière Venise,'' ''Gênes, la cité de porphyre,'' ''Florence, ingrate patrie de Dante,'' ''Rome, deux fois reine du monde,'' and other enchanted places. Bankruptcy drove Crémazie into exile in 1862; settling in Paris, he witnessed and recorded for his family in Quebec the Siege of Paris during the Franco-Prussian War in an articulate diary of great documentary value.[3]

Similarly, James De Mille, a professor of literature, history, and rhetoric at Dalhousie University, used observations made on an 1850 *grand tour* through Scotland, England, France, and Italy in his many novels.[4] In *The Martyr of the Catacombs: A Tale of Ancient Rome* (1865) and *Helena's Household: A Tale of Rome in the First Century* (1867), he narrated tales demonstrating the purity of early Christianity, an ideal he felt ought to be emulated in Canada. He voiced Canadian Protestants' support for Italian unification in a fictionalized travelogue, *The Dodge Club; or, Italy in MDCCCLIX* (1869) and in the adventure story *The Babes in the Wood; A Tragic Comedy: A Tale of the Italian Revolution of 1848* (1875). *A Comedy of Terrors* (1872), published only one year after the Franco-Prussian War, combines De Mille's own tourist's impressions of Paris with the sensational events of the Siege of Paris—bombardment, starvation, Commune, and escape by balloon—to create a topical suspense novel, but also to express his horror of revolution. In adventure stories for boys, De Mille familiarized his young readers with ancient and contemporary Italian history. His books *Among the Brigands* (1871) and *The Winged Lion; or, Stories of Venice* (1877) describe settings and plots which outstanding Canadian pupils had learned to expect in books offered as school-prizes: for special diligence in his studies, an Upper Canada Collegian might receive A. J. Church's *Two Thousand Years Ago or, the Adventures of a Roman Boy* (London, 1885) or Alfred Elwes' *Frank and Andrea or, Forest Life in the Island of Sardinia* (1860).[5]

De Mille provided information, moral edification, and sensationalist enjoyment in the tradition of best-selling historical novels. More sophisticated fare on Europe was available to the subscriber to *The Week* (Toronto, 1883-96), an exceptionally cosmopolitan publication, in travel sketches, essays, and book reviews. Alice Jones, a novelist from Halifax, contributed pieces on Winchester, Venice, Florence, and Rome, imitating in focus and style the aesthetic pilgrimages of W. D. Howells and Henry James; Goldwin Smith reported on economics and architecture in England; Gilbert Parker introduced Canadian artists living in Paris. There were literary discussions of Robert Browning, George Eliot, Petrarch, and Dante, essays explicating the theories of John Ruskin and Walter Pater, biographical sketches of Savonarola and Count Cavour. Among the books reviewed were *The Boy Travellers in Great Britain and Ireland*, Margaret Vere Farring's *Fra Filippo Lippi*, Mrs. Schuyler van Rensselaer's *English Cathedrals*, Clara Erskine Clemens' *Christian Symbols* and *Stories of the Saints*, William Ralph Inge's *Society in Rome under the Caesars*, and many others.

Among these pieces, travel sketches about European sights and scenes took a privileged place, partly because they did not bear the stigma of fiction, a genre which remained suspect to puritanically minded readers all through the Victorian Age. Combining the immediacy of an eyewitness report with useful information, travel sketches exploited, as Paul Rutherford has argued in *A Victorian Authority: The Daily Press in Late Nineteenth-Century Canada* (1982), "that sense of wonder believed common among the classes and masses,"[6] among educated and less educated readers alike.

Indeed, travelogues occupy a position between high and popular culture, and part of their appeal to the researcher of nineteenth-century Canadian culture resides in the broad variety of their expressions. Thus, travel reports were a favourite subject for invited lectures on both formal and casual occasions. In 1898 Judge Adolphe-Basile Routhier spoke to the Fellows of the Royal Society of Canada about his visit to London during Queen Victoria's Diamond Jubilee; James Le Moine delivered a speech entitled "Edinburgh, Rouen, York: Glimpses, Impressions, Contrasts" in his inaugural address as president of the Literary and Historical Society of Québec (1881); Henry Mott, assistant librarian at McGill, entertained a meeting of the Montreal Women's Club in 1896 with "Snap-Shots at London," and if one is to believe Sara Jeannette Duncan's semi-fictional *A Social Departure: How Orthodocia and I Went Round the World By Ourselves* (1890), travel reports also served as popular entertainment in ladies' sewing circles.

Personal travel-reports enlivened images of famous European sights and artwork preserved both in expensively bound albums and as part of public education and entertainment. In small villages, a pedlar might enthrall children and adults alike with *laterna magica* slides; in his *Mémoires intimes* (belatedly published in 1961), Louis Fréchette remembers such a *montreur de villes* who presented images of Rome, Mount Vesuvius, Napoleon, and "Le Juif-Errant."[7] *Eaton's Catalogue* was to continue this tradition by offering stereoscopic views of "A Visit to Rome and Venice. 25 views of Rome and Venice which are simply magnificent and gorgeous," "A Tour through England and France. 25 views of the most historical and celebrated places in both of these interesting countries," and "Wonders of the Old World. 25 views taking in all the great sights of the Old World."[8] In the larger cities, the *laterna magica* was replaced by the panorama, cyclorama, and diorama, Victorian forerunners of the cinema, all of which continued the tradition of the street-ballad on a grand scale. *The Montreal Gazette* advertised, in 1841, the presentation of a "Grand Moving Diorama of the Coronation of Victoria . . . painted on nearly 2,000 square feet of canvas" and featuring "1500 mechanical figures of ingenious instruction." Even more spectacular was a first introduction to air-travel, when "the Aeronautikon" appeared in the following year, "illustrative of Mr. Geo. Green's Aerial Voyage from London to Germany in the Monster Balloon," a feat depicted on an oil-painting of more than 11,000 square feet.[9] Travel continued to be a favourite subject of moving panoramas, their photographic realism sometimes a substitute for journeys never undertaken. In 1900, the citizens of Victoria, British Columbia, were invited to attend, for the price of ten cents, a panorama direct from the Crystal Palace in London, simulating a voyage around the world by way of a gigantic canvas covered with paintings of famous sights and slowly unrolled to the sounds of a piano before the astonished eyes of the audience. A spectator eager to learn more about the cities presented might choose a fifteen-cent volume from Robertson's Cheap Series, which offered (in newsprint) such works as James Montgomery Bailey's *England from a Backwindow: With Views of Scotland and Ireland* (1878).

Not content with an occasional display of images, the Loyalist William Croscup of Granville Ferry, Nova Scotia, hired an itinerant sailor to paint large pictures of Trafalgar Square, St. Petersburg harbour, and the British Royal Family directly onto the walls of his parlour in images which have been traced back to illustrations in the *Illustrated London News*, a publication which inspired the *Canadian Illustrated News* and the *Dominion Illustrated Monthly*, both avid reporters of European events.[10] Priests and students at the Séminaire de Québec were surrounded daily by engravings and photographs of classical sites displayed in the corridors, classrooms, and refectories in great profusion.[11] Libraries were well supplied with picture-books such as a two-volume work entitled *La Grande Ville: nouveau tableau de Paris comique, critique, philosophique . . . illustrations de Gavarni, Victor Adam, Daumier, d'Aubigny, H. Emy, Naviès, Boulanger, Henri Monnier et Thénnot* (1844), recommended by the priest Charles Honoré Laverdière in his "Catalogue des ouvrages propres à former une bonne et riche bibliothèque."[12] Outstanding students might even be rewarded with such a publication, as were Gentleman Cadet Horatio B. Preston, who received Dumont D'Urville's *Voyage autour du monde* at the Royal Military College in 1848, and a pupil at the Ottawa Ladies' College, who was awarded *London Town* in 1884.[13] Sumptuously produced albums were available to the wealthy who displayed the three volumes of Appleton's *Picturesque Europe* (1875-79) on their parlour tables or subscribed to William Notman's *Photographic Selections* (1863) which, besides presenting choice Canadian landscape paintings by Way, Duncanson, and Fraser, also reproduced works by famous Italian Renaissance painters, such as Raphael's *School of Athens*, side by side with more contemporary pieces by Turner, Holman Hunt, and Landseer.

As well as the traditional attractions of famous scenery and artworks, the wonders of modern technology and the amazing comforts of nineteenth-century travel further added to the popular interest in the travel-book. Although *The Week*, which frequently defined itself as a corrective to popular taste, condescendingly reviewed Sandford Fleming's *England and Canada: A Summer Tour Between Old and New Westminster with Historical Notes* (1884) as hopelessly *démodé* ("Mr. Fleming must be aware that detailed information about staterooms, steward's fees, extra payments for wine and beer, the large consumption of coal by the steamer, the dinners, the seasickness, the habits of the passengers, and the saloon provided for ladies when suffering from nausea or depression might have been interesting forty years ago, but are now only too familiar''),[14] readers could not hear enough of the sleek beauty and mighty power of the great liners covering the distance between North American and Europe in less than a week, the luxurious fittings of the cabins and dining-rooms, the efficiency of the trains, the splendour of the grand hotels springing up everywhere, and the conveniences of Cook's organized tours. Authors prided themselves on the scientific basis of their observations. New metaphors taken from recent inventions like the daguerrotype and photograph underlined the technological wonders of modern travel and the scientific exactitude of authors' observations. Charles Roger, an Ottawa civil servant, journalist, and historian, significantly modified the *apologia* traditionally introducing travel-writing as casual work when he prefaced his *Glimpses of London and Atlantic Experiences* (1873) with "[These letters] are mental photographs,"[15] thus claiming conscientious reporting as a basis for his book and echoing an eleven-volume *Cyclopedia of Modern Travel: A Record of Adventure, Exploration and Discovery, for the Past Fifty Years, Comprising Narratives of the Most Distinguished Travellers since the Beginning of This Century* (Cincinnati, 1856), which claimed, somewhat unjustly, that previous travellers had been primarily interested in reporting the tales of "gorgons, hydras, and chimaeras dire," whereas "in the accuracy of their observations the travellers of modern times are pre-eminently distinguished. It is no longer the testimony of a pair of eyes which is offered to us; it is also the confirmation of instruments as unerring as natural laws, which *photograph* for us the climate, the conformation, the scenery, and the inhabitants of distant lands (emphasis mine)."[16]

Such developments acquired special importance for imperialists who praised improvements in travel and observation as important contributions to the cohesiveness and power of the British Empire. In *England and Canada*, Sandford Fleming, engineer-in-chief of the Canadian Pacific Railway and inventor of Standard Time, compared its system of railways, bridges, roads, and naval routes to the communications net of the Roman Empire; French-Canadian readers, by contrast, may have found solace in detailed descriptions of modern transport because it facilitated liaison with France, particularly after the arrival of Captain Belvèze and the French naval vessel, *La Capricieuse*, following the 1855 World Exposition in Paris, signalled the renewal of diplomatic and economic connections with the former motherland.[17]

But the travel-book was also used to criticize modernity, a function confirming W. L. Morton's conclusion that "religion—not wealth, and not politics—was the chief concern, the main ideal occupation of Canadians, both British and French."[18] Theologians like the Methodist ministers William H. Withrow and Hugh Johnston or the Abbés Léon Provancher and Henri Cimon warned their flocks against the excesses of modern life; to them, a journey to Europe seemed an exodus into the depraved wilderness of spiritual decay, and reminiscences of the Roman Empire here implied the impending decline of a civilization too proud of its material resources. Methodist publisher William Briggs reached a wide readership with several such travel-books, some of them having previously been serialized in the *Christian Guardian* or the *Canadian Methodist Magazine*; the Abbé Henri Cimon's *Notes de voyage*, first published as letters to the *Courrier du Canada* in 1873, then as a book in 1876, were followed by *Impressions de voyage de Québec à Rome* in 1895; popular in parish libraries and as school prizes, Cimon's works went through several new editions and reprints (the last in 1917), thus influencing generations of readers with their pessimistic visions of European civilization.[19] An ever-increasing number of journalists provided readers of the Canadian daily press with reports on European cities' civic problems, problems looming large in Canada's own future development: the *Toronto News* informed its readers in 1887 about "the slums and social problems of the metropolis of the world,"[20] and in the 1890s, the *Mail and Empire's* famous "Kit" Coleman roamed London's worst quarters gathering information for her depictions of poverty, alcoholism, and crime.

It is a truism that most travellers anticipate their responses to people and places; indeed, most travelogues under consideration here confirm the cultural preoccupations, prejudices and myths current in the group with which the author identified himself. In keeping with the generic characteristics of the travel-book, authors often heightened, by satire or other means, scenes like chance encounters on board ship, in the train compartment, or at the *table d'hôte*, and in so doing, revealed their own allegiances. Canadian travel-books, for example, habitually ridicule American tourists observed *en route*; clergymen with an amateur interest in botany and zoology predictably enter discussions with a godless "Darwinist," and so forth. Rarely is there a sense, in the published travel-books, of spontaneous and potentially controversial responses. Private letters and diaries, however, do contain such comments; and wherever possible, I have included unpublished sources to obtain both official responses and personal interpretation, prescribed itinerary and individual deviation from the norm. Thus, contrasting with the more or less polished works by lawyers, clergymen, teachers, and journalists are the grim notes of John Ashworth, a civil servant with the Post Office

Department in Ottawa, who, in 1862, jotted down about Cologne, "Rhine a muddy stream," about Paris, "Notre Dame under repair. Could not get in. It is on an island in a dirty part of town," about Venice, "Canal smells," and about Florence, "Cathedral dumo [*sic*] very plain, all marble . . . sick of sightseeing."[21] There are also Urgel-Eugène Archambault's letters from Paris where he had travelled to supervise the Canadian display in an educational exhibition: soon bored with conventional sightseeing, Archambault begged his wife to write more often, longingly gazed at sculptures of children because he missed his own brood so much, and assured his family in frantic notes that—contrary to alarmist reports spread in Montreal—he was alive and well.[22] Most moving is the diary Gertrude Fleming kept during her honeymoon journey with Sandford Fleming, junior, pages filled with homesickness and anxiety and a growing aversion to ruins and monuments.[23]

With the exception of Archambault's letters, I have had regrettably little access to such material among French-Canadian travellers. I particularly deplore the absence in this study of letters or diaries written by contemporary French-Canadian women. It might have been illuminating to know Madame Routhier's private thoughts when she accompanied her assertive husband on his numerous journeys to Europe, journeys followed by a steady stream of books; Marie Clorinde Routhier was, after all, president of the Quebec branch of the National Council of Women and "a lady whose virtues and varied accomplishments . . . made her name a 'household word' in Canadian society."[24] Or, it would have been interesting to hear from Angéline, Routhier's academically gifted daughter, who attended a boarding-school in Paris. Published travelogues by French-Canadian women are also extremely rare in this period. John Hare's bibliography *Les Canadiens-français aux quatre coins du monde* (1964) lists only one, Célina Bardy, the elegant and eloquent daughter of a Quebec physician, who appears to have devoted her literary efforts to the memory of her idolized father. Another woman, Caroline Dessaulles-Béique, president of the Ladies Auxiliary of the Association Saint-Jean-Baptiste de Montréal and the first president of the Fédération nationale Saint-Jean-Baptiste, is so reticent about her wedding journey in 1875 as to make her memoirs *Quatre-Vingt Ans de souvenirs* (1939) practically useless in the present context. As in other areas of their lives, French-Canadian women on their travels largely acquiesced, even more than their English counterparts, in the paternalist principles of their society. Writing about the bicycle—welcomed by feminists as a vehicle of freedom—Madame Raoul Dandurand, highly active in the Canadian National Council of Women, expressed her aversion to such emancipation: "Que deviendront les arts gracieux entre ces mains alourdies? Que deviendront le piano, le pinceau et l'aiguille? . . . Et quel pire sort t'attend encore avec le démembrement des familles dont le culte du sport nous menace!''[25] Daughter of a premier and wife of a senator, Madame Dandurand defended the conservative Christian family as the mainstay of her culture, with women as the self-effacing guardians of morality. At the end of the century in 1900, she accompanied *La Patrie's* ''Françoise,'' journalist Robertine Barry, to the World Exposition in Paris, but as her two male colleagues also sent in voluminous reports, there was little left for Barry to cover except society news.[26]

All of the unpublished diaries held at the Archives du Séminaire de Québec were, of course, composed by priests who, although sometimes more emotional in their diaries than in their published work, still remained fairly close to official form and language, partly because their records were meant to prove to their superiors that the seminary's money had been spent on a deserving individual. Only very occasionally are there more private records, such as the letters Abbé Ovide Brunet wrote to his mother during a trip he took to Europe in 1861-62 to study methods of botanical research and garden design, which contain more mundane information about his health and meals than his simultaneous progress reports to Archbishop Taschereau. Priests also contribute a large number of texts to the published travelogues listed in Hare's bibliography; French-Canadian travel literature about Europe is, then, predictably more homogenous than English sources, the moreso since ''dissenters'' from the conservative, Catholic norm have left behind only largely indifferent or very brief travel reports. Honoré Beaugrand, notoriously anticlerical founder of the liberal *La Patrie* and sometime militant Freemason, published surprisingly colourless *Notes de voyage* in 1889; Arthur Buies, who audaciously joined Garibaldi's red-shirts when conservative Quebec supported the pope's cause, produced only sketchy remarks about his European travels. In formulating my conclusions, I sometimes sympathized with Reginald Martel, who, in a review of Victor-Lévy Beaulieu's *Pour Saluer Victor Hugo* upbraided the author for researching nineteenth-century views of Hugo in Quebec, most of them conservative and condemnatory, although ''Les vrais Québécois . . . sont morts, anonymement.''[27] Or, certainly, they died without obliging a contemporary researcher with writing what he or she would have liked them to write.

Victorian Canadians of all backgrounds read Europe as if it were a history-book with lessons to be learned or refuted in the development of their own new nation. On no occasion, however, were they called upon to formulate their own identity more clearly than at the many world expositions, where Canada's exhibit was visibly juxtaposed with the achievements of other nations. Encyclopedias of, and *grand tours* through, nineteenth-century culture, world expositions epitomized both the glories and the ambiguities of the age. Intimately linked with the beginning of organized and mass travel, the Great Exhibition of 1851 provides a logical starting-point for this study, especially because it almost coincides with the beginnings of regular steam-travel between Canada and Europe. The 1900 *Exposition universelle* in Paris not only marks both the apogee and the beginning decline of the century's faith in its achievements but also yet another revolution in transport, the arrival of the motor-car. Occasionally, however, earlier and later dates and places other than Europe are significant; certain typically Victorian characteristics of world expositions, for instance, continued well into the twentieth century, and their competitiveness and interdependence necessitate comments on American fairs as well as European ones.

The travel-book had become practically obsolete by the end of the century, as a contributor to *Scribner's* wrote sadly in 1897: "Who but protesting sentimentalists care a rap for the lost art of letter-writing now that a telegram of ten words answers as well all practical purposes, and is besides infinitely better than the mails? The book of travel is only a longer letter, and like it often the product of a laborious conscientiousness, a sense of responsibility for special opportunities. Indeed, the new attitude toward travel marks the atrophy of the 'travelling conscience,' that monitor insistent that this, that, or the other must be seen from a sense of duty, because one may never be twice in a given spot."[28]

But no "atrophy of the 'travelling conscience' " afflicted two Canadian travellers, one a barrister from Woodstock, Ontario, the other a priest from Quebec, who each spent four months in Europe in 1880-81 and 1881-82 respectively, leaving behind conscientiously kept and eloquently written diaries. Following Fred C. Martin's and the Abbé Nérée Gingras' journeys at some length, makes it possible to share the expectations, joys, and frustrations of two Victorian Canadians visiting the Old Country.

2

The Journals of Fred C. Martin and Nérée Gingras

On 21 May 1881, a train of the Great Western Railway steamed out of the Woodstock train station. On board were Fred C. Martin, lawyer, and his wife of three years, Louisa.[1] Leaving behind a one-year-old son, the couple set out on a delayed honeymoon, which was to take them to England, through the Continent as far south as Venice, and, on the return journey, to Ireland. Travelling by way of Toronto and Montreal (where they inspected the magnificent new Windsor Hotel), the Martins reached Quebec, where they boarded the *Parisian*, the latest addition to the Allan Line. Unfamiliar with the city, they hired a cab for a romantic drive through the old town and to Montmorency Falls. The ancient buildings, picturesque surroundings, and old-world courtesy of Quebec's inhabitants seemed more a part of the continent the Martins were bound for than the one they were about to leave; charmed, the lawyer commented as if he were already in a foreign land: "every child salutes you with a very low bow a characteristic of the French people so our Hibernian driver told us." A tourist attraction itself, a kind of miniature Europe popular for wedding journeys and other excursions, Quebec was the place where the outward-bound Anglo-Saxon practised his superiority over the proverbial charm and superficiality of the French and assumed a feudal attitude confirmed by Lord Durham's report and canonized by *Baedeker's* first guide to Canada (1894): "the advent of the tourist has not robbed the native of his simplicity of character. . . . He is the type of a peculiar people . . . their condition of life is not such as conduces to refinement, but they have much of that true politeness which is dictated by sincerity."[2]

With satisfaction, Martin scanned the cabin passenger list. Among the one hundred and fifty names, he spotted lesser celebrities like the Reverends Edward H. Dewart and James Croil, both well-known authors, and also the Prime Minister and Lady Macdonald, whose presence undoubtedly added to the excitement of the occasion. Shortly before departure, the decks assumed a festive air, rather like a ballroom, as ladies strolled about, holding large farewell bouquets in their hands, a particularly magnificent one having, of course, been sent to Lady Macdonald. Martin observed his fellow passengers with a sharp eye for social comedy; there were "a matronly old woman annoying the stewards about her luggage and . . . boxes," determined-looking men marching about as if they were practising for a walking match, young women burying their noses in the latest novel, and "a 'pair' of ladies of an uncertain age that would be a terror to a census taker but from the number of interrogatories they put to every one they meet would make excellent enumerators." Even as the boat began to sail down the St. Lawrence, accompanied by the boom of a cannon from the Citadel, the scene on deck continued to resemble an elegant parlour; no sooner had the ship weighed anchor than nearly everyone withdrew into a corner to write letters to the loved ones just left behind. The letters were picked up at Rimouski; at the same time, the steamer accepted a large quantity of mail. Ever intent on examining matters of organization and administration, Martin noted that there were so many parcels and letters that the clerk would be kept busy sorting for the remainder of the voyage. Martin also found out all there was to know about tonnage and passenger capacity of the *Parisian*, jotted down her measurements, and announced with considerable satisfaction that she had so little roll that seasickness was probably a thing of the past.

Once arrived in Liverpool, the Martins took the train to London, admiring the garden-like countryside of Derbyshire from the window. Their compartment was shared by three inquisitive gentlemen plying their travelling companions with questions about Canada. Although the three were friendly, drawing the Martins' attention to places of interest to be seen from the train window, their questions also placed the couple in an uncomfortable position. Whereas in Quebec and on board ship, Martin still confidently classified classes, ethnicities, and temperaments, he was now himself classified as an exotic stranger. Revealingly, he commented with irritation on the overwhelming presence of fast-spending American tourists in London, their assertive behaviour an additional threat to his self-confidence. He sought to compensate for a vague sense of obliteration— increased by the fact that their hotel reservation had not arrived on time—by asserting his skills as a tourist and demonstrating his superiority over a London cabby who would be ill-advised—as Martin explained at

A.   Allan Line, brochure advertising
Royal Mail steamships to Europe.

length—to mistake him for an ignorant country cousin from the colonies. Martin's sense of identity was assaulted from two directions, then, the American and the British, and his declared allegiances shifted accordingly as he sought to find his footing. Having criticized the Americans, he also affirms that London's glamour has been overrated: "they have no bright pretty theatres like those in American cities and Toronto."

Their self-confidence as Canadians and North Americans bolstered by aggressive criticism of everything and everyone, the Martins set out to explore London and its environs. Avid theatregoers and music-lovers, they attended performances by the Spanish coloratura soprano Adelina Patti, admired Quebec's own prima donna Madame Albani in Verdi's *Rigoletto*, sadly missed the English tenor Sims Reeves, applauded Sarah Bernhardt, Edwin Thomas Booth, Sir Henry Irving, Ellen Terry, and Helena Modjeska on the stage. Sandwiched between opera and drama was a visit to Charles Haddon Spurgeon's Metropolitan Tabernacle, where the immensely popular Baptist preacher attracted crowds of six thousand at a time with his lively, plain-spoken, often humourous evocations of contemporary problems and personal salvation. Always blissfully nonchalant about punctuation, Martin attempted a synopsis of the sermon, but being an Anglican, he probably observed Spurgeon's performance with more detachment than did many of his Baptist and Wesleyan compatriots: "[it] was peculiar to his style of preaching and was not without some slang. He gave us 40 minutes of it. He gives you an idea that it is time we are all sinners but not such a bad lot after all but still great room for improvement goes upon the ground that all men have a work to do and should do it. That when they sow the seed (as in the parable of the sower) they should not expect to see it grow the next day but be content to wait and . . . to bring forth 'the corn in the ear.' "

Such spectacles satisfied Martin's hunger to witness world-famous celebrities; despite its poorly lit theatres, London was still an English-Canadian's most important cultural centre, and Martin prepared to carry mementoes apart from his diary away with him. From a workman at Westminster Abbey, he obtained "a relic of the oldest part of the Abbey," a souvenir of dubious authenticity; and he searched for the genealogical roots of his family in Somerset House where he ordered copies of a document describing his great-grandfather's mill.

Martin's imperialist pride was also fired by the sight of the Princess of Wales driving through the streets of London. Citizen of an age in which photographs, *cartes de visite*, and stereographs provided dozens of images of famous people and places, Martin compared Princess Alexandra's real appearance with her photo and, satisfied, noted: "We . . . had a splendid view of her. She is very like the photos of her." Fascinated with royalty, Martin proudly related a chance encounter with Eugénie, ex-empress of the French and in exile in England since 1870. In 1873, the Ottawa journalist and civil servant Charles Roger was part of the delegation representing the Canadian government at Napoleon III's funeral, an event Roger described in *Glimpses of London and Atlantic Experiences*. Now, in 1881, following the death of the Prince Imperial in the Zulu War, Eugénie was building a memorial in St. George's Chapel at Windsor; the Martins saw her on one of the occasions when she came to inspect its progress. The couple must have been enchanted as she boarded the same railway carriage, looking "tall and slight and . . . beautiful . . . but sad." Like the Princess of Wales, Eugénie was a famous sight ("We had a very good view of her"), the more gratifying because her appearance—wrought with the thrilling aura of personal and national tragedy—was unexpected, hence a special bonus on the itinerary. Reminders of recent French history followed the Martins everywhere on their sightseeing; at Madame Tussaud's, they admired the "carriage used during the Franco-German War by the late Emperor Napoleon III in which he was driven through the Prussian lines on his way as a prisoner of war to Germany after his surrender to the King of Prussia at Sedan." Later, in Paris, they were to view a panorama of the Siege of Paris, "really too natural to be pleasant." Napoleon I and the Battle of Waterloo still loomed large in everyone's mind as well; Napoleon's carriage "taken at Waterloo" and the camp bedstead on which he died in St. Helena were displayed side by side with artifacts relating to the fall of the Second Empire. From Brussels, the Martins made an excursion to Waterloo. With the "British Lion . . . on a Pedestal [with] one of his paws on a Cannon Ball [looking] as though he defied anyone to touch it," Britain must have appeared to the couple like a bulwark of security and peace, ready to receive the royal casualties of the continent's fallen monarchies.

From England, the Martins made their way to Italy by way of Brussels and the Rhine Valley. Travelling on the steamer *Kaiser Wilhelm* among the romantic castles along the river, Martin was soon at war with the officers on board for giving him no answers, or very insufficient ones, to the historical information he requested. He found solace in his *Baedeker*, which released him from the duty of commenting on the scenery in his own words, and he praised the virtues of the guidebook, its profusion of reliable facts and figures. Martin's knowledge of literature provided a complementary kind of guidebook; thus, forgetting that Desdemona perished in Cyprus, he gleefully observed that she was strangled in the very room "in which we breakfasted and lunched" in Venice, and in Lausanne historical associations were served, free of charge, with his boiled egg and morning paper in the Hotel Gibbon, named after the famous author of *The Decline and Fall of the Roman Empire*.

Tyrannized by their *Baedeker*, the Martins dutifully visited ancient art "till I was completely exhausted and felt as if I didn't care if I never saw another painting." The lawyer seemed much happier, however, when he concerned himself with the evidence of modern industry. At an exhibition in Milan, he compared the displays with similar ones he had seen five years earlier at the Centennial Exhibition in Philadelphia, and commended the Italians for their excellence in silk-making and in the production of carriages, furniture, china, and glass. With equal interest, he inspected the Galleria Vittorio Emmanuele, an imposing shopping arcade and national monument completed only three years earlier and boasting, since 1880, in the Caffè Gnocchi, the first room in Milan with electric light; later on, in Glasgow, Martin approvingly commented on the attractive Victorian arcades of that city as well. Martin's interest in both useful and ostentatious architecture reflected a concern for appropriate forms of national self-representation, a concern which was also expressing itself in Canada in the building of banks, railway stations, post offices, and hotels.

Although they were seasoned travellers by now, the couple gladly left the impressive new buildings of Milan and Paris behind and rejoiced to be back in London "where everyone speaks English." Their first errands included a trip to the bank to pick up letters from home. Always anxious to present a precise account of their venture, to offer proof of its usefulness and perhaps instruction to future travellers among their own family, Martin still briefly drops the mask of the methodical Victorian tourist when he lambastes his diary: "What 'a pest' you have been to take care of . . . and if ever I go again I certainly shall not take you or any of your family."

Years later, Martin found a poem expressing his own relief at reaching familiar ground again, and an endearing self-irony speaks out of his having preserved the clipping along with the diary:

HOME AGAIN AT SMITH'S CORNERS.

                                        Mrs. Benjamin Boodle loquitur.
Well! we're come from our journey, thank Heaven!
    We've had a be-youtiful trip.
How many days passage? Oh! seven,
    And not a soul sick on the ship.
Are we tuckered? Well, rather. Remember
    We've only been three months away—
Let's see—July, August, September,
    Without even resting a day.

Yes—travel's the best education,
    And this was a capital chance.
Where we've been? Oh! all over creation,
    To England and Scotland and France,

To Brussels, Berlin and Vienner,
  The Danube 'way past Booderpest,
To Munich and over the Brenner,
  To Vennis, Milan and Tree-est.

Talk the language? Well, no, I should rather
  Say not. But our money was good,
So we hadn't the least bit of bother
  In making ourselves understood.
We went to Mount Blank and Chamooney—
  To Thoon, Interlaken and Burn,
And the girls—well, they really got spooney
  At the sight of the Lake of Loosurn.

Like the People? No! Begging their pardons
  They are a lazy and indolent lot,
Sitting round in their caffy's and gardens,
  And drinking up all they've got.
At a concert one night—in a "Keller"
  They called it—at Munich, my dear,
We saw quite a likely young feller
  Drink seventeen glasses of beer.

New dresses? Yes, nineteen or twenty
  From Paris. Such creppy de Chin!
Such laces and trimmings in plenty!
  I know that it does seem a sin.
Boodle swore—but I will not repeat it—
  When the dressmaker sent him the bill;
But at last he consented to meet it.
  You will admire them—I am sure that you will.

Glad we're home? Yes, indeed! We are nearly
  Worn out with the journey, and strife
With conductors and porters. Sincerely,
  I was never so glad in my life.
Let others write poems and ditties
  Of wandering over the sea—
Let them boast of those big foreign cities,
  But—good old Smith's Corners for me!
                    George L. Callin in *Paris American Register*,
                          Zurich, September, 1888.

Martin was to become a respected citizen of Woodstock, entering partnership with Robert Bird to form the law firm of Bird and Martin, with offices above the handsome Imperial Bank on Market Square. His home at 126 Graham Street survives today as a distinguished boarding house in the heart of old Woodstock. When he died in 1908 following a fall off an electric car, his obituary praised his "kindly smile and cordial clasp of the hand."[3] In an 1890 photograph, he looks at us with large clear eyes, a portly man, repectably buttoned into his coat.

Should our second traveller, Joseph-Nérée Gingras, have accidentally shared a table on board ship with Fred C. Martin, the former would probably sooner or later have recoiled with horror. His ring designated Martin as a prominent Freemason, who later served two terms in the Worshipful Master's chair, as well as filling the position of Grand Registrar and sitting on the Board of General Purposes; shortly before his death, "he received the high honor of being appointed Grand Representative in Canada of the Grand Orient of Belgium."[4] To conservative Catholics, Freemasonry seemed a satanic conspiracy to de-Christianize the world with its faith in science and rationalism; to Gingras, Martin might have appeared like the living incarnation of such a threat. At the time of his journey to Europe from 7 October 1882 to 10 February 1883, Gingras was the priest of the parish of Saint-Gervais, Quebec. He was fifty-eight then, having been ordained in 1848. Among his early teachers and friends was Charles Chiniquy who left the priesthood in 1858 to become a Presbyterian minister and notorious critic of the church. It is unlikely that their relationship survived Chiniquy's apostasy, although one of Gingras' postings included Kankakee/Illinois, coincidentally the hometown of Chiniquy's wife. No such hereticism appears to have troubled Gingras' career: besides Saint-Gervais and Kankakee, he faithfully served parishes at Percé, Saint-Raphael-de-Bellechasse, Saint-Edouard-de-Lotbinière, and Baie-Saint-Paul, before he obtained his final parish, Saint-Gervais, where he died in 1893, after having founded his own parish of St. Nérée. Descended from an ancient family settled in Quebec since the seventeenth century, Gingras shared his name with a number of distinguished ancestors and cousins, such as the Abbé Léon Gingras (1808-60), author of *L'Orient, ou Voyage en Egypte, en Arabie, en Terre-Sainte, en Turquie, et en Grèce* (1847) and the Abbé Joseph-Apollinaire Gingras (1847-1935), a poet and essayist.

For Nérée Gingras, Quebec was, of course, not the picturesque tourist-land it had seemed to Martin; in fact, the priest may well have agreed with Napoléon Legendre, who complained in 1877 that too many tourists inundated Quebec every summer and besieged its inhabitants.[5] For Gingras, Quebec was home, and nostalgia set in even as the ship, the

Allan Line's *Peruvian*, inched its way along the St. Lawrence, repeatedly stopped by thick fog.[6] Winter was around the corner, and soon travellers would have to board their ships in Portland, Maine, or New York. Accompanied by five other priests, all—like him—in plain clothes, Gingras continued his spiritual régime on board, honouring Sunday as he had always done. Although he instantly stereotyped the English passengers as cold, overly punctual, and serious, as well as "gras et rouge" in appearance, he still observed them with a mixture of benevolence and compassion because, as Protestants, "[ils] ne connaissent pas la vérité, ils ont été élevés dans l'erreur"; still they were to be commended for their observance of Sunday Service. They were, in any case, dearer to God than the "méchants Français" who had forsaken their duties as Christians since the Revolution and desecrated their churches. One day they would be punished, Gingras predicted, his prophecy firmly achored in the idea of providential history; in contrast, the Protestants, innocently immersed in their benighted beliefs, might eventually be rewarded for their piety.

After a rough crossing, with the *Peruvian* battling high winds like a valiant stallion, "tout bouillant de chaleur et de sueurs," Gingras and his companions arrived in Ireland, where—on stops in Armagh and Dublin—they contemplated the fate of the Irish Catholics and mournfully visited churches appropriated by the Protestants. Momentarily tempted to return instantly to St. Gervais because his luggage had been misplaced and his spectacles stolen, Gingras still quickly settled into a familiar routine by saying mass on the first possible occasion. In London, Gingras briefly visited Cardinal Manning, famous convert to Roman Catholicism, who endeared himself to French-Canadian ultramontanists with his staunch support of Papal Infallibility at the 1869-70 Vatican Council.

Gingras, however, soon travelled on to Paris, where he visited Judge Adolphe-Basile Routhier's daughter Angéline in the boarding-school of the Couvent du Sacré-Coeur. Routhier, a key-figure of nineteenth-century French-Canadian conservatism, journeyed frequently to Europe; the ubiquitous judge and his family—several travellers describe chance meetings with him in Paris, Rome, even Algiers—provided a kind of substitute home, a reliable point of reference, for some of his compatriots who sought the company of their own abroad more than most of their English-Canadian counterparts; the journalist Jules-Paul Tardivel, for instance, stayed at the Pensione Lavigne in Rome, a meeting-place for travelling French-Canadians: "J'y ai trouvé plusieurs compatriotes: M. le curé Dupuis, de Saint-Grégoire, M. l'abbé Jeannotte, supérieur du collège de Sainte-Marie de Monnoir, qui arrivent de Terre-Sainte; M. le curé Bélanger, de Saint-Roch, M. l'abbé Laflamme, professeur à l'université Laval, M. Leduc, de Montréal, et plusieurs d'autres encore."[7]

Like Martin, Gingras visited the panorama depicting the Siege of Paris opposite the Palais de l'Industrie. Through his impassioned description of the scene speak not only the humiliation and pain Quebeckers felt at the defeat of the French, but also the widespread conviction that the agnosticism of France had attracted the wrath of God.

Gingras marvelled at the life-like, photographic allure of the panorama: "nous voyons toutes les horreurs du siège, et cela, comme si c'était naturel, et nous croirions à la réalité; nous voyons les blessés que l'on porte sur les brancards, une bombe qui éclate au milieu d'un peloton de soldats, un mur qui s'écroule, des officiers qui pointent des canons pour la défense, nous voyons des maisons à qui les boulets ont mis le feu, et l'on jurerait que tout cela se passe au milieu de nous!" Seven years later, the writer Faucher de Saint-Maurice was to describe a panorama of Jerusalem located a few steps from Sacré-Coeur, the latter built—partly with funds contributed by French-Canadians—to commemorate the Franco-Prussian War and to atone for the horrors of the "insurrection," the Commune. Both vivid and monumental, panoramas served as important popular extensions of historical painting, keeping alive traumatic events for years to come: the idea of juxtaposing a view of the holy city of Jerusalem with a reminder of the Franco-Prussian War imbued plans for future revenge with the aura of a holy, chivalric duty.

Even if a panorama was not available to remind a traveller of a horrendous historical event, an animated scene could be easily invented by an imaginative diarist. Gingras does not appear to have visited Waterloo, but two decades earlier Monsignore Benjamin Paquet had, and anticipating the 1870-71 War, he pitted the Prussians against the French in the following scene: "Je suis demeuré près de deux heures sous la gueule du Lion et mon imagination s'efforça de rassembler dans cette vaste plaine, maintenant si tranquille, si 'morne' les légions de toute l'Europe qui s'y donnèrent jadis rendez-vous. J'y vis l'Anglais, l'Hanovrien, l'Allemand, le Prussien, etc—J'y vis la phalange jusqu'alors invincible de Napoléon— je vis le grand capitaine lui-même—Au point du jour je vis toutes ces legions s'ébranler, se ranger au bataille—J'entendis donner le signal du combat— . . .—Quand je reconnais les Prussiens et que je les vis attaquer si vigoureusement les Français, ne me possédant plus, je criai de tous mes poumons—*Grouchy*—Grouchy—ou` est tu? que fais-tu?"[8]

Reinforced by the panorama he had seen in Paris, memories of the Franco-Prussian War continued to haunt Gingras as he travelled along the Rhine Valley, and he heaved a sigh of relief when he reached Bavaria, "pays bien Catholique . . . le plus catholique de l'Europe." The Bavarians seemed a morally robust and healthy people to him, commendable for their good manners if not for their incomprehensible dialect. By contrast, the population of the Abbé's next stop, Venice, appeared decadent, sad, demoralized: "l'on se fatigue en le voyant." In his assessment of Venetians (and, as we shall see, of all Italians), Gingras formulated a stereotype common among members of his ideological background: he juxtaposed the healthy North with the weary South, but because of recent political events, he had to be careful to specify one particular region of Germany which met his requirements. Such topical modifications of commonly accepted national stereotypes sometimes also significantly altered a traveller's itinerary, even if he was not forced, as tourists were during the Franco-Prussian War, to travel to Biarritz via Germany, Switzerland, and Italy: during the Boer War, for instance, patriotic British and Canadian travellers avoided Switzerland because its government supported the Boers.

In Rome, Gingras privately commemorated the day of the Immaculate Conception, a particularly popular dogma among devout French-Canadian Catholics. After its introduction by Pius IX in 1854, Romans celebrated this day with great solemnity during his reign, with Rome's grand buildings illuminated "comme par l'enchantement." Now, in 1882, the lights were extinguished, both in the windows and in the hearts of the Romans. Pius IX's successor, Leo XIII, had lost virtually all of his temporal power, living as "the prisoner of the Vatican" since the passage in 1871 of the Laws of the Guarantees, which severely curtailed the pope's realm of influence. The Quirinale Palace, now occupied by Umberto I, king of Italy, was, to Gingras, purloined from the pope. Still, the Abbé briefly forgot his scorn of the *parvenu* monarchy when the fourteen-year-old crown prince drove past because young Vittorio Emmanuele reminded Gingras of the courteous manners he left behind in Québec: "Il salue à droite et à gauche, il ôte sa casquette, juste comme un jeune universitaire salue les Dames qu'il rencontre dans les rues de Québec!" Despite Rome's spiritual decline, Gingras was hopeful about the pope's eventual victory. Saying mass in a church built on the ruins of an ancient temple dedicated to Minerva, the Abbé observed that the church had also triumphed over the demons of the pagan world. As he said farewell to Rome, Gingras' xenophobia and hatred of Republicanism broke forth, projected onto the very appearance of the city and of its inhabitants: "Comme ville, Rome n'est pas une belle ville, les rues sont étroites, sales, on y est mal! La grande masse de la population est détestable, c'est un peuple abruti, et dégénéré, des figures d'hommes et de femmes impossibles! C'est un peuple tapageur qui vit, en grande partie, dans la rue, qui passe ses nuits à crier et à chanter."

These two diaries share a number of obvious similarities. They were written at approximately the same time and hence respond to some of the same politico-cultural developments. Both cover four months of travel pursuing a similar itinerary. Their professions—priest and lawyer— trained Gingras and Martin to use language with relative ease and generally with the intent of impressing large or imposing audiences; neither diary dwells extensively on intimate, personal response, and probably both authors intended to share their written impressions with others, if not to publish them. Differences between the two documents are, however, equally apparent. Gingras is inspired by the special messianic fervour often found among French-Canadian clergymen of the period; Martin is an Anglican who happens to be primarily interested in secular and administrative matters and who keenly explores recent developments in industry and science. Although impressed with advances in science, such as the photographic accuracy of the Paris panorama, Gingras is almost exclusively concerned with religious topics. So, although their itineraries are alike, the emphases placed on various states of the journey correspond to the two authors' specific concerns; for Martin, London is the focus, and he spends more days there than anywhere else on his trip; for Gingras, Rome, or more correctly, the idea of Rome as an Augustinian City of God, assumes that position.

The lawyer and the priest not only observe different things, they also perceive them in different ways: Martin kept a factual record, relying strongly on empirical observation. Even imaginative areas, like literature, or spiritual ones, like religion, are translated into sense perceptions: Spurgeon is described as delivering his sermon with effusive gestures and in slang; *Othello* is said to have taken place in the hotel where Martin eats his breakfast and lunch. Gingras, on the other hand, tends toward allegorical interpretations of landscapes, cities, people. The narrowness of Rome's streets, their dirt and noise reflect the spiritual decadence of a people who have forsaken the Holy Father; London and Paris seem wastelands with a few true believers tucked away in oases of faith. The ''plot'' of Gingras' journey imitates a pilgrim's progress through the slough of despondency of impious Europe, its superficial dreariness juxtaposed with a spiritual subplot envisaging the ultimate triumph of the church. Martin's trip, a middle-class version of the gentlemanly *grand tour*, represents status symbol and educational experience at the same time. Gingras ''reads'' Europe as if it were a contemplative text; Martin implicitly pursues the tradition of Protestant account-taking: only the sum total of conscientiously recorded observations permits general conclusion and justifies the enterprise of the journey, although Martin occasionally allows his *Baedeker* to do his work for him.

Middle-class professional men, Martin and Gingras are representative of the majority of Canadian travellers who will be encountered in this study: clergymen and lawyers lead among the writers of travel narratives, closely followed by journalists in ever-growing numbers. Few reports exist, for obvious reasons, by those whose business required them to cross the Atlantic many times. A memoir like Conyngham Crawford Taylor's misleadingly entitled *The Queen's Jubilee and Toronto "Called Back" from 1847 to 1887* (1887) is very rare indeed. A drygoods salesman, Taylor frequently travelled to Britain and the Continent to buy linens in Ireland, tweeds in Scotland, embroideries and silks in Switzerland, velvets and woollens in Germany, and artificial flowers in Paris, collecting a host of intriguing information on the business practices in the countries visited.

Not quite as homogeneous as class and profession are the travellers' ethnic backgrounds: British-Canadians were clearly not members of a cultural monolith but proudly insisted on their English, Scottish, or Irish origins. The Reverend Moses Harvey—himself a native of Armagh, Ireland, before he settled in St. John's, Newfoundland, and became an authority on its history and natural resources—observed how colourfully varied the accents spoken on board were as his boat departed for "a trip to the Old land": "Very interesting it was to listen to the buzz of conversation in the saloon, and to note how the English, Scotch and Irish accents blended—the English deep, stomachic, musical; the Scotch broader, stronger, rougher, more emphatic and more thoracic; the Irish soft, sibilant, dental, and when not too pronounced, quite mellifluous."[9] Rather more poignant is the ethnic element in Kathleen Coleman's work; passionately Irish, Coleman still had to remain as neutral as possible as columnist of the *Mail and Empire*. Always shrewd, she archly asserted her identity by juxtaposing her own temperament, that of "a wild and untutored Celt," with the subdued English as she described the pageantry of Queen Victoria's Diamond Jubilee to her readers: "Calm English girls tilted their sailors to the proper angle, and gave vent to their feelings so far as to exclaim, 'How interesting!' when a convoy of gloriously-jewelled princes passed us on the road at a gallop. . . . You may imagine, therefore, the brilliancy of the scene when the Saxon was thus forced to expression over it."[10] Moreover, Coleman invented a travelling companion named "Theodocia," an arrogant and ethnocentric Englishwoman, and gleefully watched her defeat by Irish beggars, a defeat hinging on a separate dialect and an episode worth quoting at some length for its subtle strategies of ethnic subversion:

> "Gracious! What do you want, my good woman, and why don't you ask for it in English?" this to a tattered, forlorn-looking old creature, who with a thin shawl over her head and nothing on her feet and legs, was asking charity, "in honour of God and the blessed Virgin." Theo

is a good soul, though she does say a sharp thing now and again, and is absolutely devoid of "sentiment" . . . so of course she gave something to the pathetic old figure in the rags and tatters. I knew what would happen, for I'd been there before; but I hold that when people travel they should have as little to do with guide books as possible, and should not be given to informing each other about the habits and customs of different places and people if one of them happens to know something of the same. Experience is a fine thing, and the dearer you buy it the less you are apt to forget it. When Theodocia shut up her purse again and hurried away from the praises and prayers of the relieved one (which were hardly congenial, seeing that "May the hivins be your bed this night, yer honour, an' may ivery hair of yer head be turned into a mould candle to light ye to glory;" is hardly a thing to be desired . . .), she found herself surrounded by beggars that beggar description. The halt, the lame, and the blind, they were all there, all shrieking at her in Irish to "help their necessities," and one and all promising her such speedy departure to a better land, and such extraordinary comforts when she got there, that she turned to me in despair, and pathetically entreated me to put forth my best Irish and rout the enemy, which was done after a judicious distribution of halfpence.[11]

If, after this scene, the reader needed any further indication about Coleman's allegiances, they must have become finally clear to him after her moving description of Parnell's grave in the same pages.

Ethnic backgrounds apart from the ones mentioned were rarely in evidence, except for the distinctly German education of Maria Elise Lauder, author of *Evergreen Leaves; or, 'Toofie' in Europe* (1884). Rivalry between the English and French, however, also persisted into their travels abroad, despite the political rapprochement initiated by the alliance of France and Britain during the Crimean War, Queen Victoria's visit to Paris—coincidental with the victory of Sebastopol—during the 1855 World Exposition, and the arrival of the *Capricieuse* in Quebec and Montreal, an expedition enthusiastically received by the French and politely condoned by the English. If, in the following pages, I often describe Canadian travel to Europe as imperial travel, I am alluding to a double plot: the confirmation of the British Empire and the longing, largely unfulfilled, for a new French Empire. The shadow of Napoleon—revered in Quebec as the successor of France's most powerful monarchs—continued to loom large, and the reign of Napoleon III, particularly as long as he styled himself a protector of the endangered papacy, renewed hope for French supremacy. The birth of the Prince Imperial was welcomed as a promise of continuity, and the historian Jean-Baptiste-Antoine Ferland glowingly described the many festivities surrounding that important event in a letter from Paris to his Canadian friends.[12] English-Canadians watched the rising self-assurance of the French with some alarm, as did James Douglas from Quebec, professor of chemistry and a distinguished mining expert, who observed with concern the appointment of Napoleon III's "most eminent diplomats" to the post of consul-general of Canada, the arrival of Prince Napoleon "in a warship to unveil the statue of Bellona which crowned a monument over the dead that fell at the battle of Sainte-Foy in 1760," and the involvement of enthusiastic French-Canadian youths in the defence of the Emperor Maximilian, the doomed ruler of Mexico: "[Napoleon III] certainly revived in the French-Canadian imagination a keener sense of affiliation with their old country than had existed for several generations."[13] To French-Canadians, Napoleon III's defeat at Sedan was a double tragedy because hopes for a legitimist, Catholic French Empire now seemed permanently buried; Octave Crémazie correctly suspected his English compatriots of secretly rejoicing over the outcome of the Franco-Prussian War because with Teutonic supremacy Britain's too seemed confirmed.

Naturally, Canadian travellers preferred Britain and France to all other countries, closely followed by Italy and Palestine as the lands associated with classical education and Christianity. The Lowlands, Germany, and Switzerland remained largely the *pays de passage* they had always been on the old diligence routes; few travellers ventured into countries off the beaten track such as Spain and Eastern Europe. Scandinavia appears to have held even less interest although the indefatigable Sandford Fleming (reprimanded in 1880 in the House of Commons for his frequent absences "during which time the railway work was unconsidered, and his responsibility neglected")[14] visited Denmark and Sweden in 1892 in the company of Sir Charles Tupper, commenting that he found the countryside to be much like Nova Scotia.[15] Travellers' expectations were largely focussed on the cities of London, Paris, and Rome, with Jerusalem serving as an important metaphor highlighting and, to a certain degree, subsuming encounters with European cities. Although many travellers recorded their responses, a select group of individuals whose biographies seem especially representative and whose writing is both articulate and interesting, will dominate the following pages: Judge Adolphe-Basile Routhier, Jules-Paul Tardivel, the Abbé Léon Provancher, the Reverends William H. Withrow, Hugh Johnston, and Moses Harvey, and the journalists Kathleen Coleman and Andrew Learmont Spedon. First, however, the practical aspects of nineteenth-century Canadian travel to Europe must be put in perspective.

3

The Modernization of Travel, Guide Books, and Travel Satire

Improvements in transport and the introduction of organized travel and reduced return fares made journeys to Europe increasingly attractive to Victorian Canadians in the second half of the nineteenth century. In international travel the sailing-ship had, after many years of experimenting, finally been replaced by steel-hull, screw-driven vessels, but Canada took longer to adopt steamship travel than its sister colonies because the St. Lawrence and the east coast presented exceptional difficulties with their treacherous terrain, ice, and fog. Despite the work of earlier seafarers like Jolliet, Cook, and Desbarres, there were few navigational aids for the ordinary merchant ship. After 1850, however, the St. Lawrence was cleared of dangerous rocks, and excavations were conducted in preparation for extensive ocean traffic. Charts, sounding systems, pilotage service, and the magnetic compass were improved, and additional buoys and lighthouses were installed. By the 1890s, a Canadian could travel overseas on three different lines serving Montreal and Québec: the Beaver, Dominion, and Allan lines. Of these the Allan Royal Mail Line, property of a Montreal shipping magnates' family and so called because it had been awarded the Atlantic mail contract by the Canadian government in 1855, was to become the most influential.[1] In his book *England and Canada: A Summer Tour between Old and New Westminster, with Historical Notes* (1884), Sandford Fleming underlined the importance of a sophisticated and extensive communications network for a powerful British Empire; in 1874, Queen Victoria knighted Hugh Allan in recognition of ''his successful efforts in establishing steam communication between the

Mother Country and Canada, and for the remarkable increase in Imperial trade that had been the result of his labours."[2] Royal visitors to Canada preferred Allan liners for the crossing; Allan's ostentatious hospitality in his mansion "Ravenscrag" to the Prince of Wales, the Princess Louise and her husband, the Marquis de Lorne, and the Duke of Connaught regularly made the headlines in the Dominion. At the beginning of his overseas service during the Crimean War, Allan had proved his patriotism by leasing his ships, the *Canadian* and the *Indian* to the British government for the transport of troops, weapons, and horses, a service he was to repeat during the Boer War, although—being a shrewd businessman—he generally charged higher prices than other fleets.

Allan's imperial convictions were reflected in the record-breaking efficiency and the splendid fittings of the more luxurious ships in his fleet. The *Sardinian*, built in 1875, crossed the Atlantic in an unprecedented eight days in 1879, its passengers as a result even being somewhat disappointed on arrival because "they were . . . far from having got through the occupations usual on an Atlantic voyage."[3] Cabin passengers stood in awe before the salon, "a gorgeous palatial apartment," where glittering lights illuminated the "ceiling . . . delicately panelled in French white, enriched with gold mouldings."[4] The panelling—walnut, rosewood, and teak—combined with "handsome fluted columns of ebony, with rich gold capitals"[5] created an atmosphere at once elegant and comfortable. A piano and a well-stocked library were at the disposal of passengers, who reclined on red velvet sofas; those in need of privacy could withdraw to a "ladies' sitting room or boudoir" or to "a charming snuggery."[6] Although contact with second-class and steerage passengers on board Allan liners was kept at a minimum, Sunday Services united all classes and creeds, when "through the open doors came the steerage passengers, men and women, neatly dressed and leading the little children gaily decked in their best for church, with those from the first and second cabin, all on equal footing."[7] The *Parisian*, the first Allan liner to be equipped with bilge keels to prevent the roll and with "a double bottom, divided into watertight bulkheads"[8] to increase safety, inspired confidence with its 5,359-ton bulk although she was still much smaller than later ships, such as the 12,099-ton *Scandinavian (2)*, built in 1898 for the White Star Line and purchased, in 1912, by the Allan Line. When the *Parisian* first arrived in Montreal, its citizens were invited to see for themselves how safe and comfortable trans-Atlantic travel had become; a coloured advertisement later featured the *Parisian* as "slicing easily through a lumpy sea under steam and sail."[9]

By the end of the century, passengers could choose between eleven different steamship companies departing from New York or Montreal's winter port, Portland, Maine, during the long freeze-up of the St. Lawrence. *Baedeker's London and Its Environs: Handbook for Travellers* (1892) listed the fastest and most luxurious among these as the Inman Line's *City of New York* and the *City of Paris*, Cunard's *Etruria* and *Teutonic*, and the White Star's *Majestic*. In 1900, cabins were available for 80, 90, or 110 dollars, a return ticket for 130 to 150 dollars. Crossings generally took six to ten days then, but the *Teutonic* had established a record in 1891 with five days, sixteen hours, and thirty-one minutes.

Such speed and comfort were a far cry from historian François-Xavier Garneau's experience in 1831, when he sailed for England on the *Strathisla*. The boat was at the mercy of wind and weather from the day of its departure. Having left on 20 June, she was forced by a lull to cast anchor shortly thereafter near the Ile-aux-Grues, and Garneau, the captain, and the pilot whiled away the time visiting a rustic and hospitable family on the island. When a favourable breeze arrived, the *Strathisla* continued along the St. Lawrence and into the open ocean until the 25th, when she was blown off course into one of the bays of Newfoundland. On the 27th, she passed Newfoundland and continued smoothly for a week, with Garneau immersed in the works of Byron and Newton. On 4 July, the boat was hit by a violent storm, "toutes les voiles hautes furent serrées, tous les ris furent pris dans les voiles basses, au bruit toujours croissant des flots et de la bourrasque."[10] On the 11th, she reached the Channel, blown back and forth by a temperamental breeze; a few days later, Garneau finally reached his destination after a crossing still to be considered speedy compared to Susanna Moodie's nine weeks on board in 1832. Yet, despite his unreliable and leisurely mode of conveyance, Garneau inadvertently announces a new age of travel. In his travel book *Voyage en Angleterre et en France dans les années 1831, 1832, et 1833* (1850) he uses the word "touriste," a neologism not acknowledged by the Académie française until its use in Stendhal's *Mémoires d'un touriste* in 1838.[11]

The signs of an impending revolution in transport were even stronger in 1838 when Joseph Howe, accompanied by his friend Thomas Chandler Haliburton, sailed to England to attend Queen Victoria's coronation. Twenty days into a tedious voyage, interrupted only by scribblings in his diary and by meals "repairing the waste which ennui and vexation, rather than any healthy exertion of mind or body, had occasioned,"[12] Howe and his fellow passengers were lured away from their dining-table by the exciting news that the *Sirius*, an English steamer, was ahead, ready to take on the mails from Halifax and inviting anyone interested to come and investigate the ship which could be expected to complete a crossing in twelve to fifteen days. To Howe, the *Sirius* seemed the noble harbinger of a new age, moving "in gallant style with the speed of a hunter,"[13] while the

Tyrian lumbered along "with the rapidity of an ox-cart loaded with marsh mud."[14] There was a rakish look about the *Sirius*; painted black and red, she was enveloped by an aura of power and elegance. Ever intent on the advancement of his home province, Nova Scotia, Joseph Howe instantly speculated on the advantages to be gained from a regular steamship service between Halifax, New York, and Liverpool, and he used his stay in England to lobby for such a scheme. On 18 March 1839, Samuel Cunard of Halifax formed the British and North American Royal Mail Steam Packet Company, and in 1840, the first Cunard liner, the *Britannia*—the ship by which Charles Dickens was to sail to America—made its maiden voyage. The railway had conquered the vagaries of natural time and space; travel by sea was to become regular and punctual as well and provide, as Cunard envisaged it, an "ocean railway." He too was knighted for his services in steam transport both for civilians and the Crimea troops. Howe's and Cunard's dreams of making Halifax and Boston into busy international ports failed, however, because Montreal and New York offered richer hinterlands. In 1867, Cunard liners stopped calling at Halifax, and they were generally boarded in New York.[15]

The improvements of ocean travel ensured that instead of sinking into the tedium of a lengthy voyage, passengers engaged in studied leisure, with pseudo-activities planned for every hour of the day; the grand liners, akin

B.   "Dinner-Time on a French Liner," *The Dominion Illustrated.*

to floating luxury hotels, catered to every imaginable need or whim.
Thomas C. Watkins, a business man from Hamilton, Ontario, was
determined *not* to sink into sloth. A prominent member of the Methodist
Church and "a total abstainer from the use of tobacco and alcoholic
liquors,"[16] Watkins rose at 5:30 every morning while on board the
Cunarder *Gallia* to take his daily sea-bath, frowning at the lazy or seasick
who slept in till ten o'clock or later and even had breakfast in bed.
Mealtimes for the self-disciplined were set for seven, one, six, and nine
o'clock. Watkins roamed the ship with a stern eye, observing the other
passengers in their activities, "employed as usual in reading, writing,
playing the piano, conversing, promenading, attending concerts, playing
cards, dancing while the sailors' band plays lively airs, singing, courting
occasionally, playing shuffleboard, pitching quoits, betting on the run of
the ship, smoking and, last and worst, gambling, at which many young
men are sadly victimized and deprived of the money they want badly by a
lot of blacklegs, who seem to make a busines of going back and forth for
this purpose."[17] Watkins himself preferred to spend his time studying
astronomy and reading Burton's *India, Arabia and Egypt*, although he
was prevailed upon to watch the American passengers' festivities on the
Fourth of July, when "a young lad dressed up so as to represent Liberty"[18]
was paraded about the ship. In courtesy to the Canadian passengers, the
celebrants cheered both the president and Queen Victoria before settling
down to an evening of music and oration.

But even the astounding achievements of nineteenth-century technology
could not always be relied upon. Three days after leaving New York, the
ship suddenly shuddered violently and then stood still: the shaft was
broken. Passing steamers tried to take the *Gallia* in tow, but failed. Ship
engineers toiled for five days to repair the damage; on Sunday, work was
completed, and Watkins pestered the crew for details of the operation:

> The shaft is an enormous beam of iron in seven sections, weighing
> about twelve tons each, united by bolts passing through the flanges. It
> was the second section from the screw which broke. In breaking it bent
> another section and the bolts between nearly all the sections. Most of
> the bearings on which the shaft revolves were torn away and the tunnel
> badly damaged. To make repairs five sections had to be disconnected
> by driving out the bolts, which took nearly three days. Fortunately the
> break was oblique. The sections had to be brought into line,
> reclamped and bolted, and the broken section clamped over the break
> with three iron clamps, each about four inches wide and one and a half
> inches thick, bolted together in the strongest manner. New bearings
> had to be constructed and new connections made. The work continued

night and day for nearly five days in a small tunnel, without ventilation, except what could be obtained from air-shafts to the deck far above.[19]

At last, the work was done, and Watkins announced that the result was "an unequalled triumph of engineering skill on the ocean, almost entirely due to the indomitable pluck and energy of our engineers, for whom the passengers raised a purse of one hundred and twenty-five pounds, to be divided between them and who so nobly seconded their efforts and the captain was presented with a gold watch on arriving in Liverpool."[20] Faith in the attractions of modern ocean travel was restored, and the passengers gathered in a rapturous thanksgiving service after having whiled away five anxious days with watching whales, porpoises, and sharks and attending old Mr. Anderson's funeral at sea. Thoughts of death may well have lingered in everyone's mind when the regular copious meals were reduced to two per day, and even the ascetic Watkins experienced sudden cannibalistic urges: "there are some stout old ladies and gentlemen on board, who, if not too tough, might supply us with a few good meals."[21]

Not all ocean voyages tested the passenger's faith in technology as severely as did Watkins' eventful crossing in 1885: many travellers remained in awe of the conveniences of modern ocean travel. The railway, by contrast, had almost become a commonplace by the second half of the nineteenth century. Canadians reached the ports of Montreal and Quebec by way of steadily expanding railway and steamship routes; with the building of the Grand Trunk Railway, a direct connection was provided via the Victoria Bridge from Montreal to Longueuil, with an extension to Portland, Maine. The construction of the Victoria Bridge between 1854 and 1859 was welcomed as the symbol of Canada's firm integration in Britain's communicative system, and the bridge gained at least part of its glory from association with other feats of engineering in the British Empire such as the Aswan Dam, the Ganges Canal, the Indus Basin Scheme, the Grand Trunk Road through India, and the steel railway bridge across the Zambezi River; on his visit to Canada in 1860, the Prince of Wales duly evoked comparisons with the Roman Empire when he celebrated Victoria Bridge—"that immortal monument of Stephenson's skill, of British capital, and Canadian industry"—as "unsurpassed by the grandeur of Egypt or of Rome."[22] Sandford Fleming, who firmly believed in the harmony of technology and nature, declared the railway equal in cultural importance to the discovery of America, the development of the Gutenberg press, and the Reformation. Travel, once the privilege of the wealthy, was now accessible to all members of the Empire, making them true citizens of the world.

Canadians, proud of their own growing railway system, compared the extensiveness and comforts of North American and European services. The closest parallel seemed to be Italy, whose unification, like Canada's nationhood, was dependent on a railway, a development much delayed under the rule of the conservative Popes Leo XII and Gregory XVI. *Murray's Handbook for Travellers in Northern Italy* of 1877 gave extensive details on the Mount Cenis Tunnel, completed in 1871 to connect France with Italy; such information would have been almost as interesting to a Canadian traveller as reports on the progress of Victoria Bridge in his own country. The tunnel, moreover, created a direct connection between London and Brindisi, the port of embarkation for travellers to Egypt and India, thus opening an important route for officials in the service of the Empire, who could even have their luggage sealed to avoid customs *en route* through Italy. Despite the modernization of travel in the Italian kingdom, however, travellers were urged not to expect British efficiency: "The traveller is strongly advised to be at the Station in good time. Except at Genoa, and one or two important terminal or international stations, there is only one *guichet* for all classes, and no official in attendance to preserve order and prevent crushing and confusion. The arrangements, in short, at most Italian stations, are in this respect by no means creditable to the authorities."[23]

Besides requiring punctuality, travelling Canadians kept a sharp eye on the amenities offered on board European trains and riverboats. Sandford Fleming, jr., and his young bride telegraphed ahead for a luncheon basket to be delivered at a railway station on the way to London and were delighted with their order ("everything tasted so good, little crusty loaves, hot steak and potatoes, butter, cress, and cheddar cheese with a little flask of sherry"),[24] but Edmund Allen Meredith, then assistant provincial secretary, Canada West, was little impressed with the Rhine steamers in 1853, finding both their fittings and cuisine inferior to those of the pleasure craft plying the Saguenay, the St. Lawrence, Canada's many lakes, and the Mississippi and Hudson.[25] Attractive tourist facilities were an important commodity, he knew; appropriate means of conveyance and a good meal would make even the most spectacular scenery more appealing, a factor to be earnestly considered for Canada's own burgeoning tourist industry. But some tourists, well into a bottle of Rhine wine or two, forgot to speculate about the national usefulness of tourism; travelling down the Rhine in 1860, a tipsy George Munro Grant, freshly ordained minister of the Church of Scotland and principal-to-be of Queen's University, neglected his otherwise painstakingly recorded expenses for a while and drowsily jotted down the occasional pleasant thought as the wooded hills and castles passed by.[26]

Along with the modernization of transport, tourist accommodation underwent significant changes. The grand hotel, the nineteenth-century replacement of the traveller's inn, originated in the United States, with the New York City Hotel (1794-96), the Exchange Coffee House in Boston (1806-09), and Tremont House in Boston (1828-29) as pioneering constructions.[27] Closely connected with the building of the railway and western expansion, the grand hotel (featuring a central lobby, double and single rooms, handsomely appointed public rooms, as well as baths, lavatories, gas light, free soap, and a different key for each bedroom) became a symbol of national achievement, and cities across America competed in erecting palatial hotels, a development to be duplicated in Toronto's King Edward Hotel and Montreal's Windsor (where the Martins spent the night) and, later, the Canadian Pacific Railway chain built in the style of French *châteaux*. In the second half of the nineteenth century, large luxury hotels were regularly built to receive the crowds of world expositions and to serve, in a sense, as major exhibits of the architectural and mechanical ingenuity, the organizational efficiency, and the flawless hospitality the host-country had to offer. Judge Adolphe-Basile Routhier, travelling in style in the early eighties, chose the Langham Hotel in London, the Grand Hôtel du Louvre in Paris, and the Albergo della Minerva in Rome. Both the Grand Hôtel du Louvre and the Langham had been built for world expositions, the first for 1855, the latter for 1862. Situated on Portland Place, the Langham boasted a façade combining Italian Gothic and French Renaissance, and it featured 400 beds, 300 water closets, two libraries, a hydraulic lift, "and a courtyard enlivened with fountains, flowers and a band that played on summer evenings."[28] Managed at the beginning of its existence by an American, it attracted many American tourists who flocked to Europe in droves following the Civil War and relished the hotel's American-style services. Opened in the presence of the Prince of Wales, the Langham obviously sought royal approval, as did the Grand Hôtel du Louvre on the Rue Rivoli, which emulated the style of Napoleon III's Second Empire; arriving after the events of the Franco-Prussian War, Routhier must have keenly felt the irony of an architectural style surviving its perpetrator.

Not all Canadian travellers could or would, of course, afford such luxurious accommodation. The lawyer Thomas Langton affectionately welcomed his bed in an Italian *pensione* like a dear acquaintance ("they act like a sandbag, punch a hole in them and it stays a hole till you punch another one, so when one gets in one moulds one's shape in the mattress"),[29] while Edmund Allen Meredith was unpleasantly reminded of the days of the traveller's inn with its often dubious sanitary arrangements when he spent the night in a London bed-and-breakfast place: "Oh horror of horrors! on awakening in the morning we beheld the pillow covered alive with bugs! I expostulated warmly with the landlady's representative, Miss Bath, who promised to have the bedstead taken down the following morning and thoroughly cleaned, and recommended the burning of a light during the ensuing night."[30]

With the increasing speed of travel and the growing numbers of passengers to be transported from place to place, new logistical problems were created. National celebrations such as the Queen's Golden and Diamond Jubilees were increasingly used as tourist attractions, and Conyngham Crawford Taylor, drygoods salesman from Toronto, had a taste of the attendant exigencies of organization when he witnessed the victory celebrations in Portsmouth following the Crimean War:

> The streets were filled with people who seemed totally at a loss how to spend the night. Tired groups might be seen wandering from street to street, making fruitless attempts at admittance at various houses, where the price seemed too exorbitant to any but millionaires. While wandering about the streets in this way the writer had offers of beds at a guinea apiece, or to be rowed over to the Isle of Wight for the same price, but the appearance of our soliciting friends not bespeaking extra accommodation, we declined their kind offer, and the night being fine, with the exception of a rest on a chair at an hotel, was spent in promenading the city.[31]

Goldwin Smith, reminiscing about his youth, might well nostalgically remember the peaceful days before missed train connections, lost luggage, and unconfirmed hotel reservations began to haunt his holidays,[32] but modern travel was here to stay, and Canadians were beginning to respond to some of its unexpected complications. R. Vashon Rogers, barrister-at-large at Osgoode Hall, sensing a new and lucrative field for legal practice, published an exhaustive treatise entitled *Wrongs and Rights of a Traveller by Boat—By Stage—By Rail* in 1875, in which all possibly conceivable travel calamities (involving tickets, baggage, accidents, and so forth) and their legal implications were explained to the anxious tourist.

For those who felt that the intricacies of modern travel as a whole were too much to bear, organized travel was an attractive alternative. Thomas Cook's package tours, originating in organized excursions to temperance meetings in the 1840s, began to blossom in 1851, when he transported thousands of modest income visitors to the Great Exhibition in London. *Grands tours* to the famous cities of the continent were advertised in 1856, with Swiss and American tours and a Conducted Crusade to the Holy Land soon to follow. Cook's services quickly included all aspects of travel;

he provided train, boat, and hotel reservations, reliable guides, interpreters, and guidebooks, and gave expert advice on proper travelling gear.[33] Cook's methods became the gospel of travel organizations; *Voyages-Rivet*, a Montreal travel agency specializing in pilgrimages to Lourdes, Loretto, and the Holy Land, advertised its services in 1900 as based on Cook's approach. Many Canadians trusted, and were impressed with, Cook's efficiency. J.-C.-K. Laflamme, professor of science at Laval, enlisted the agency's services for a ticket taking him to Paris, Berlin, Constantinople, and Genoa, when he attended a geological congress in Turkey in 1897.[34] His colleague, the Abbé Léon Provancher, a widely travelled naturalist, appreciated Cook's cheap fares, even imitated his methods in organizing

C.   Murray's Handbook Advertiser.

several pilgrimages from Quebec to Jerusalem.[35] An anonymous contributor to *Belford's Monthly Magazine* felt like a well-tended child when, clutching "a ticket for a circular tour [of the Continent], divided into three parts, each part comprehended in a book of coupons, and the three books put up in a convenient little green cover, kept together by an elastic band," he was met at the wharf by the proprietor of the New Bath Hotel to prevent him from going astray.[36]

Many old copies of *Baedeker's* and *Murray's* guidebooks in Canadian libraries testify that few travellers, grateful for the host of useful information the guides contained, ventured forth without them or their *Murray's Handbook of Travel Talk*, containing "Dialogues—Questions—Vocabularies in English, German, French and Italian" and praised by the *Saturday Review* as keeping "steadily in view the actual needs of travellers; for it is absurd to put a manual of polite conversation on literature, art, science, philosophy, and the musical glasses [sic] into the hands of an honest but uncultivated tourist, who can only ejaculate his simple wants in inarticulate interjections."[37] *Baedeker's Paris and Environs with Routes from London to Paris of 1900*, then in its 14th revised edition, mapped out every step for the traveller arriving in Paris, in instructions assuming that he was a fortress besieged by an alien culture: "On arrival the traveller should hand his small baggage to a porter (*facteur* commissionaire; 40-50 c), follow him to the exit, where an *octroi* official demands the nature of its contents . . . and call a cab (*voiture de place*). The cab then takes its place in the first row, which is reserved for engaged vehicles. After receiving the driver's number (*numéro*), the traveller, if he has any registerd luggage, tells him to wait for it ('*restez pour attendre les baggages*'). Hand-bags and rugs should not be left unguarded in the cab, at any rate not without making the driver notice the number of articles, as there are numerous thieves always on the lookout for such opportunities."[38] The remainder of the anticipated arrival was planned with military precision to give the tourist the feeling that although he was exposed to a foreign language, currency, and mentality, he was in full control of the situation. A tourist's luggage—imposing trunks and portmanteaux perhaps purchased from Barrington and Son, Dessaulles, or Kraft in Montreal, all of whom exhibited well-made trunks at the 1878 Paris exhibition as samples of Canadian manufacture—contained the proof of his respectability; J. E. Costin's *Le Guide du voyageur de Montréal à Paris via Liverpool et Londres* (Montreal, 1899) listed essential items to preserve a gentleman's dignity in any situation: two suits, one for the journey, another for special occasions, one coat, a raincoat, a pair of galoshes and one pair of shoes, two changes of underwear, a dozen handkerchiefs, half-a-dozen detachable collars, one nightshirt, towels, soap, scissors, a penknife, a mirror, a small glass, a corkscrew, a comb, a toothbrush, pins, needles, buttons, thread in different colours, pencils, pens, ink, paper, envelopes. For seasickness, Costin recommended flasks of brandy and wine as well as a few potions.

In encouraging defensive behaviour, guidebooks also enforced ethnocentricity, advising travellers to consort with their own kind and avoid undue contact with the natives. *Murray's Handbook for Travellers in Central Italy* of 1856 advised visitors to Rome to take lodgings in the Piazza di Spagna, where they could expect the comforts of English company; the dangers of the Roman climate were pointed out to "delicate invalids" and "nervous persons"[39] and precise instructions for appropriate housing given. Protestants were advised not to display their criticism of "Roman Catholic errors"[40] by misbehaving during mass; they were urged instead to prove their superiority with gentlemanly behaviour. Jules-Paul Tardivel responded to such arrogance by declaring Baedeker and Joanne guides satanic instruments; yet his own letters to *La Vérité*, later collected in *Notes de voyage*, influenced hundreds of readers with his own hysterical phobias of Liberals, Jews, and Freemasons. Guidebooks provided itineraries and lists of churches, monuments, artwork, and scenery to see and firmly advised the traveller to reject his *cicerone*'s suggestion to take him elsewhere, "for he has no notion of the value of any object; and caprice, or some plan of his own, or mere laziness will often make him try to put you off."[41] Only if ample time was left, should the tourist permit himself to be led astray to see some object or sight not sanctioned by the guidebook.

The editors listed useful books to read before travel and thus significantly shaped the appreciation of art in the age of mass travel, the moreso since editors' choices of things to see followed the hierarchies established by popular art historians. Among the works most frequently cited were Franz Kügler's *Handbuch der Geschichte der Malerei von Constantin dem Grossen bis auf die neuere Zeit* (1837), translated and published in two volumes 1842 and 1846 respectively as *A Hand-Book of the History of Painting, from the Age of Constantine the Great to the Present Time*, Lord Lindsay's *Sketches of the History of Christian Art* (1847), Anna Jameson's *Sacred and Legendary Art* (1848; 1850; 1852) and *Memoirs of the Early Italian Painters and of the Progress of Painting in Italy: From Cimabue to Bassano* (1845), and John Ruskin's many works, especially *The Stones of Venice* (1851-53). All of these favoured the art of the Middle Ages and the early Renaissance over later developments because the former seemed a pure expression of Christianity devoid of the sensual paganism of the high Renaissance and the Baroque. Whereas in the 1830s François-Xavier Garneau still preferred the classicist architecture of the Madeleine in Paris, Canadian tourists of the second half of the nineteenth century, both Protestant and Catholic, could be trusted to praise gothic churches and express displeasure with Renaissance and Baroque buildings, to prefer, with the righteous satisfaction of an activity sanctioned by respected historians, Raphael's, Fra Angelico's, or Botticelli's work to that of Michelangelo and Veronese.

Amateur art historians like Emeline A. Rand (wife of Theodore Harding Rand, professor at and chancellor of the newly constituted McMaster University) generally duplicated these views; her *In the National Gallery: Four Letters on the Development of Italian Art* (1894) concludes with a dismissal of the Mannerists and "Naturalists" who "regarded art till it became a medium for the representation of the follies and vulgarities of human life rather than a divine speech of souls moved by moral earnestness and uplifted by the noblest aspirations."[42] Throughout her *Letters*, Rand insisted on a "life-like" depiction as the hallmark of great art, but her concluding remarks clearly indicate that she dismissed realism without the saving grace of spirituality as much as did her mentors. Judging from the *Revue canadienne*'s essays on ancient and contemporary art, conservative French-Canadian criticism shared with the English a strong emphasis on the moral and spiritual qualities of art, but it went considerably further in demanding an almost purely symbolic approach. "La vie est elle-même invisible et ne saurait tomber sous nos sens," wrote Alphonse Leclaire in 1895 (basing his conclusions on the work of philosophers Simon-Théodore Jouffroy and Victor Cousin, as well as the theologian Félicité-Robert de Lamennais), "Hélas! il est vrai, nous sommes condamnés à n'en rien voir ici bas que des signes ou des caractères expressifs; et c'est ce qui nous explique comment il se fait que nous trouvons bien souvent une beauté plus grande et plus parfaite dans des oeuvres d'art qui n'ont certainement pas la vie, que dans les réalités vivantes qu'elles représentent."[43] Leclaire prefers painting to sculpture because the former is "plus immatérielle,"[44] and he grants the highest place to music, "un signe tout aérien, presqu' immatériel."[45] The *Revue* regularly printed reproductions of paintings from the 1890s onwards, accompanied by evaluative essays. Much attention was paid to the German Nazarenes, a group of early nineteenth-century painters who, now often considered the German Pre-Raphaelites, attempted to duplicate the life and work of medieval religious communities and whose ascetic work seemed to express a newly revived ideal of primitive Christianity. Less favourable were discussions of neo-Renaissance work excelling in the brilliant rendition of shapes, textures, and colours and, most objectionably, occasionally usurping a religious subject: Carl Becker, an academic painter favoured by the Imperial Court in Berlin, was reprimanded accordingly for his "Ave Maria in Venice": "Becker s'abondonne au faste du décor, au brillant des draperies, des étoffes . . . la forme extérieure, l'effet sensoriel sont plus sa préoccupation que l'impression religieuse elle-même."[46]

An artist's exemplary life also enhanced the value of his work; the *Revue* printed idealizing biographical sketches of the painters covered, and most travellers were familiar with Giorgio Vasari's *Lives of the Artists*, tirelessly repeating his most famous stories of Giotto, Raphael, and Botticelli in their own accounts. Further interest in artists' lives and the lives of other historical figures, not so much as impeccable moral *exempla* but as human beings of considerable psychological complexity immersed in their historical periods, was evoked by George Eliot's historical novel *Romola* and Robert Browning's verse. So many English-Canadians saw Italy through Browning's eyes that his work too became a kind of guidebook, especially since *Murray's* consistently pointed out landmarks associated with the poet's life and work. Emerging from Florence's Via dei Servi onto the Piazza SS. Annunziata, for instance, the tourist was to contemplate "a fine bronze statue of Grand-Duke Ferdinand I" because it was the inspiration for Browning's "The Statue and the Bust." Briefly summarizing the poem's story, *Murray's* reminded the reader that "Browning teaches that vice hindered by indolence may be more criminal than vice accomplished."[47]

The educated Canadian sometimes resented the tyranny of such itineraries and selections, and his travel commentary occasionally assumes the form of a dialogue with criticism or even satire undercutting the assertiveness of the guidebook. Ruskin was a favourite target; his moral earnestness appealed to many Canadians, but his return to medieval ideals seemed anachronistic to others. Some travellers were not amused when they found themselves staring—with growing resentment—at mosaics or paintings which Ruskin had ordered them to find uplifting. Thomas Langton, an eminent lawyer from Toronto, cursed the Englishman for luring him into Pisa, "a beastly hole,"[48] and Constance Rudyard Boulton, a Manitoba newspaperwoman, cycled into Padua in pouring rain and "puddled miserably about . . . all that afternoon, seeing the sights. We did our little best to admire Giotto's frescoes in the chapel of the arena (knowing that Ruskin would crush us sooner or later if we did not) while the water squeezed up and down our boots, and ran out of our hats down our necks."[49] Independent and adventurous travellers scorned the predictability of tourists' responses trained by guidebooks and popular authors. Thus, in *A Voyage of Consolation* (1898), a fictionalized travel narrative, Sara Jeannette Duncan depicted her heroine Mamie Wick as confiding "spontaneous impressions" to her diary, in reality clichéd and plagiarized literary effusions dictated by her mother. The Wickses, in hot

pursuit of the trails mapped out for them by *Murray's*, *Baedeker's*, and
Ruskin's *Stones of Venice*, engage in serious conversation with a group of
travelling maidens over the business of travel: "Do you gloat on the
medieval?" inquires Miss Cora of the Senator. "We're perfectly prepared
to," he replies, "I believe we've got both Murray and Baedeker for this
place."[50] Jules Fournier, an outspoken journalist, chose a different venue
to mock Adolphe-Basile Routhier, an inveterate traveller whose books
became authorities quoted by many subsequent tourists,for his presump-
tuous judgements on people and places. In mercilessly dissecting
Routhier's diction and conclusions in a bookreview, Fournier not only
wrote an amusing *compte rendu* but also attacked the bourgeois
self-assurance of a generation of travellers whom he considered obsolete
and whose accounts increasingly belaboured the obvious: "Au cours de ses
explorations, M. Routhier a découvert une mer importante: L'Adriatique;
des îles qui paraissent assez considérables, entre autres Madère et les
Açores; deux villes qui ont noms respectivement Gênes et Naples; un pays
qui s'appelle l'Italie, et une ville qui s'appelle Rome."[51]

The collection of picture postcards Routhier brought back from his
travels seemed to Fournier special evidence of the judge's mechanical
approach to foreign environments. Photography, elsewhere praised as the
quintessence of new, scientifically precise reporting, also became the
hallmark of consumer tourism. Thomas Langton, a passionate photog-
rapher, used an increasingly aggressive vocabulary to describe his
activities: "I prowled for an hour in search of genre pictures," or "I
stalked one nun unsuccessfully till I believe I frightened her."[52] Although
Langton gently mocked his own work, which was, moreover, rarely blessed
with the results he would have liked it to have, he still pointed toward an
increasingly exploitative element in photography in particular and in
tourism in general, an element he sharply satirized in his description of the
Baron Wilhelm von Gloeden, a German with "golden hair and beard,
handsome features, sloping shoulders and graceful feminine action" whom
he met in Taormina. Van Gloeden's depictions of sultry Italian youths
posing in the nude or wrapped, *à la grecque*, in bed sheets, gained
considerable fame among contemporary tourists and coincidentally
produced several extraordinary examples of nineteenth-century homosex-
ual photography.[53]

Some critics of modern travel may well have been appalled that yet
another prerogative of the élite—moneyed and/or intellectual—had been
taken over by the mob. A certain snobbishness does indeed prevail in the
Canadian novelist Grant Allen's *Historical Guides*, handbooks (possibly
inspired by Ruskin's *Mornings in Florence* (1881-83), an art historian's
selective answer to Murray's all-inclusive guides) on Paris, Florence, the

cities of Belgium, Venice, Rome, Dresden, and Nuremberg, which carefully abstain from any practical information or any comments on the more popular sights: "The Crystal Palace and Madame Tussaud's are good amusements for children, but are no more necessary for adults than the Pantomime. Windsor Castle, half an hour by rail, is ancient in form, but has been so much restored that it possesses little real interest. Hampton Court is somewhat better; but I do not recommend you to go out of your way to see it. As for the theatres and other casual amusements of London, they are a matter of taste. Baedeker and the daily papers will tell you all about them."[54] Similarly, Chester Glass, a Toronto barrister, pursued a formidable itinerary around the world in 1879-80, described in his *The World: Around It and Over It. Being Letters Written by the Author From England, Ireland, Scotland, Belgium, Holland, Denmark, Germany, Switzerland, France, Spain, Monaco, Italy, Austria, Greece, Turkey, Turkey-in-Asia, The Holy Land, Egypt, India, Singapore, China, Japan, California, Nevada, Utah and New York*, taking pains to assure his incredulous reader that he did not rush through his programme pulled along by the exigencies of a Cook's ticket, but that he belonged to an earlier class of leisurely travellers "staying long enough in each country to see its cities and its people, to understand the leading features of its history and to participate in the amusements and modes of life of the natives."[55]

Even individualists, however, had to observe the political realities of Europe, and they were well advised to check the most recent guidebook for current regulations. In the 1850s especially, before the unification of Germany and Italy, travellers had to be prepared for the tiresome complications of crossing many different borders. John Ashworth, obtaining a passport in 1862 for his trip to Northern Italy from the Austrian ambassador in London, realized that he was preparing to enter a world of the past when he was confronted with a gentleman in a powdered wig.[56] By arranging for his visa in London and by confining his visit to Austrian territory, Ashworth spared himself the almost inconceivable complications involved in travelling through the different Italian states before unification. A tourist in 1854 had to be prepared to deal with five different currencies (the Austrian or Milanese *lira*, the Tuscan *zecchino*, the Tuscan *scudo* of 10 pauls, the Roman *doppia*, and the Neopolitan *oncia* of ducats), and *Murray's* recommended that he carry a sufficient supply of *Napoléons d'or*, a generally acceptable currency. In order to negotiate successfully with his *vetturino*, the tourist needed to be familiar with the different measures of distances used: the French *myriamètre*, the Piedmontese mile, the Milanese mile, the Venetian mile, the Parma and Piacenza mile, the Tuscan mile, the Roman mile, and the Austrian mile. Only if he knew the proper conversions for all of these could he be sure that his driver would transport him a predictable distance for a fixed price. With the unification of Italy, currency, measurements, and weights were decimalized and passports were no longer required, although *Murray's* continued to advise that British subjects furnish themselves with "*this important certificate* of nationality."[57] Customs formalities on the border were now judged "generally lenient and formal,"[58] and *Murray's* dissuaded travellers from attempting to bribe the officials of the new Italy. Tourists were also urged to check coins left over from pre-1862 trips carefully because several had been declared obsolete. The change of times announced itself especially in "Francs and Soldi bearing the Pope's head": these were now "of no value, except as handsome coins."[59] *Murray's* adopted a tone of muted respect for the Italian government toward the end of the century, and disparaging comments on local *ciceroni* were now kept at a minimum. By 1899, no passports were required by British subjects entering Italy, Holland, Denmark, Sweden, and Norway; those who chose to carry one anyway for security reasons owned their passport for life, its lasting value signalled by its often luxurious fittings: "[it] can be mounted on Muslin or Silk on Roan, Morocco or Russia Case,"[60] advised Edward Stanford, London agent for the sale of the Ordnance and Geological Survey Maps. This friendly arrangement was to be painfully terminated by the First World War; Paul Fussell describes in *Abroad: British Literary Travelling between the Wars* (1980) how the reintroduction of passports in 1915 generated an identity crisis among a generation who had grown up considering themselves citizens of the world.

4

The Travellers: Social and Cultural Aspects of Travel in Victorian Canada

Scrutinizing his fellow-passengers in 1867, Andrew Learmont Spedon, a school-teacher and journalist from Montreal, observed the following classes of travellers, most of them "British Canadians": "wealthy farmers going to purchase cattle for the improvement of their stock:—others, simply on a visit to their native country; some for the renovation of their health; and a few to see the Paris exhibition [that is, the 1867 *Exposition universelle*]; also two or three English families homeward bound after a few months sojourn in Canada, perfectly disgusted with the country and its people . . . also a few elderly virgins who had emigrated from Scotland a few years before for the benefit of a change, and to show their good graces to the Canadian youths; but were also returning disaffected with the country—its bachelors in particular."[1] Adding to this list young men setting out on their *grand tour*, young women on their way to a finishing school, painters and musicians embarking on a year's study with renowned masters in Paris, Rome, and Leipzig, students and professors bound for universities and congresses, booksellers determined to replenish their stock with the latest European publications, journalists on special assignment, priests and clergymen undertaking a pilgrimage to the Holy Land, and diplomats and politicians on their frequent travels produces a more or less complete cast of Canadian travellers on their way to Europe in the mid-and late-Victorian era. With such disparate backgrounds, the purposes of these tourists were naturally varied.

"Young man, *go to Europe!*"[2] Grant Allen exhorted in *The European Tour* (1899), a book advertising the *grand tour* as an empirical lesson in

language and history, an appropriate form of travel for an age proud of its
scientific approaches to the acquisition of knowledge. If chemistry could
only be learned in the laboratory, geology in field work, and biology at the
dissecting table, then cultural accomplishments too had to be acquired *sur
place*. As in the regular classroom, no time was to be wasted with irrelevant
material. Allen considered England, France, Italy, Greece, Egypt, and
Assyria "the lands which lie in the direct line of ancestry of our own
civilization."[3] Algeria, Russia, Norway, Denmark, and Spain were only of
marginal importance, while China and Japan could be dismissed
altogether because they did "not form links in the immediate genetic chain
of European and American civilization."[4] The tourist should concern
himself with the typical features of each country, study Allen's *Historical
Guides* for information on buildings, monuments, and paintings, and not
waste his time on modern atrocities like Madame Tussaud's, the Crystal
Palace, or even the city of Berlin. A best-selling novelist and journalist who
was born in Canada but spent most of his life abroad, Allen addressed
himself to Canadians, but his book was clearly directed at an American
audience, from whom he anticipated opposition to his travelling scheme as
a betrayal of American self-sufficiency and national pride; hence perhaps
his belligerently utilitarian tone and his studiedly flippant treatment of
England: "if you see England at all, see mainly the country. . . . The

D.   "Cloisters, Westminster Abbey" from the George Reid Scrapbook.

country is the most smiling and gardenlike in Europe. If it were mere fields, I would not recommend you to see it. But it is an artificial product, the one really admirable artistic outcome of the British idiosyncrasy.''[5]

No such detached reasons for travel to England were advanced by a contributor to the *British American Magazine* in 1863, who interpreted a young Canadian's *grand tour* as a strengthening of the bond between colony and motherland to whom the colonist "owe[s] and cheerfully acknowledge[s] a profound allegiance.''[6] Diligent preparation would make the journey profitable, with the study of "surgery, chemistry, geology, botany, [and] mineralogy,''[7] a thorough knowledge of European history and biography, as well as of the French, German, and Italian languages considered essential prerequisites. Exploring the success of "Canadians

E. "Italian Altar" sketch by Ottawa architect Thomas Seaton Scott.

Abroad'' in the *Canadian Magazine* in 1896, Frederick Clement Brown, an insurance manager from Toronto, found the key in their Anglo-Saxon hardiness and loyalty: steeled in body and mind, a young Canadian was unlikely to succumb to the temptations of foreign cultures and could be expected to extract only their useful teachings.

Among well-connected and wealthy Canadians, a journey to Europe traditionally completed a young man's or woman's education. ''Elegant Canadians'' followed the traditional itineraries of the *grand tour* to acquire the cultural and social polish which would make them fully functional members of their class. In this group, there are many famous names of the Canadian establishment. At seventeen, Thomas Stinson Jarvis, offspring of one of the most powerful and staunchly Loyalist Family Compact families, ''was sent away for a year's travel, his father judging this to be more profitable than a Univ[ersity] course,''[8] at least for the time being. Jarvis—a graduate of Upper Canada College—later attended Osgoode Hall, became an eminent lawyer, and published a number of successful novels. His lively and opinionated letters describing his travels were published in 1875 as *Letters from East Longitudes: Sketches of Travel in Egypt, the Holy Land, Greece, and Cities of the Levant,* including sketchy remarks about travel in Europe and a rainy winter spent in Italy. His reports proved to his family that their son was using his moral and cultural training well in exploring foreign lands: allusions to the Bible and John Bunyan, William Warburton and Byron pervade his letters, and the cadences of eloquent sermons ring through his sentences: ''There she stood enrobed in splendour—the splendour of the lily—immaculate, pure and undefiled, she lay before the eye as a transient vision—the unpeopled city of the brain; or as a light of heaven flashes through the dying mind, ere the spirit leaves the clay to there abide,''[9] he exclaims, looking down upon Jerusalem in the snow. Precociously self-assured in his assessments of people and places (listening to Arab music, he suggested that the singing sounded like grunts ''emitted by some beasts''),[10] Jarvis still suffered the pangs of adolescence, and some of his effusions—thinly disguised as learned commentary—reveal his not-so-scholarly preoccupations and frustrations. ''The wind generally produces indescribable effects upon the poor half-clad women,'' he muses in Egypt, ''among the young disclosing forms of matchless symmetry, while in the aged exposing only hideous deformity'';[11] a visit to a monastery elicits a heartfelt ''Woman, with all her beauty, with all the happiness she imparts to man, brings a corresponding and a greater amount of trouble with it,''[12] and toward the end of his journey, he jealously observes ''that a couple of engagements had sprung up between some young spinsters and bachelors of our party, and we could not go in any direction to rest in perfect solitude, without seeing these unfortunate people sitting very close together out on the crags.''[13] Jarvis's juvenile misery was often exacerbated by homesickness; he anxiously awaited the mails from Toronto, attached himself to Canadian tourists or benevolent elderly travellers wherever he could find them, and habitually drew parallels, some of them very startling indeed, between his homeland and the exotic lands he was visiting: entering the Grand Mosque in Cairo and "tying on the huge slippers," he was "reminded . . . of the Canadian snow-shoeing parties, often enjoyed at that very time of the year."[14]

Despite Jarvis's continual search for suitable companionship, he travelled mostly on his own; in a bourgeois reinterpretation of the *grand tour*, his father may have expected his son to gain independence, robustness, and prudence in financial matters, a utilitarian outlook shared by Costin's *Le Guide du Voyageur de Montréal à Paris via Liverpool et Londres* (1899), which had equally useful advice to offer to aspiring professionals: "Le voyage devient de plus en plus une partie essentielle d'une éducation libérale, c'est une nécessité de notre époque. Pour celui qui pense et étudie, cela lui ouvre un champ plus vaste à ses investigations, toujours nouvelles, et pleines d'intérêts." Once successful, a businessman might reward himself with a journey to replenish his health: "pour celui qui est dans le commerce, dans une profession ou une industrie, cela lui fait un changement salutaire à sa santé."[15]

Jarvis's letters gave his parents little cause for alarm. In contrast, William Henry Parker, who was to become a lumber merchant at Hunterstown, Quebec, may well have made his father wish he had never let his son out of his sight. Travelling through Italy in 1855, young Parker gleefully reported that he had chosen a route "much infested by bandits," whom he intended to fight with "colts [and] revolvers" should they become "bould" [sic], and that he intended to deal similarly with any offensive Arabs during the later stages of his tour.[16] Nor did young Parker convince his family that he was deriving much educational benefit from his journeys when he had little else to say about Jerusalem than "[it] is the most outrageously funny city I ever dreamt of in an ugly dream."

Other parents wisely anticipated such problems and preferred to supervise their children's education at all times. Egerton Ryerson, then chief superintendent for education, Canada West, tutored his son Charles, barrister-to-be, on his *grand tour* in 1866, attending theatre, opera, and oratorio performances in London and Paris with him and visiting the galleries of the Vatican. Plans to travel on to Florence, Bologna, Venice, Trieste, Vienna, Prague, and Berlin were made, but apparently not executed. Ryerson was an anxious parent, concerned that "Charley" should benefit from his journey and become a responsible, god-fearing citizen. Whereas the tutors of eighteenth-century aristocrats often complained about their charges' incorrigible laziness, Ryerson and his son duplicated the educational regime of the Ruskin family: they studied the plays of Racine and Molière in the original before going to the performance, attended church services and public speeches held in French, and employed a language tutor for an hour every day during their three-month stay in Paris. During his many previous journeys to Europe, Ryerson had formed numerous illustrious and useful connections; Charley was introduced to all of these and urged to imitate the more industrious and successful among them. Although a dedicated Methodist, Ryerson had widened his circle of acquaintances on his travels to include some surprisingly unorthodox individuals. During a stay in Rome in 1856, Ryerson had fallen ill and was faithfully visited by Augustin Theiner, a church historian, who was also keeper of the Archives of the Vatican and Librarian to the Pope, but who eventually lost his offices because of his controversial views on the dogma of Papal Infallibility. Charley was introduced to Theiner, watching with horror how the old man, a neglected and smelly eccentric, warmly greeted his father by kissing him on both cheeks. Ryerson's determination to give his children both a strictly Protestant and a cosmopolitan upbringing occasionally incited the wrath of his fellow-Methodists, who objected to his daughter's dancing and music lessons as worldly and corrupting. Ryerson (who also had choice wines shipped from Europe) may well have himself perceived such ambiguities in his approach; a passionate educator, he agonized over the proper instruction for his children, wondering sometimes if worldly knowledge would not spoil their faith. Thus he wearily discusses Charley's progress with his "dearest Sophie," his favourite daughter, in a letter from Paris:

> I am determined not to spend money to make an *idle* & free living gentleman of him. He certainly likes to spend money, as well as to make objections to what I propose to do. Yet he has many amiable qualities, & I am here living & travelling for him, & him alone, as I would not have undertaken this journey, nor would I now go one foot to Italy, were it not for him. At my age I feel that sightseeing, & especially going to countries & places that I have seen before, is lost time to me, & beyond what I ought to do. If I am successful with Charley I shall be amply rewarded; but if it makes him more captious & vain, & less industrious, it will cast a dark shadow over my last days.[17]

Ryerson took pains to educate Sophie as well as his son, but naturally young women from Canada's high society were even more protected on their travels than Charley had been. Completely sheltered from any responsibilities, the pretty Ethel Davies, daughter of Sir Louis Davies, chief justice of the Supreme Court of Canada and premier of Prince Edward Island, toured Europe with her family in 1899-1900, observing the "natives" at arm's length, but enthusiastically commenting on the events of the Boer War and decorating her diary with patriotic mementoes such as scraps of clothing worn on days of British victories.[18] The daughters of Robert Bell, eminent geologist and sometime acting director of the Geological Survey of Canada, attended a finishing school in Karlsruhe, Germany in the 1890s, from where they made numerous excursions into the famous cities and spas of Europe. Under the guidance of one Fräulein Nödel, the Bell sisters were introduced to the mysteries of German idioms, grammar, composition, and conversation, but they also received instruction in chemistry, physics, history, and sports, besides being thoroughly prepared for their role as débutantes in London and Ottawa with lessons in music, drawing, and deportment. The day was planned from nine in the morning till eight at night, with breaks for meals and walks, but all the activities still seem to have left time enough for Margaret Bell to read the occasional trashy novel by Eugenie Marlitt, a nineteenth-century German bestselling author, and to attend performances of Wagner operas. Robert Bell's daughters, extremely well-connected teenagers who sent greetings to Wilfrid Laurier and Annie and Achille Fréchette through their father, were as anxious as Fräulein Nödel to keep the Karlsruhe school an enclave for the élite. In a letter of 6 May 1897, Margaret reports that the granddaughter of the chancellor of Edinburgh University has been admitted, whereas another girl has been refused entry because Nödel deems her socially undesirable. The letters contain numerous schoolgirlish descriptions of outings in and around Karlsruhe; in Bell's view, shaped by class and age, Germany remained a romantic country with quaint villages and princesses—albeit eccentric, "emancipated" ones as Margaret points out to her father—stationed at every street-corner. Their own imperial connections were duly honoured on the day of Queen Victoria's Diamond Jubilee with a personal note of congratulations from Baden-Württemberg's Grand-Duchess.[19]

Thomas Stinson Jarvis, William Henry Parker, Charles Ryerson, Ethel Davies, and the Bell sisters went to Europe to acquire a cultural and social polish they felt was not yet available at home; equally nervous about Canadian resources were travellers who journeyed to consult European physicians. John Ashworth brought his wife Julia in 1862 to have her examined by three different specialists in Britain for what appears to have been an ovarian tumor. Obsessed with the womb and its disorders, nineteenth-century American gynecologists prescribed local treatments ranging from leeching and injections to cauterization, with almost any

kind of concoction— including water, milk and water, linseed tea,
"decoction of marshmallow . . . tepid or cold"[20]—used for medication.
John Ashworth duly jotted down the cures suggested for his wife's
disorder, but they do not provide convincing evidence that British
gynecology was necessarily farther advanced than North American: Dr.
Simpson diagnosed "an ovarian tumor," Dr. Bird an "inflammation of
the cellular fibre," and Dr. Clay of 101 Piccadilly, Manchester, stated
categorically "that there is not the slightest sign of ovarian, but that it is
inflammation of cellular coating of the womb." Dr. Bird prescribed
injections of iodine and worked out a diet plan for the ailing Mrs.
Ashworth: she was to be allowed beer, port wine, beef and mutton, but
urged to avoid fresh bread at all cost.[21]

Both men and women arrived in Europe seeking remedies for
tuberculosis, a disease assuming almost epidemic proportions, particularly
in Quebec. In 1850 James Douglas, a physician from Quebec City and
first superintendent of the Beauport Lunatic Asylum, prescribed winters
in Italy for himself when he acquired "a troublesome cough which he
could not shake off."[22] The teacher Urgel-Eugène Archambault had his
Canadian surgeons' diagnosis of tuberculosis confirmed in 1883, spending
long wistful months in the hot climates of the south of France, Italy, and
North Africa.[23] W. C. Caldwell, a wealthy businessman from Lanark,
Ontario, and owner of flour-milling, textile-manufacturing, lumbering
and mining enterprises, consulted physicians in Edinburgh and London
for severe chest pain in 1874, his reviews of famous London preachers—so
common in English-Canadian travel-books of the time—assuming a rather
more lugubrious tone than usual under the circumstances.[24]

Very occasionally, even a less affluent patient could afford to consult a
famous European specialist. The painter Robert Harris, afflicted with
poor eyesight, had been diagnosed as suffering from a "congestion of the
optic nerve" by his Charlottetown physician, Dr. Dodge, who prescribed
leeching and a pair of spectacles. Once in London for his studies, Harris
consulted a Dr. Boroman, famous "oculist," but he panicked at the
sumptuous furnishings of his practice: "I felt rather afraid of his charges
which of course I expected would be very high . . . you go through the
hands of a footman, a sort of half secretary, and an assistant oculist who
sends a report, and then the doctor himself." But Harris need not have
worried: after telling the young painter that he was very "long-sighted,"
Dr. Boroman refused to take any fee, "which rather took [Harris's]
topsails back."[25]

Travellers on their *grand tour* or on their way to medical specialists were
occasionally motivated by their lack of trust in the quality of Canada's own
resources. But prominent Canadian institutions were also sending their

members abroad to be trained, with public funds, to contribute to Canadian self-sufficiency, even excellence in medicine, education, urban planning, art, architecture, and other important areas. The Séminaire de Québec regularly sent prospective instructors to be trained at appropriate institutions; thus, the organ of the seminary, the *Abeille du Petit Séminaire de Québec*, announced on 5 June 1879, "Départs pour l'Europe," adding that "Depuis la fondation de l'Université Laval, le Séminaire de Québec a envoyé se former en Europe la plupart des professeurs qui occupent actuellement les chairs des facultés de théologie, de droit, de médecine et des arts. Paris, Louvain, Londres sont les principaux centres où l'on est allé étudier les diverses sciences qui s'enseignent maintenant à l'Université."[26] Jean-Jacques Lefebvre has compiled a selective list of Canadian students at foreign universities between 1760-1850 (that is to say, just prior to the period considered here), including Jacques Labrie, founder of the *Courrier du Canada*, who completed a medical degree in Edinburgh in 1807-08; François-Olivier Doucet, who studied medicine in Paris before practising in Chambly; Kingston, Ontario; New York; France; and Vera Cruz, Mexico; Guillaume-Henri D'Eschambault, who obtained his doctorate in law at Louvain; and a number of other pioneers of medicine and law in Canada.[27] Lefebvre's list contains forty-three entries, but there is evidence from notices placed in contemporary newspapers and other sources that dozens, perhaps hundreds, of professional Canadians completed their higher education abroad.

Educators in charge of designing educational programmes at home travelled through Europe in search of inspiration, models, and teaching aids. Thomas-Etienne Hamel, who, after completing a degree in mathematics in Paris, was to become one of Laval's most eminent professors of science, as well as its rector in 1871-80 and 1883-86, shopped for bunsen burners, prisms, barometers, and microscopes during a visit to London and Paris in 1854-55.[28] The newly acquired scientific equipment might be demonstrated in a lecture given by the charismatic Joseph-Clovis-K. Laflamme, also professor of science and rector (in 1893-99 and 1908-09) at Laval and a much sought-after public speaker; on 17 September 1896, the diarist of the Séminaire de Québec noted: "Mgr. Laflamme a fait quelques expériences avec les rayons X devant un certain nombre d'anglais, protestants, médecins, et autres. Ils ont eu l'air fort intéréssé."[29] Collections of mineralogical, geological, botanical, and zoological specimens had to be assembled to instruct students in taxonomy. Hamel admired the Crystal Palace's geological garden in Sydenham and investigated the classification systems at a museum of zoology and botany in Dijon, jotting down measurements and sketches for future use at the seminary. Ovide Brunet, priest and botanist, travelled to Europe in 1861 for a year-long study of botanical centres in London, Paris, Florence, Bonn, Hamburg, Amsterdam, Leyden, Rotterdam, Nantes, and Angers before establishing a botanical museum at Laval containing more than ten thousand different plants.[30] Laval's instructors found additional inspiration for the scientific research and teaching at international conferences. J.-C.-K. Laflamme attended conferences in France, Germany, Romania, Russia, and elsewhere, angrily reporting to his colleagues at home that serious work was obstructed by delegates who had come for a cheap holiday, not serious work.

Concerned not only with the proper upbringing of his own children, but also with the education of the entire nation, Egerton Ryerson was one of the most active explorers of the European educational system. On his first educational tour in Europe in 1844-46, Ryerson pursued a formidable itinerary inspecting schools in Belgium, France, Italy, Bavaria, Austria, the German States, and Switzerland, noting down their teaching and disciplinary methods. In Paris, where he studied French and attended a variety of lectures just as he was to urge his son Charley to do twenty years later, he investigated "several schools of the Protestant dissenters in Paris," and the entry typifies the kinds of items of which Ryerson took particular note: the architectural design of the school, its spiritual régime, and the political aspects of denominational teaching (a matter close to Ryerson's heart since his famous polemic with Bishop Strachan over the privileges of the Anglican Church in Upper Canada). He writes: "The first was the Female Normal School, containing nineteen pupils. I was impressed with the admirable arrangement of the school and its appliances, as well as the taste and neatness of the botanical garden. The dormitory was plain, neat, and airy; in it on the wall were pasted the following passages of Scripture, viz., Psalms xv.9, Amos iv.12. There were two schools for boys and girls attached to the institution, but these several departments constitute one school—all Roman-Catholic children taught by Protestants, on strictly Protestant principles. The priests make no opposition. People independent of the priests."[31] From 1851 on, Ryerson took advantage of world expositions in Europe to acquire display objects for his Educational Museum, in which the country's natural history and its mechanical and agricultural improvements as well as specimens of its burgeoning art production were to be exhibited. At the 1855 exposition in Paris, using his talent for making and maintaining useful connections, Ryerson obtained an introduction to the officers of the British Royal Geographical Society, who promised him "a splendid collection of several hundred Maps and Charts."[32] He also purchased, from the Austrian exhibit, several hundred prints "of Objects of Natural History, especially Botany,—prepared by a new process, which will make them look better than the plants themselves for teaching purposes,"[33] and "a series of Plates in relief, (extremely cheap), for teaching the Blind."[34] Ryerson coveted globes from the Prussian exhibit, acquired seeds and grains from all of the countries represented at the exposition, and ordered special thermometers, "as those made and used in London and Paris do not range low enough for the Winter climate of Canada."[35] Furthermore, Ryerson returned from his 1855 tour (which included visits to London, Paris, Brussels, Antwerp, Florence, and Rome) with two hundred paintings and close to one thousand plaster casts of famous antique statuary packed away in crates, artwork which he and his daughter Sophia—conscientiously following the guidelines laid out by Franz Theodor Kügler's *Handbook of Painting* (1842), a generally acclaimed work of reference—had carefully selected from renowned copyists all over Europe, among them Antoine-Sébastien Falardeau, a native of Quebec who had settled in Florence and married the pope's niece. Of particular note among the plaster casts were the many portrait busts of ancient philosophers and politicians. Other statuary, according to a letter from Munich of 1 January 1856, included portrait busts and statuettes of "twelve of the celebrated German Emperors, and some thirty of the most distinguished German and Italian Artists."[36] In an age which interpreted history through the biographies of eminent men and women, portrait busts were considered important educational material, especially with the new "science" of phrenology seeking to determine a person's mental and emotional gifts from the formation of his skull. In order to reap maximum educational benefit, paintings were to be arranged in a kind of nineteenth-century version of the Great Chain of Being, with those "of a Scriptural character" ranking highest, followed by "important events of History and celebrated Characters," "*genre*-paintings," including land- and seascapes, paintings of animals, and "Fruits and Flowers, in undecaying beauty and brilliancy, the latter sometimes animated with examples of Insect Life."[37] From the establishment of such a collection, Ryerson expected to reap larger social benefits: not only would the statues and paintings provide useful and pleasing instruction to the populace, but also their impact would—he hoped—even improve the working-classes: "in places where such Museums of Art exist and are accessible to the public . . . I have observed an order and propriety of conduct in the labouring classes, a gentleness and cheerfulness of manners that I have not observed among the same classes elsewhere."[38] In a sense, Ryerson's collection was meant to educate English Canadians as the Desjardins collection had inspired the population of Quebec. In 1816 and 1821 two French priests, Philippe-Jean-Louis and Louis-Joseph Desjardins, acquired more than one hundred and twenty paintings removed from French churches during the Revolution or

from the Louvre to make room for paintings requisitioned during
Napoleon I's Italian campaign. The Desjardins collection formed the basis
of the first Canadian public art gallery, opened in 1838 on Quebec's Rue
de Buade by the painter Joseph Légaré and an associate. Closed in 1855,
the collection was later acquired by Laval, although several fires destroyed
valuable parts of it. Since nineteenth-century painters like Légaré and
Antoine Plamondon learnt their profession by restoring and copying these
paintings, the traditions of the art of seventeenth- and eighteenth-century
France continued in nineteenth-century Canada. Like the Desjardins
paintings, Ryerson's collection confirmed a colonial tendency toward
imitation and traditionalism, but because Ryerson's journeys and pur-
chases had been financed from public funds (a procedure eventually
leading to an investigation of Ryerson's spending), it also set an important
precedent for the official support of the arts in Canada.

Eager to forge a national art, Canadian painters and sculptors travelled

F.   ''Paris 1888'' from the George Reid
Scrapbook.

abroad to gain technical proficiency and exposure to both traditional and innovative art forms. Lists of Canadian artists copying famous works in the Louvre survive in its archives as do catalogues containing the names of Canadian artists exhibiting their work in the "salon officiel de Paris." Of the eighty-five Canadian artists studying in Paris between 1800 and 1905,[39] most arrived after the 1878 Centennial Exhibition in Philadelphia, where France had made an especially strong showing. Writing in *The Week* in 1891-92, the novelist Gilbert Parker noted that there were approximately twenty-five Canadian art students studying in Paris at the time. Impressed with the monumental figure painting of the Academic masters, the religious mural decorations of Puvis de Chavannes and Hippolyte Flandrin, and the work of the Barbizon painters, artists like Wyatt Eaton, William Brymner, Robert Harris, Paul Peel, Blair Bruce, Charles Huot, Ludger Larose, Joseph Saint-Charles, Ozias Leduc, Marc-Aurèle de Foy, Suzor-Côté, and such women artists as Mary Bell, Florence Carlyle (grand-niece of Thomas Carlyle), Mary Ella Dignam, and Harriett Ford studied at Colarossi's or Julian's, the latter so popular with Canadian artists that Sara Jeannette Duncan used it as a setting in her novel *A Daughter of Today* (1894). Among the attractions of Julian's were its famous visiting professors (Bouguereau, Boulanger, Laurens, Lefebvre, Robert Fleury, Constant and others), flexible hours, and low tuition fee. Founded in 1868 by a prize-fighter who knew nothing about art, Julian's eventually encompassed ten different studios in Paris, three exclusively for women, whose male models were required to pose in bathing trunks. More than a hundred students often crowded around the models, the heat was stifling, the noise deafening, and practical jokes the rule: an enraged James Wilson Morrice left Julian's when a French student smashed a *baguette* over his head. Most Canadian artists travelled to Paris using their own resources, but sometimes study in Paris, like Etienne Hamel's and J.-C.-K. Laflamme's educational tours, were conducted with official patronage: Ludger Larose, J.-C. Franchère, Charles Gill, Henri Beau, and Joseph Saint-Charles, all students of the Abbé Chabert at the Ecole des Arts et Manufactures in Montreal, were funded by clerical authorities to study religious mural art in Paris in preparation of the decoration of Sacré-Coeur Chapel (1892-94) in Montreal's Notre-Dame.

The presence of Canadian artists in Europe gave rise to a Jamesian theme of North American innocence exposed to the wiles of wicked Europe in fiction and art criticism. The Halifax novelist Alice Jones—herself an artist— set her novel *Gabriel Praed's Castle* (1904) in the painters' and antiquarians' milieu of Paris, and Gilbert Parker felt that Canadians, regardless of the overwhelming presence of European tradition all around them, see "things with no intervening mist of conventionality . . . ;

[Canadians are] bade to be independent and free from [their] youth up, in the ordinary colour of life when every day's work is nation-making."[40] Ironically, even works expressive of Canada's harsh and rugged environment were occasionally created, composite-fashion, in foreign studios. Ernest Thompson Seton painted one of his most famous canvasses, the haunting "The Triumph of the Wolves," using a dog carcass, a skull and bones, a bucket of blood from a Paris slaughter-house, and borrowed peasant clothes, with the woods of St. Cloud as a backdrop. Getting rid of the cadaver after the painting was completed proved even more difficult than acquiring all of the paraphernalia: Seton was pursued all over the city by a suspicious policeman observing his repeated attempts to throw a large bundle into the Seine. Amusingly, "The Triumph of the Wolves" became a *cause célèbre* on the occasion of the Chicago World Fair because its realism seemed too gruesome to the organizing committee to promote Canada to the world.[41]

Few records appear to have survived of Canadian artists' impressions of Europe (one of the most prolific painters of European scenes, James Wilson Morrice, has left no written record of his extensive travels), but among them are W. L. Forster's autobiography *Under the Studio Light* (1928), Robert Harris's *Some Pages from an Artist's Life* (1910), William Blair Bruce's letters, and Joseph St. Charles's correspondence. Particularly rich and revelatory of the mutual fertilization of European tradition and Canadian national fervour is the work of Napoléon Bourassa, one of the founders of the Royal Canadian Academy. A painter and sculptor, Bourassa also distinguished himself as a journalist (he was a co-founder of the *Revue canadienne*), novelist, and one of Canada's first art theoreticians. During his European studies in 1852-55, Bourassa explored, in Paris, the work of Hippolyte Flandrin, a pupil of Ingres and a religious painter, who had decorated the ancient church of St.-Germain-des-Près in Paris with murals acclaimed for their simple religiosity. In Rome, Bourassa reputedly met, and was influenced by, Johann-Friedrich Overbeck, the founder of the Nazarene Brotherhood. From Flandrin and the Nazarenes, Bourassa received important inspirations for his fresco work in Quebec churches and cathedrals, work designed to make art an organic component of public and sacred buildings once more, rather than leaving it as a preserve of the wealthy or embalming it in galleries. Bourassa wrote extensively about his travels, publishing essays on "Naples et ses environs" and "Le Carnaval à Rome," reporting to the Royal Society of Canada, and communicating with his family in letters later published in *Lettres d'un artiste canadien* (1920). As in his paintings, which prefer pastels to colourful oils, flatness to sensuous plasticity, and symbolic content to realism, an ascetic mind speaks through Bourassa's writing. He is, for instance, scandalized at the abandoned excess of carnival in Rome. He would rather follow a funeral, he claims, because he understands "plus que jamais la sagesse de L'Eglise, qui, aussitôt après ces jours de gloire, appelle tous ses enfants pour leur répéter que les jouissances des sens s'en vont en poussière."[42]

Bourassa was impressed with both the Nazarenes' style of painting and their ideal of communal art, a concept realized on a more worldly level when Ludwig I of Bavaria invited some of them to embellish his capital, Munich. This communal appeal of mural painting also fascinated George Reid, a painter who travelled widely and repeatedly in Europe. In Paris, he saw the new Hôtel de Ville, where not only famous painters like Puvis de Chavannes, Jean-Paul Laurens, and Constant, but also younger artists had been allotted panels, just as sixty sculptors and painters from across America had been involved in the decoration of Washington's Library of Congress. It took, however, many years to persuade the Toronto City Council to permit a similar scheme for the Toronto City Hall; Reid only succeeded when he offered to complete two murals depicting scenes from pioneer life, free of charge, by himself in 1897.

If Canada's painters and sculptors considered London, Paris, Rome, Venice, and Florence the Meccas of their art, then book-lovers and aspiring authors—their itineraries often maps of Canadian literary taste—found theirs in the regions and cities associated with their favourite authors. Few travellers to Scotland forgot Walter Scott, the "Wizard of the North," a writer much beloved by Canadians both English and French.[43] On his pilgrimage to Scott's famous residence, Abbotsford, Andrew Learmont Spedon, born in Edinburgh, proudly announced that his father had been one of the stonemasons employed in building it. James Elgin Wetherell, principal of the Collegiate Institute of Strathroy, Ontario, undertook a literary journey to Britain in 1892, after having edited high-school texts of Walter Scott, Tennyson, Longfellow, and Wordsworth, and he described his itinerary through the "Land of Burns," Walter Scott country, Stratford-upon-Avon, and "Tennyson Land" in *Over the Sea: A Summer Trip to England*. Few lovers of literature were, however, as fortunate as the poet Louis Fréchette, who, after corresponding with Victor Hugo during his exile on Guernsey, was finally admitted to the home of his literary idol in 1880, an historical experience Fréchette celebrated in a speech to the Royal Society of Canada: "A l'époque ou j'eus l'honneur d'être reçu chez lui, il emplissait le monde de sa renommée. Il était entré en France en triomphateur, après vingt années d'exil qui avait entouré son front de l'auréole des martyrs et des prophètes. Et il vieillissait dans l'austérité d'un travail persistant et plus fécond que jamais, caressé par ses petits-enfants, idolâtré par son grand Paris,

acclamé par la France, salué par l'Univers entier.''[44] Hugo welcomed
Fréchette as a child of France's old colony, lost owing to "les folies de Louis
XV," and seemed surprised at the large number of Frenchmen populating
America. A journey to America had always been his dream, he said, but
sensing that death was near, he preferred to concentrate his energies on
completing his literary opus. When Hugo's body lay in state beneath the
Arc de Triomphe four years later, two other Canadian travellers, the Abbé
J.-B. Proulx and the Curé Labelle, used the occasion to express their
displeasure with Hugo's liberal politics and anti-clericalism, by ostentatiously
visiting in the Montparnasse cemetery the humble grave of Louis Veuillot,
ultramontanist editor of *L'Univers*, a man revered, even sanctified, by
Quebec conservatives.

Probably the only French-Canadian ever to meet Hugo in person,
Fréchette experienced his meeting with him not only as a personal
privilege, but also as a proxy for his fellow countrymen, at least those with
a similar passion for Hugo's work. Journalists covering special events in
Europe assumed a comparable role; generally not members of a privileged
social class, they were delegated to observe and interpret events for their
readers, according to their paper's policies: as photography was not yet
widely used in newspapers and periodicals, demands on a journalist's
evocative powers could be considerable. Whereas Fred C. Martin's and the
Abbé Gingras's notes were only accessible to an intimate circle and books
of travel were generally too expensive to be bought by many, journalists
and editors like Goldwin Smith, Andrew Learmont Spedon, Alice Jones,
Sara Jeannette Duncan, Honoré Beaugrand, Jules-Paul Tardivel, Arthur
Buies, Faucher de St.-Maurice, and others reached large readerships with
their serialized travel reports. Especially successful ones were also issued as
books, like Tardivel's *Notes de voyage*, based on letters to *La Vérité*, or
Goldwin Smith's contributions to *The Week*, later gathered in *A Trip to
England*.

Walter Harte, an American journalist writing in the *New England
Magazine* in 1891, found that journalism had not yet become a respectable
profession in Canada because newsgathering continued to be associated
with "bohemianism" and because few papers required their contributors
to sign their work.[45] Yet there were pioneers whose inspired, sometimes
daring, work legitimized, even glamourized, journalism, among them a
remarkable number of women: Kathleen Coleman, also known as "Kit,"
of the *Mail and Empire* travelled to Europe to cover the Queen's Diamond
Jubilee in 1897; Agnes Scott of the *Free Press*, who called herself
"Amaryllis," reported from the 1900 World Exposition in Paris; Grace E.
Denison, the "Lady Gay" of *Saturday Night*, explored hospitals and
slums in Europe's cities. It was still considered proper for women

journalists to write under fanciful pseudonyms—and Sandra Gwyn's remarkable sleuthing work on "Amaryllis" proves just how successfully anonymous a writer could be—but some, like "Kit," also became extremely well known as individuals. Together with a few other outstanding professional women, Coleman was even given a biographical entry, with photograph, in Henry Morgan's *Types of Canadian Women* (1903), a biographical dictionary mostly featuring society women displaying their prettiest ballgowns.

Journalists were funded in their travels by their papers and their subscribers; clergymen and priests, too, were occasionally dispatched to Europe by their congregations to restore their health and replenish their spirituality. Preachers could benefit for years to come from a rich store of illustrative material gathered during a pilgrimage to the Holy Land or elsewhere. In an age when sermons were considered part of public entertainment, with editors like Edmund E. Sheppard of Toronto's *Saturday Night* carefully reviewing Sunday sermons for style and delivery, parishioners had a vested interest in keeping their clergymen up-to-date. Thus, the congregation of St. James Street Methodist Church, Montreal, offered an overseas ticket to Hugh Johnston, who regularly sent letters home to the *Christian Guardian* during his journey, before publishing *Toward the Sunrise: Being Sketches of Travel in Europe and the East* in 1881, a book successful enough to go through at least three editions. Even years later, Johnston's sermons benefited from his travel experiences: when, in 1886, for example, he inveighed against the dangers of liquor, card-playing, dancing, and theatregoing, he juxtaposed "the suffering son of God hanging in helpless agony upon the Tree; His arms extended wide, and at the centre of each open palm a huge iron nail forced through the quivering flesh and lacerated veins" with the "grand hotels and lovely gardens,"[46] the orange blossoms and dancing orchestras of Monaco's gambling paradise to shame his audience into abstinence. While Johnston returned from his journey more energetic than ever, his famous travelling companion, the Reverend William Morley Punshon, a widely acclaimed Wesleyan preacher, failed to regain his health and died *en route*. Johnstone's book was undoubtedly made even more attractive because it also contained a fervent eulogy for his fellow Methodist.

In even greater numbers than their Protestant colleagues, French-Canadian priests undertook pilgrimages, either to the holy shrines of Europe or to Palestine, subsequently publishing works like *De Québec à Jérusalem: journal d'un pèlerinage canadien en Terre-Sainte en passant à travers l'Angleterre, la France, l'Egypte, la Judée, la Samarie, la Galilée, la Syrie, et l'Italie*, as did the redoubtable Abbé Léon Provancher in 1884. Pilgrimage became military expedition when seven contingents of

French-Canadian papal *zouaves* were dispatched to Rome to assist Pope Pius IX in 1868 in his defence against Giuseppe Garibaldi and his red-shirts. Enthusiastically acclaimed by the conservative French-Canadian press, the *zouaves* often wrote letters and journals containing radically selective descriptions of Rome as a sacred city; letters not pursuing that image were apparently censored or even confiscated. The *zouaves* perceived themselves as crusaders, dedicated not only to preserving the *status quo* in the Vatican, but also to gaining Europeans' respect for the Christian idealism surviving on the shores of the St. Lawrence. Such propaganda filtered into efforts to attract future emigrants to Canada. The Curé Labelle addressed the ''Congrès catholique'' in Paris in 1885, assuring his audience that the British conqueror had not succeeded in imposing his ideal of commercial and industrial education on French-Canadians who continued to adhere to ''la noble . . . la vigoureuse . . . la chrétienne et catholique éducation française''[47] and that, un-afflicted by gallicanism, Canada offered a sanctuary to Frenchmen desiring to return to a pre-revolutionary society.

French-Canadian nuns had diligently prepared the uniforms and banners for the papal *zouaves*, and the press commended the soldiers' mothers for their patience and sacrifice. As it had been during the Crusades of old, a woman's place was at home, and even during ordinary—not military—travel, female tourists still posed special problems.

5

Women Travellers

1. GERTRUDE FLEMING'S HONEYMOON

The *Parisian*'s passenger list for its sailing at the end of May 1881 includes besides the name of Fred C. Martin also that of Mrs. Martin. This listing and the pronoun "we" in Martin's diary are, however, the only indications of her presence. In most Victorian-Canadian travelogues, women lead a shadowy existence; their husbands planned the itineraries and formulated the impressions. Adolphe-Basile Routhier, accompanied on most of his travels by his wife Marie Clorinde, let his female readers know what *he* thought of equality when a performance of Molière's *Les Précieuses* in Paris reminded him of the contemporary "fléau féminin," the blue-stocking: "Suivant la comparaison d'un spirituel écrivain, un petit cercle est semblable à un grand cercle, mais ils ne sont pas égaux"; and, he added patronizingly, "je me garderai bien de vous dire, lectrices, lequel des deux sexes est le grand cercle."[1] The reader of John Ashworth's diary only gradually realizes the presence of a wife as the details of her gynecological disorders occur among equally pithy observations on the rams and sheep he intended to buy for his household. Women travelling on their own, especially spinsters, often attracted ridicule. Thomas Stinson Jarvis encountered the proverbial old maid on the boat to Palestine: "Two very thin, unmarried and aged sisters also adorn the decks. They wear long brown cloaks to their ankles, of which too much are generally seen; they have such a bird-like appearance that I am doubtful from what ornithological museum they have escaped. Rather a hard look out for the boys, is it not?"[2]

Ladies were a liability to their male companions, considered too frail to tolerate rough company and dubious accommodation. *Murray's Handbook for Travellers in Northern Italy* of 1877 urged that "only . . . a single male traveller" ought to travel in a *vetturino* because "his companions are frequently disagreeable; and none of the regulations which prevent annoyance in a diligence apply to these private vehicles."[3] Travelling with ladies was more expensive, for "if any ladies are of the party, no house except a first-rate one should be used; but bachelor travellers may frequently be comfortably accommodated, and at a lower charge, at houses of a second grade."[4] Women, then, seemed a cumbersome and luxurious piece of luggage labelled "handle with care"; if due caution was not applied, she might—in an age of tight corseting and heavy clothing—retaliate with fits of fainting or "neurasthenia." A mysterious nervous disorder, "neurasthenia" especially afflicted middle-class English and North American women of the mid- and late Victorian Age, one of the best-documented cases being that of Alice James, sister of Henry and William.[5] Forced to live out an ideal of sexual romanticism, the affluent woman assumed the role of a beautiful, delicate child incapable of any serious thought or occupation; the pressures of self-control and the boredom of idleness found their vent, as Barbara Ehrenreich and Deirdre

FASHIONS

G.   "Travel Fashions," *Canadian Illustrated News.*

English have argued in *For Her Own Good: 150 Years of Experts' Advice to Women* (1978), in psychosomatic illness usually manifested in "headache, muscular aches, weakness, depression, menstrual difficulties, indigestion . . . and usually a general debility requiring constant rest."[6] Ironically, a woman's invalidism confirmed her role as a romantic heroine; thus, Susan Sontag has demonstrated the morbid attraction which nineteenth-century literature perceived in terminal tuberculosis, especially in women and children.[7]

If the pressures of everyday middle-class life often produced depressed and languoruous women and overprotective husbands and brothers, then the exigencies must have been even greater on a journey, when immaculate appearances and an even temper could be difficult to maintain. On an extended honeymoon trip, a young bride—required to perform instantly and to perfection as an adoring wife, decorative hostess and eagerly listening companion—might well feel overtaxed; likewise, a new husband could be overwhelmed by his sudden tasks as paternal protector, lover, and cultural instructor in constantly changing settings.

Gertrude Fleming née Mackintosh, Sir Sandford Fleming's daughter-in-law, wrote a diary chronicling such a honeymoon. Obviously the daughter of loving and generous parents, Gertrude introduces herself as a high-society bride, accustomed to flirtatious but decorous attention from the men in her company, to painstaking observance of social etiquette, and to a constant supply of fashionable clothing, jewellery, and entertainment. In the beginning of her wedding journey with Sandford, jr., known to his family as "Bob," life seems to be a continuation of her life as an Ottawa débutante, with dashing young men courting her and showering her with bouquets wherever she goes, well protected by her husband of a few days, who appears to have observed his young wife's social success with considerable satisfaction. All through their journey, Gertrude is most at ease with men who either worship her politely or treat her, paternally, as if she were a helpless child, reinforcing the attention of her parents, who maintained contact with their daughter with a steady stream of letters, telegrams, and flowers. But their reassurance proves not sufficient: soon fatigue and homesickness, together with intense feelings of guilt and inadequacy, invade her bliss. More and more frequently, she refers to herself as Bob's "invalid wife," craves privacy, and—in stark contrast with their glamorously extensive itinerary—withdraws into enclosed spaces like her hotel drawing-room, her train compartment (preferably one with a lock), the shelter of curving mountains, and vine-covered village lanes. Bob does much of his sightseeing alone, while Gertrude writes letters home or cries herself to sleep.

Confessing that she likes men better than women, she only feels comfortable with Anglo-Saxon men of her own class. Others she watches keenly from her window or in the hotel lobby, commenting with telling details on their repulsive appearance, their very conspicuousness perceived almost as a physical assault. Smell especially appalls her as an offensive invasion of her privacy. Perhaps such outbursts are oblique commentaries on her own sexual initiation, which, of course, is never discussed openly. Perhaps the repulsive obtrusiveness and self-confidence she notes in European men reflects her experience of a shockingly new aspect of her well-bred husband, one for which she had not been adequately prepared. And perhaps, considering her fascination with presumably repulsive men, she is also shocked at the discovery of her own sexuality. Revealingly, she flirts with a monk on the Riviera while her husband busily investigates a church: with a celibate, she feels in control, even enjoys his "leer."[8]

Gertrude's diary, engaging, moving, sometimes delightfully amusing, best speaks for itself. Gratefully, I quote from it at length, leaving her diction and erratic punctuation intact, and only editing exceedingly repetitive passages, because repetition as such is part of the Flemings' dilemma: a journey, which was to proceed purposefully, if leisurely, instead evolves in often monotonous circles.

The year 1891 was eventful in Sandford Fleming's family: a day after Sir John Macdonald's death in June, Fleming's daughter Lily received "a kind thoughtful note from Lady Macdonald asking her not to postpone her wedding,"[9] which was duly performed shortly thereafter; in October, Fleming's ninety-year-old mother passed away; and in November he inserted a clipping in his diary announcing "an important society event in the marriage of Miss Gertrude Dickinson Mackintosh, daughter of Mr. C. H. Mackintosh, M.P. to Mr. Fleming, the eldest son of Mr. Sandford Fleming, C.M.G." Sandford, Sr., had reason to be pleased with his son's choice and promptly sketched the more impressive branches of Miss Mackintosh's family tree into his diary, among them Captain Duncan Mackintosh ("of ancient Scottish lineage and a relative of 'The Mackintosh,' chief of clan of Moy Hall, Inverness")[10] who had married a sister of the Earl of Desart before settling in Ireland, where Gertrude's grandfather, Captain William Duncan Mackintosh, was born, later an attaché of the ordance branch of the Royal Engineers of Canada. His bride was Leonora Raffles Dickinson, niece of Sir Stanford Raffles, founder of the port of Singapore, whose name survives today in one of the world's most glamorous grand hotels.

By 1891, Gertrude's father had already proven himself fully worthy of his lineage and become one of the Dominion's most versatile and energetic men. Forced to leave school when his father died, he became a literary and entrepreneurial prodigy at thirteen, "writing dime novels for a Boston publishing house and having them accepted.''[11] With his earnings he entered the study of law, a career he exchanged for journalism at the age of twenty when he began to rise rapidly in the publishing world as the editor of several important newspapers including the *Ottawa Daily Citizen*, and of *The Canadian Parliamentary Companion*. One of John A. Macdonald's favourite protégés, he was both a member of parliament and mayor of Ottawa, before being appointed Lieutenant-Governor of the North-West Territories in 1893. A fervent imperialist who, at seventeen, offered ''a book of original poems'' to the Prince of Wales on his visit to Canada, and who published a history of the Dominion since Confederation entitled *Canada's Diamond Jubilee* a year before his death in 1931, Mackintosh was as concerned about developing Canada's infrastructure as Sandford Fleming, and delved into questions of transport as president of several railroad companies, and of natural resources as managing director of a mining company in British Columbia, a post he accepted following his term as Lieutenant-Governor.

Judging from the warm affection his daughter Gertrude expresses for him and her mother, Mackintosh managed his family life with equally fervent commitment. Father of at least seven children at the time of his daughter's marriage, he still kept in close contact with her all through her wedding journey, travelling to Montreal with another daughter to receive her as she stepped off the train bringing her back to Canada.

The Mackintosh family had spared no effort to give their child a wedding day worthy of their love and their position, and the *Ottawa Daily Citizen* paid tribute to its editor-in-chief by printing a lavish account of the festivities. As carriages ''with white wedding favours on the drivers' whips''[12] crowded the streets, a large congregation filled the pews of St. Alban's, marvelling at the bright flower arrangements and pretty gowns which ''made a general effect of gay colour and animation.'' The bridal music from *Lohengrin* announced Miss Mackintosh's arrival, resplendent ''in her gown of white merveilleux satin, gracefully draped with white crepe, and trimmed with orange blossoms and pearl *passementerie*.'' Her six bridesmaids, sisters all, ''wore grey cloth gowns, relieved by pink and grey velvet and trimmed with silver *passementerie*.'' As the Rector of St. Alban's, the Reverend J. J. Bogert, began the wedding service, ''the November sun shattered a few long arrows of gold against the shining western windows of the church.'' This magic moment coincided with the exchange of the wedding vows, and soon after the couple walked down the centre aisle to the strains of the Wedding March. Over three hundred guests gathered at the Mackintosh home on Daly Street, with many Ottawa dignitaries in attendance, before the newly-weds—Gertrude smartly dressed in navy blue and gold, with a hat ''of blue velvet trimmed with gold braid and yellow osprey''—boarded the train to Montreal: "The newly married couple sail for England on the *Teutonic* on Wednesday week," concluded the *Citizen*'s social reporter with an almost audible sigh.

Gertrude Fleming and her husband of a few hours entered the dining-room of Montreal's Windsor Hotel. A guest, recognizing the couple, "dashed at us with loud congratulations, making me very miserable and self-conscious. ; . . . We both grew orientally red." Having triumphantly labelled her diary "Gertrude Fleming—Married Woman!'', the twenty-one-year-old bride still hoped that "the 'newly-married feeling' will soon wear off—I am ill at ease." Memories of the wedding in Ottawa lingered in her mind, "everyone so kind and happy. . . . Why all that rice? it was detestable." The next morning, the couple awoke to a congratulatory note from the Montreal Football Club shoved under the door, bearing the additional news that "Montreal defeated Ottawa College 17-6," "hence" Gertrude concluded, "much jubilation." Soon Bob's passion for football was to come in handy. Meanwhile, she spent her first Sunday as a married woman writing a letter to her mother; letters and telegrams from all of her family arrived the day after: "They miss me."

On their way to board a steamer to Europe in New York, the couple stopped over in Boston: "It was frightfully damp and rainy but I went out to get some flowers—violets and huge chrysanthemums. They make me *happy*." In the evening, the Flemings tried to amuse themselves at the Tremont with an American play called "The City Directory." Gertrude did not enjoy her evening: "It must have been funny as everyone roared with laughter—It bored me to distraction. . . . We left at the end of the 2nd act. Never saw such a large and enthusiastic audience and am wondering if I have no sense of humour." She was, however, not at all bored watching "a most extraordinary oldish man" and his antics in the dining room the following morning and recorded the little scene with a delightful sense of social comedy: "It was 9:30 in the morning I will have you know and when we got in he was just finishing a brandy and soda! After that he ordered a pint of . . . hock which he consumed with large quantities of biscuits and cheese! Still feeling rather low he called for a green chartreuse (it *was* green I heard him myself) after finishing that—he paused and seemed to taste. His face became purple with rage and he roared to the waiter in a passion 'What the Hell do you mean bringing me green when I ask for 'brun' chartreuse? The unfortunate waiter in a frenzy of fear dashed for the brun—I couldn't leave until I saw him drink *that*—I was thrilled to the core. When Bob tore me reluctantly away—He was tipping the waiter for the third time—I really grew quite fond of that little man in spite of his vinous tendencies. It was a glorious day. . . .'' This bit of social comedy, as well as thoughts of home and of her life as a girl, kept Gertrude happy for the remainder of the day: she bought "a little violet enamelled pin set with a tiny diamond" for a friend's or relative's birthday. Over dinner, she was introduced to a "Mr. Hacketts or Bracketts, a beautiful young Harvard man who was by way of being extra nice to me!" The beautiful young man offered to call in the morning and take the Flemings to Harvard. Gertrude mused: "I hope he won't forget."

Mr. "Hacketts or Bracketts" turned out to be a Mr. "Haskell" when he called early the next morning: "wasn't it lucky he sent up his card and I didn't have to ignominiously ask him his name after all his devotion last night! What a knockout it would have been and he so beautiful!" More beautiful young men were in store for Gertrude at Harvard, where Mr. Haskell conducted the Flemings to watch a football match "against Princeton or something": all the young men were "so polite and [had such] hand-on-their-heart-manners!" The young woman walked away bedecked with violets offered by the enraptured Mr. Haskell: "I forgot I *was married*—that's a pretty bad beginning."

Indeed, Sandford Fleming, jr., became somewhat irritated and "poo-poohed all Mr. Haskell's advances for the evenings." Still in a glow from her Harvard adventure, Gertrude enjoyed another play in the evening featuring "real live chickens, dogs, cows, geese and pigs! A horse-race—real horses—seven of them." More violets, "heaps of them," arrived from Mr. Haskell the next morning, enhancing Gertrude's childish joy over the show. But the couple were due to leave Boston that day; Gertrude, feeling "tired and not very well" prevailed upon her husband to wait till the afternoon. Exhausted, she reached New York and, after a supper of devilled kidneys and champagne, went to sleep complaining: "I haven't been sleeping well and can't get rested."

Letters from her family greeted Gertrude the next morning, with news about the days after the wedding, and she sighed: "they all miss me frightfully and won't be happy until I am safely back with them.—My *dear* ones!" A drive through Central Park cheered her up; there were carriages and horses and "nice men" to admire: "They *all* look very fit and well-groomed. Clean with glossy, straight, well-brushed hair." Instantly afterwards, she announced abruptly, as she was to do frequently from now on, "I am quite ill and wretched," before returning to New York's elegant strollers on Fifth Avenue: "the women wear lovely clothes with beautiful furs. Sable and mink seem to lead—but I also saw Chinchilla and silver fox." Most of her time, however, was now taken up writing and reading letters: "It is the only way I can get near them all!" On board ship, with a telegram and flowers from home waiting in her cabin, she mailed a last letter to her mother: "am I 'grown-up'? I am too nervous for words—afraid of being ill!''

After a seven-day crossing on board the White Line's *Teutonic*, Gertrude had reason to congratulate herself: "I am so pleased with myself and the way I have stood the voyage—*Only once!* and there was every excuse for it—rough, choppy sea with rain and sleet the first day out." Again, she enjoyed watching people, as usual preferring the men to the women: "There are some nice people on board—principally men the women are all uninteresting except one and she is only interesting because she looks quite bad. My particular friends are all men—First, as he is the best-looking, comes Mr. Lidderdale, an Englishman, he is young, *beautiful*, fairly clever and nice. Next comes a Captain Caddell. He is in the Royal Engineers and rather a dear—entertaining but ugly—another friend is a Mr. Johnson—heaven knows who or what he is—Bob knew him before somewhere—He is an Irishman and has a sort of way with him. An Englishman a Mr. Hamilton, who lies of course—but is amusing make up my 'steady' quartette." Gertrude detested change: whenever it came to leaving one hotel and a circle of acquaintances for another, she panicked. Now too, as the boat docked in Liverpool, she was loath to leave her "quartette" behind although in New York the idea of the crossing had filled her with unspeakable anxiety: "We have all sworn eternal friendship. . . . The men all gave me 'souvenirs'—dear of them."

A cable from her father awaited Gertrude at the Lancashire and Yorkshire Hotel in Liverpool; at once, she prepared to create yet another nest for herself: "The hotel is very quiet and comfortable and we have delightful rooms." The Flemings ventured forth to dine, but Gertrude shuddered in the cavernous dining-room: "badly lighted . . . . Eight or ten lonely and sad-looking people—all in evening dress—eating in solemn silence at different tables either in 'couples' or alone. The creak of the pantry-door, gentle as it was got on my nerves and sounded like the crack of doom!" Overcome by homesickness, Gertrude cried all the next day, wishing she "had never left my home or my Mother!!" But there was London to look forward to and having written letters home, she swore to "amuse myself and never, never, never be blue again."

From now on, Gertrude began to watch her moods carefully, congratulating herself for "amiable" days and feeling guilty for attacks of depression. The couple wandered through Liverpool, admiring the "lovely fruit and flowers" in the market, but judging the city itself "abominable very large, dirty and dismal—the people all looking like shopkeepers or *Canadians!*" Although Gertrude fastidiously dissociates herself from her average fellow countryman, she is nevertheless shortly thereafter identified as a Canadian, possessed of a charmingly soft voice with "a resonance."

En route to London, the Flemings tipped the conductor to keep other passengers out and to Gertrude's delight they were "*locked* in to a quaint little compartment only opening to the outside" where they picknicked on a luncheon basket delivered to their railway carriage halfway to London. A similarly cosy setting awaited Gertrude in her suite at the Metropole Hotel, featuring a "sitting room [with] a piano . . . and fresh flowers." Still, Gertrude felt tired and miserable and was persuaded only later in the evening to go out for a ride in a hansom cab.

The days in London were filled with her usual activities: window-shopping, watching people—especially handsome men, dining with numerous acquaintances from Bob's "former" life, going to the theatre (most of which bored her "to the verge of imbecility"), and showing off a new lavender and white dress with yellow touches. Sightseeing never seems to have entered Gertrude's mind, except for one visit to Westminster Abbey, where she "claimed an ancestor in Sir James Mackintosh." Repeatedly, Fleming set off to lunch or for a drive by himself because his young wife was once again busy writing letters or feeling feeble. As in Boston, she perked up over a chance meeting with an old adorer by the name of Percy stationed at Woolwich, who had "got so English that I absolutely felt gauche and rough beside him!" Another old flame suddenly appeared at The Haymarket; he, "it appears . . . never took my engagement to Bob very *seriously*!! and he is so naif!" Yet he impressed her with his man-of-the-world's air, and she remained amused and interested all evening. Flowers arrived the same evening from another admirer, Mr. Lidderdale, one of the "quartette" at the captain's table on the *Teutonic*.

Almost at once, however, Gertrude's condition deteriorated. She felt weaker and gloomier every day in the grey London drizzle, fainted during a dressmaker's fitting, and two weeks after her arrival in London, on the day of their projected departure for France, "succumbed at last to the inevitable! I am now in bed under Dr. Cheadle's care." Dr. Cheadle (a close friend of her father-in-law and renowned London physician, who had also made a name for himself as a member of Lord Milton's expedition to the North West Territories in 1862) stayed with her for several hours during the night, treating her "like a baby" and saying she "should have laid up long ago." He ordered burgundy, and Gertrude felt "quite drunk half the time." In the mirror, she saw a thin and yellow-looking person, "with green shadows around my eyes," scolding herself for being "full of self-pity." Leaving Fleming behind in the hotel, Cheadle persuaded Gertrude to go for a drive; he offered "much good advice, seemed sorry for me and was altogether dear." Although she had been longing for the sun and the French Riviera since her arrival, she now dreaded leaving London and her newly found confessor and paternal counsellor.

Armed with Dr. Cheadle's instructions, the Flemings departed for Paris with a week's delay. Gertrude settled into the cosiness of her rooms at the Grand Hôtel, leaving her husband "to his own devices" and enjoying the home-like comfort of coffee and rolls in bed. She blossomed in Paris, however, agreeing to brisk walks through the Tuileries gardens and to lengthy excursions by boat along the Seine. A hairdresser persuaded her to have "a little curl in the middle of my forehead—all the French women are wearing it and it looks too wicked!" She did not take to French men, however: "Such mincing shrugging acting popinjays. Perfect little monkeys! And they look at women with such an air of conquering hero that I long to box their little French ears—Horrid little trousers and hats and frockcoats. I hate them. They don't look real."

Fleming decided to take "his invalid wife" south to Nice as soon as possible; predictably, she enjoyed the journey on the *train-de-luxe* because it allowed her to withdraw into a private, sumptuously furnished shell, a "delightful little compartment with comfortable brass bed and quite private I had a lock on my door—delightful!" Nice welcomed them with "the bluest most heavenly sea . . . the balmy summer air all smelling of flowers and green things growing the soft *purr*—it is so gentle and evanescent—of the waves—and perfection is reached at least it seemed to me that just breathing and seeing and feeling was all life really meant—and that brains were a distinct detriment." Gertrude at once ventured forth for a walk by herself and promptly got lost. Her husband located her after some searching; then, on the drive back, "it got so dark and drear, chill and miserable as soon as the sun got safely to bed that it brought one to earth with a sickening sinking of the heart," and Gertrude once again went to bed "early being still an invalid!!"

Still, she was happier on the Riviera than anywhere else during her honeymoon journey. She often experienced a feeling of *déjà vu* among the flowers and fragrances of the Mediterranean and the fairy-tale air of its faded off-season guests, a Russian princess and a French marquis, "all very grand but very decrepit and rather shabby!" Children by the roadside showered the Flemings in their carriage with blossoms and the couple in turn "bombarded them . . . with 'coppers.' " Glamourous plans for the remainder of the journey were being made as letters arrived from an acquaintance, a military attaché in Cairo, offering to procure rooms for them at the famous Shepheard's Hotel and to serve as their guide. The Flemings' *bonne entente* is only briefly interrupted at a performance of Meyerbeer's *L'Africaine*, when a "naked" ballet and the smell of *chypre* drove Gertrude, nauseated and faint, out of the theatre.

Christmas was close and Gertrude steeled herself for days of homesickness. Instead, she walked about as if in a trance: "I know in future days I *will* only have to shut my eyes tight and be transported back again to the south with the soft smell of the eucalyptus and roses in my nostrils and the soft touch of wind in my face." The landlord ("or whatever he is called in France") woke her up on Christmas Day, carrying a tray with coffee and rolls, a large bunch of *La France* roses, and stacks of cables and letters from home. Her stocking, a "long yellow one for good luck," was filled with "a crimson-silk sunshade, a fan, a miniature, a pair of cuff-links and red silver snuff-box, a gold hat-pin, nougat, a basket of candied fruits and a bushel of crimson roses." Gertrude much enjoyed shopping for "Bob's" Christmas presents, describing it—as always—as a playful and half-forbidden extravaganza. For the first and only time in her diary she used the endearing "Bobby": "Bobby got a gold ring, a turquoise pin, pearl shirt buttons, some silk socks, which I got in Paris and sweets galore—he is greedy really for them!" However, a service at the English church of Nice brought tears to her eyes, and she felt "unhappy and so lonely: There is a wail for home and Mother smothered in my heart and a lump that won't melt in my throat!" Later in the evening, she rewarded herself for bravely suppressing her tears all day by writing long letters to her family.

Pouring rain and a return of "neuralgia" drove her deeper into misery during the next few days, but with the return of sunshine, Gertrude revelled in watching peasants in their quaint Sunday clothes and "little French soldiers who are drilling all over the place." In their shabby clothes, the soldiers looked "real" to her, an adjective she uses repeatedly to convey an impression of sordidness. The soldiers' unkempt appearance made them look human and vulnerable, the perfect antidote to their superiors whom, with a telling shift in pronoun, she described as "the most impossible little creatures, all curled hair, oiled to a dazzling radiance, moustaches fierce with wax, and His eyes bulging at women and stinking of scent. I can actually smell him as I write!" Later, she flirted with an old priest at a monastery in Cimiez, asking him, "Do you like being a priest?" and receiving the answer that, sometimes, he did not, "with quite a leer at me." "Wasn't it delightful of him," she concluded triumphantly, accepting a bottle of violet scent as he asked whether she would come back.

Other excursions took the Flemings away from the sea and into the mountains. Gertrude, initially afraid of losing sight of the ocean, liked "the deep dark woods and the smell of the dear earth and green things better than the sea!" The same maternal and womb-like safety of enclosure enchanted her at another spot, where, surrounded by mountains and chasms on all sides, she gazed at the "deepest blackest purple with a rosy mist and the shadows all pearly" till she longed to put her head down in her "mother's lap and cry." Emotion strained her so that she turned "quite white"; Fleming administered a quart of wine, but she still spent all of the next day in bed, half encouraging herself that some day soon she would be "so sensible" and half giving in to feelings of inadequacy and guilt. Later, in San Remo, she wandered through the old streets of the town rediscovering some of the safety of her enclosed mountain retreat in the "tall sad houses clinging to each other and clasped to each other by arches connecting them across the street" and among the luxuriant trailing vine covering houses and arches.

On 31 December, the Flemings travelled on to Monte Carlo, awash with the smart set in evening-dress and dinner-coat, and Gertrude decided to compete with her new frocks, one in "bright dark blue . . . trimmed with lace and a white hat" and another "mauve crêpe de chine all pailleté and embroidered in white and a silver violet toque I had got in Paris." A prince instantly followed her into the lift, but she kept her eyes firmly fixed on the floor: "I *know* he's a beast." The couple strolled over to the Casino; the gambling seemed "so real and sordid" and the gloomy darkness of the rooms frightening. Still, Gertrude was persuaded to try her luck and won seven pounds, assisted by a "nice American man." Several days later, she passed the "little suicide graveyard"; as the light faded over the neglected garden, she swallowed her tears and "said a little prayer for them and got altogether serious and uncomfortable." In the evening, they arrived in the Casino shortly after a man had shot himself in despair; in hysterics, Gertrude has "to be almost carried back to the Hotel by Bob!"

Sunny days in San Remo followed, with Gertrude's birthday on 4 January bringing letters and presents, "a lovely old brooch set with amethyst and brilliants, and all sorts of mosaic work," a gratifying day almost immediately followed by the Flemings' departure for Genoa, a traumatic leave-taking for Gertrude only softened by the arrival of more letters from home. Genoa swarmed with deformed people, she found, "mis-shapen dwarf men and women—usually broken out in spots— begging at every street corner"; feeling faint and ill, she fled back into her hotel. Smell always affected her deeply, and Genoa stank "bad, really nasty." In one of her rare and always delightful flights of humour, she adds "no wonder Christopher Columbus left it and discovered America."

In Pisa, the Flemings start up a vigorous round of sightseeing, Gertrude all the while congratulating herself secretly on her stamina, but refusing to climb the leaning tower of Pisa with Bob. "He says there is a glorious view from the top and great bells the largest weighing six tons!" Despite Gertrude's uncommon perseverance, Fleming had to finish the afternoon by himself, *Baedeker* in hand; tired and bored out of her wits, his wife returned to the hotel to wait for him there.

"Black skies" and "a chilly wind" wait for them in Rome; like George

Eliot's Dorothea Brooke and Charles Dickens's Little Dorrit, Gertrude shuddered at the mouldy, "catacomby" smell of the Eternal City: "We went for a drive—a cold dismal and shivery drive ending up in numbed misery at St. Peter's." Mistaken for dignitaries, the Flemings were at once escorted to the Sistine Chapel where they "heard the most glorious music and singing." Still, she concluded her entry for that day with: "a dreary day—all told." Serious sightseeing started up in the morning with Gertrude consenting to eat at *table d'hôte*, relinquishing her precious privacy in front of a fire in her drawing-room. Later in the day, the Flemings roamed through the coliseum; or, rather, Bob investigated it thoroughly, while Gertrude climbed "to the top and thought and thought and thought." Fatigued, she returned to the Quirinale Hotel for a private supper of poached eggs and cherries, while "Bob went down and spent a most entertaining evening."

Gertrude Fleming's diary breaks off on 11 January with the following entry: "Sunshine and letters the first thing in awakening! Mother, Father, Maude, and Mr. Fleming all wrote—Mother says Xmas was like a funeral without me and that they were miserably lonely—dear dear people—I was so glad—honestly and disgracefully glad at their misery! My own heart is already crying out for home again—But I mustn't tell! Dressed and out— went down and walked through the Corso—the fashionable shoppy street of Rome. It was crowded between eleven and twelve all sorts of beautiful soldier men with sort of winged helmets . . . ladies driving and walking, dressed beautifully and only looking foreign about their hair and heads. I *must* find out more about those soldiers!"

The couple's journey appears to have continued without any major mishap, for three months later Fleming senior noted their return to Ottawa, celebrated with a large tea-party in the conservatory of his house "Winterholme." This was the first of many such gatherings which were to punctuate Gertrude's life from now on: a typical entry in Sir Sandford's diary on Christmas Day 1892 reads: "At dinner Minnie Bob and Gertrude Walter Hugh Ethel Noel Elsie Smith Nellie Hall and Miss Flood governess." Proverbially fond of children, Sandford Fleming was delighted when his son and Gertrude presented him with a new grandchild, Charlie, in 1893, a daughter, Jean, in 1895, and a second son, John Archibald in 1898, with several other children to follow in future years. Charlie inherited his grandfather Mackintosh's propensity to accomplish great things at a young age, when, as a thirteen-year-old, he fished a drowning couple "paddling down from their summer home . . . to get the day's mail" out of the water "in a manner so gallant as to deserve the Royal Humane Society's medal."[13] His mother settled down to a long and apparently happy marriage, assuming the prominent position in Ottawa society her background had predestined her for. When she died in 1946 a few years before her husband, the *Citizen* eulogized her as an accomplished hostess, "an active social leader."[14] A year after the end of World War II, her house on the corner of Chapel and Besserer streets, once the property of John A. Macdonald and coincidentally the house where he had summoned her father to offer him the editorship of the *Citizen*, and where Charles Herbert Mackintosh had died in 1931, seemed a precious link to the capital's optimistic and gracious past—a grace sometimes bought, as it was by Gertrude Fleming, at great emotional cost.

2. THE NEW WOMEN

While Gertrude Fleming was wholly immersed in her role as a child-bride, other women travellers were ready to strike out on their own. Apart from meek companions, the Victorian Age also produced intrepid travellers like Isabella Bird, Frances Trollope, Anna Jameson, and Mary Kingsley. The "New Woman," exasperated with the uselessness of feminine existence in the affluent classes, proposed to acquire a profession and fulfil her life with a mission. An essential part of her emancipation was the freedom to move about at will. The "New Woman" often considered the routes and sights prescribed by the guidebooks as paternalistic straightjackets, and instead of sublimating her impatience with "serious" sightseeing into headaches and fatigue, as Gertrude Fleming did, she devised her own itinerary and her own way of talking about it. Thus, in her 1892 novel *A Social Departure: How Orthodocia and I Went Round the World by Ourselves*, Sara Jeannette Duncan sends her independently minded heroines on a tour dedicated to enjoyment, not instruction, although the women soon develop a keen interest in social reform. And although Grace Denison, social editor of Toronto's *Saturday Night* for twenty-two years, referred her readers to *Baedeker's* for descriptions of the sights of Berlin in 1890, her own way of exploring the city combined the leisurely inquisitiveness of the *flâneur* with the high social conscience of the reformer. Likewise, the *Toronto Mail*'s Kathleen Coleman affirmed that "when people travel they should have as little to do with guide books as possible. . . . Experience is a fine thing, and the dearer you buy it the less you are apt to forget it."[15]

Conservative Canadians eyed such women tourists with revulsion, often blaming their unorthodox behaviour on the negative influence exerted by American suffragettes. The Emancipated American Female or E.A.F., as a contributor to *Belford's Monthly Magazine* called her in 1878, seemed unattractive in a masculine way and Canadian women travellers were warned against her pernicious influence: "The average American girl is not altogether to blame that her chest is flat, her shoulder blades sharp and her voice nasal . . . the American lady who has travelled all over Europe, and feasted and junketed in every continental city, is apt to acquire a hardness of countenance and a raspiness of tone which do not contrast advantageously with the voice and visage of English and French sisters."[16] The question of female emancipation turned into a question of national identity; the American woman's rejection of her traditional role duplicated her nation's rebellion against the mother country, whereas Canadian women were expected to prove their country's loyalty to the Crown with a demure manner and appropriate respect for their elders. By focusing on the "E.A.F.," the Toronto lawyer C. R. W. Biggar modified the satire habitually directed at American tourists in general in Canadian travelogues: "we heard an American girl in front of the bust of Julius Caesar, looking with interest at the clear-cut, intellectual face, with its strongly marked lines, Roman nose, and sharply defined lower jaw, and saying to her gray-haired, soft-hatted companion in a tone of frank (not shy) surprise: 'But *poppa*, surely Caesar didn't believe in all those heathen gods and goddesses,' as she indicated with a wave of her well-gloved hand the adjacent statues of Mercury, Minerva Medica and Proserpine."[17] Biggar conveys his idea of the American girl's shallowness and impertinence by surrounding her with the sculpture of a political genius, her own doting father, and his, Biggar's, superior historical knowledge; her wave with a "well-gloved hand" (no other details of her physique are given) trivializes her further as an ornamental and mindless product of the "cultured New England States."[18]

Grace Denison, in contrast, carefully distinguished between "the staid, unreceptive Americanism"[19] she perceived in the stereotypical Yankee tourist and the plucky independence of American women travellers on their own. In Waterloo, she entered conversation with a wealthy American family:

> They had just come back from Waterloo, and enlightened me thus: "It was very nice. We drove out and saw the monument; it was real nice, and it was such a nice day for a drive. Sister and I thought it was all just as nice as it could be!" "And it was not strange to stand on the very site of that decisive battle—didn't it seem unreal to see everything so calm and peaceful?" I queried, digging deep for some more fitting adjective than "nice." "Oh, no" said "sister," placidly, "We did not think about the battle. It is in the English History, and at school I never took much to English History, but you might feel different, being Canadian. You'd better go to-morrow and see it yourself. It's a real nice drive."[20]

Denison indeed found these women "incongruous and unsatisfactory,"[21] but she was full of praise for three Massachusetts schoolteachers setting out on a Cook's tour through Central Germany and down the Rhine: "they were great girls."[22] Moreover, she often identified herself as American when it came to criticizing European manners and morals concerning women.

For most of the journey described in *A Happy Holiday: A Tour through Europe* (1890), Denison travelled on her own although she was by then married to Albert Ernest Denison, and she was a firm supporter of new means of transport promising greater freedom of movement. Descended from a distinguished Irish family, Denison shared with her father, the Archdeacon Sandys of Chatham, Ontario, a missionary zeal, and with her brother, E. W. Sandys, a magazine writer and editor in New York, a literary talent which made her the idol of many aspiring women authors. In 1897, she contributed a pugnacious article to *Massey's Magazine*, celebrating "The Evolution of the Lady Cyclist" and assuring her readers that the bicycle (a symbol of social and sexual equality) had made women healthier, both mentally and physically: "The triumph of the woman cyclist over prejudice, timorousness, bruises and discomfort of various sorts in pursuit of her dear pastime, has . . . brought her steady nerves, brisk circulation, lost youth, brilliant eyes and strong muscles; her lungs, her heart and her head have gained, and to those who believe health helps every way, her eternal welfare is also the surer for it."[23]

Many times during her journey, Denison described herself as a missionary bringing the gospel of women's rights to benighted Europeans, and she often juxtaposed her own busy and idiosyncratic travel programme (a fairly unorthodox itinerary through the Netherlands, Germany, Austria, Hungary, Switzerland, and France) with the mental stagnation of old world men and women. For her character cameos of European *mores*, she created brief dramatic encounters, rejuvenated versions of one of travel literature's stock scenes, the chance encounter in the carriage or inn. Wedged in between "a voluble German" and "a loquacious Frenchman" at Sunday dinner in Cologne, Denison dispensed her first lesson in proper etiquette when the two gentlemen "coolly lit their cigar when the ice cream came, and puffed me into cloudland,"[24] an impertinence she was not prepared to tolerate. Denison and the German's wife exchange furious glances in a scene reminiscent of Katherine Mansfield's acerbic *In a German Pension*; the wife urges her husband: "Smoke *thou!*" and Denison spits: "These German fraus are awful to me, they frown and grunt and put out their lips and grumble and growl to themselves like a small thunderstorm in their uncouth displeasure."[25]

Denison blamed European women's subservient role on their traditional education. On the train from Prague to Vienna, she chats with a "Venetian lady who was going to her husband in Russia,"[26] accompanied by a baby daughter and an obnoxious little boy. In the mother's indulgent response to her son's tyranny over the girl, Denison recognizes the vicious circle of women's acquiescence in men's pleasure: " 'Enough, my boy, do not annoy the little Rita! You will make her a cross child and not pleasant to play with when she is larger.' 'I shall not play with her, when she is larger!' announced this subject of the Czar. 'Not? Oh, poor little lonely Rita!' sighed the 'Mutterchen' and '*Voilà*!' the whole subject in a nutshell, of the woman question in these parts: Be agreeable, and do just as Milord tells you, and *you may play with him sometimes!*"[27] As she often does, Denison concludes the scene with a cruel caricature of her victim: "I saw the up-growing of that plain-faced young tyrant, and the up-growing nose was not pretty! His full lips and fat eye-lids and cold steel-blue eyes, his flattened nose and cruel jaw, and I prayed for his speedy removal from this sublunary sphere."[28] In Vienna, she advises a concierge wishing to emigrate to America that his treatment of the opposite sex would not do there, because "the women are first; the men where they can!"[29] and prides herself on having discouraged yet another backward Austrian from importing his ways into the progressive New World.

Besides dispensing advice to recalcitrant European males, Denison pursued her interest in social reform. Donning a maternal persona (sentimental descriptions of small children abound in her book), she visited a maternity ward in Brussels and a hospital in Cologne, ventured into slums, and, appalled, watched Belgian lace-makers at work: "I never can look at the fairy, delicate leaves and flowers of a bit of Brussels lace without feeling again the sharp, needle-like pain, and seeing the red-stained eyes of those poor lace-makers."[30]

Considering Denison's feminist militancy, it is surprising to learn that she opposed the vote for women. Her columns in *Saturday Night* were to tackle controversial issues rather more cautiously and obliquely than *A Happy Holiday* does. For most of her career, she wrote for a publication which had established a reputation for its staid conservatism. Founded by Edmund E. Sheppard in 1887, *Saturday Night* was designed to appeal to Toronto's Anglo-Saxon male business class and to cater to its prejudices against Catholics, Blacks, Jews, and emancipated women. The Woman's Page was expected to contain light society gossip; it was not the place to defend women's rights openly. Thus, in an 1899 column, Denison discussed ambition among women, suggesting that it could well be realized in supporting, and rejoicing in, a husband's or son's achievements. Cautiously, she added: "ambition centered in self is, however, not so rare as might be supposed among the petticoated ranks these days."[31]

Such an attitude of compromise also informs Constance Rudyard Boulton's travel sketch entitled "A Canadian Bicycle in Europe."[32] Boulton, who appears to have been a newspaperwoman from Manitoba, cycled through Italy in 1896, accompanied by a female friend. Not to mention the courage she proved in traversing a country popularly depicted as infested by brigands and highwaymen, the bicycle marked Boulton's excursion as a revolutionary enterprise. Yet, she too rejected the more radical accoutrements of cycling, assuring her readers that she found it unnecessary to conduct her expedition in the unfeminine uniform of dedicated cyclists—bloomers. Lily Dougall, writing about the "New Woman" in her novel *The Madonna of the Day* (1896), gave similar attributes to her assertive protagonist, a travelling women journalist: "She escaped vulgarity. There was just enough of what was well-bred in accent and aspect to make her loudness an interesting eccentricity rather than a loathsome commonplace."[33]

Not even "Kit" Coleman's considerable independence, initiative, and unconventionality were always enough to overcome the concessions to popular taste her job required. Born at Castle Blakeny, Ireland, Kathleen Blake emigrated to Canada in 1884; by the age of twenty-five, she had been widowed twice, following marriages to an Irish squire forty years her senior, who left his fortune to his mother, and to Edward Watkins, her Toronto employer.[34] In 1890, E. E. Sheppard, the editor of *Saturday Night*, bought one of her articles, a travel sketch of Paris; it attracted the attention of Christopher Bunting, editor of the *Mail*, who hired the young writer as the editor of "Woman's Kingdom," a woman's page which, even more long-lived than "Lady Gay's" society column, was to continue for twenty-five years and survive the *Mail*'s merger with the *Empire* in 1895. Though her arena was originally a conventional woman's page with random information on fashion, kitchen, and household affairs, "Kit," as the increasingly popular journalist signed her articles, soon concerned herself with a variety of social, cultural, and political issues. The astuteness of her judgement combined with the liveliness of her writing contributed to the *Mail and Empire*'s popularity; they also contributed to making journalism a respectable profession for women in Canada. A thin, red-haired woman with a striking resemblance to Sarah Bernhardt, "Kit"—Mrs. Theobald Coleman following a third marriage in 1898—entertained her readers in 1892 with travel sketches from London, Dublin, and Paris; reported on the World Fair in Chicago, and, in 1898, became the only accredited woman journalist to cover the Cuban War. Kit developed an exceptionally close rapport with her readership because in addition to such special assignments, she dispensed advice to the lovelorn, whose letters arrived at the *Mail and Empire*'s offices by the sackful. Some

of her replies try to strike a truce between emancipation and traditionalism, an ambiguity earning her the criticism of later feminists like Flora
MacDonald Denison. Determinedly liberal in her own life, Coleman
hesitated to give her own forthright views as advice to her readers either
because when she assumed—like Grace Denison—the role of substitute
mother, she felt responsible for them or because her editor kept a close eye
on her column. In questions of marital strife, for example, she generally
counselled women to be politic and not relinquish the economic safety of
marriage unless it was absolutely necessary.

Despite a busy sightseeing schedule on a journey to London, Paris, and
Dublin in early 1892, Coleman punctually dispatched a manuscript every
week to be published on page five of the Saturday edition of the *Toronto
Mail*. With the greater part of her column understandably devoted to
describing European sights and scenes, she still provided the customary
"pot-pourri," random information ranging from ways to treat acne and
dandruff to railway statistics and the ever popular "correspondence,"
Kit's replies to letters from her readers. Indeed, her columns soon
assimilated useful observations made on her jaunts through the three
cities. Thus—scolded by a female reader who signed herself "Little Nell"
for neglecting her household duties—the journalist retaliated with
homespun recipes for potato soup, shrimp salad, and oyster plant fritter, as
well as "a couple of nice plain dinner menus."[35] Yet she also introduced
Torontonians to the fare and service at Parisian chain restaurants like the
Bouillons Duval where plain, but attentive, young women decked out in "a
short black dress, white apron with bib, half sleeves of white cotton tied
above the elbow with blue ribbons, and a high mob cap of white muslin
tied loosely in a large bow under the chin" served delicious dishes of
"coquille de turbot gratin," a "mixture of fish, nutmeg, and other
flavourings,"[36] as Kit informed any Toronto cook who might have wished
to imitate the concoction.

Like Denison, Coleman shunned most of the habitual tourists' sights
and instead roamed through the market, the *abattoir*, the flower and fan
shops, the new shopping arcades and department stores, providing not
only impressionist vignettes of intriguing sights seen, but also statistical
information. Besides noting that the Bon Marché department store
employed 4,200 workers and used 1,750 horses and wagons, as well as
featuring a reading-and music-room and well-furnished and heated
bedrooms for the shop-assistants, Coleman exclaimed enthusiastically over
the freshness of the produce displayed at the *Halles Centrales* ("the
mountains of lobsters and crabs waving their claws in useless despair"),[37]
admired the robust health of the market women, and coolly inspected
efficient and painless methods of slaughter. New fashions—whether in

bonnets, fans, or flower arrangements— were sharply observed and recorded in all of their cluttered *belle époque* sumptuousness: in January 1892, Parisian women sported "bonnets, tiny creations of velvet covered thickly with gold spangles," their fans were "spangled with tiny gold, blue, green, silver, and red sequins," while dinner-tables displayed amazing centrepieces with "little Roman chariots of plush . . . holding pots of flowers in bloom."[38] Always practical, Kit noted that few muddy skirts were seen around Paris because "every Parisienne takes good care to hold up her dress as high as possible,"[39] showing off the ruffles and frills of her petticoats at the same time. Braving the occasional uncomplimentary remark on her English feet, Coleman too displayed her calves as she "valiantly gather[ed her] skirts up à la Highlander."[40] Although, as an editor of a woman's page, Coleman was expected to supply ample information on the latest in ladies' fashions, she also let her readers know in characteristically acerbic style when she thought a particular *dernier cri* unbecoming or plainly absurd. "Lots of women are blossoming out in purple," she wrote from London, "reminding one of the Liverpool fish women, and though not one woman in a thousand looks well in the colours, they will wear it, since fashion so decreed it; purple noses don't look well with purple bonnets, but some women are such fools that they don't mind looking magenta."[41] She responded equally sharply to correspondents who, fired up by her articles from abroad, intended to pack up and leave for London or Paris themselves. "It is all nonsense," she reprimanded a female reader who revealingly identified herself as "Jeanne Hugo," "What would you do in such a strange confusing place as Paris all by yourself too! My dear, you cannot get such a situation as you speak of, because you are not qualified to hold it."[42] She also snapped at a young man wishing to make his fortune in Europe, telling him to try Australia or New Zealand first. Quite obviously, Kathleen Coleman considered herself— and was generally accepted by her readers as—a moral authority with both the right and the obligation to counsel her "paper-children" well.

During her four-month stay in London, Coleman reported on current events and public debates, selected because she could expect her readers to be interested in them or because she felt they ought to be. Much sympathy could be anticipated for the news that London was in deep mourning over the deaths of the Duke of Clarence, Cardinal Manning, and the Baptist preacher Charles Spurgeon. Spurgeon's body arrived at Victoria Station on 27 February and for his many faithful followers in Canada Kit evoked the scene in a deft vignette:

I saw many women weeping. It was raining heavily, and a bitter wind was blowing, but the platform was crowded, before eight o'clock in the morning. All hats were lifted as the coffin passed across the platform to the hearse, and most of the women were in deep mourning. There were few flowers, according to express wish, but long branches of feathery palms extended the whole length of the coffin. . . . On the plate at the foot we read the inscription, 'I have fought a good fight; I have finished my course; I have kept the faith.' Mr. Spurgeon was the people's friend, and they mourn him sincerely. He was in touch with them. A great man by reason of his simple truthful teaching, his practice of the same, his great faith and undoubted sincerity. He is deeply and deservedly regretted.[43]

Perhaps not quite so much agreement could be anticipated from Torontonians for Coleman's occasional outbursts on the women's question. Outraged by an article in the *London Globe* entitled "In Praise of Ignorance," she devoted most of her 27 February column to advocating women's education, concluding sarcastically that "If a woman is clever she must repress her talent and feign ignorance on the topics of the day in order thereby to delight and rest the man who deigns to dally with her."[44] Often lulled by Coleman's expertly drawn pen-sketches of ballgowns and wedding-dresses into thinking that "Woman's Kingdom" catered exclusively to a traditional view of women, the *Mail*'s readers were regularly startled from their complacency when Kit felt that the time was ripe once again.

Of all of the nineteenth-century forms of travel-writing the newspaper serial was probably the most appropriate for the description of great cities: labyrinthine and unpredictable, the exuberant life of London and Paris wilted in carefully planned narratives, but blossomed in the meandering paths of newspaper instalments with their sudden transitions from place to place, class to class, and style to style. Kit's Saturday, 6 February, column, for instance, covers such topics as golf for women, gossip about the Duke of Clarence's death, the wedding gown of his fiancée, May of Teck, her wedding presents, Cardinal Manning's death, and January sales at Peter Robinson's and Nicholson's, all with the attendant changes in style: there are sentimental romance ("The Duke of Clarence was the Princess of Wales' favourite child. He was a shy, reticent young fellow, who did not make friends as quickly as his brother George of Wales, but who was much beloved by those who knew him well. He loved Princess May for a long time, but could not get the Queen's consent to his marriage with her till six weeks ago, which fact makes his untimely death a still more bitter blow to his grandmother"), and official obituary ("It is some seven years since I met and chatted to the late Cardinal Manning in his palace at Westminster. . . . The personal popularity of the late Cardinal with the

English people was very great, and there is probably no living representative of the Protestant Church around whose bier, were he dead, a
concourse so widely representative of the diverse ranks and steps of the
social ladder would gather''). Coleman also excels in fashion journalism
(''Feather boas are going out as rapidly as they came in, and everyone is
wearing wide silk scarfs in an immense bow under the chin'') and social
comedy (''Country cousins are here in plenty, and cabs and busses are
loaded with parcels of 'bargains' bought by fussy old country ladies, who
are forever counting them and letting them fall about one's feet in
tram-cars and other public conveyances'').[45] The Woman's Page, the
presumed reflection of the feminine mind's exclusive concern with trivial
information, often camouflaged, more or less successfully, its editor's keen
awareness of modernity. Heterogeneous, disjointed, and stripped of a
unifying vision, Kathleen Coleman's column was a more perceptive and
innovative solution than the firmly controlled narratives composed by
many of her contemporaries.

3. A RUSKINITE IN CANADA: ALICE JONES and *THE WEEK*

Practical-minded, Grace Denison and Kathleen Coleman concerned
themselves little with painting, sculpture, or architecture; extensive visits
to the galleries would probably have been too much of a concession to the
conventional sightseeing they so despised. Another woman journalist,
however, well-read in the works of John Ruskin and Walter Pater, created
word-pictures of Italy's cities and art treasures for her readers in sketches
for *The Week* which rank among the finest in Canadian travel-writing.
Born in Halifax in 1853, of United Empire Loyalist stock, Alice Jones was
the daughter of Lieutenant-Governor Alfred Gilpin Jones of Nova Scotia
and the sister of Frances Jones Bannerman, a well-known artist and poet.
In the 1880s and 1890s Alice Jones travelled extensively in England,
France, Italy, and Northern Africa, immersing herself in the study of
languages. Her love of Europe led her to move permanently to Menton,
France, where she died in 1933. Besides contributing to such periodicals as
the Halifax *Critic*, *Frank Leslie's Monthly*, the *Dominion Illustrated
Monthly* and, above all, *The Week*, she also composed several novels
(among them *Bubbles We Buy* [1903], *Gabriel Praed's Castle* [1904],
Marcus Holbeach's Daughter [1912], *Flame of Frost* [1914]), using her
experience abroad to develop Jamesian contrasts between old-world
corruption and new-world innocence, but her fiction is hackneyed
compared to her perceptive, elegantly written travel vignettes. An
important antidote to the utilitarian or perfunctory approach to art among

many of her fellow travellers, Jones's essays present impressionist scrutiny and aesthetic evaluation, both always firmly grounded in her faith. Although she advocated "loitering" among the sights instead of briskly striding past them, Jones placed the Protestant convention of self-scrutiny and relentless fulfilment of duty at the service of art: all sense perceptions must be closely examined for both their artistic and moral validity. Like Ruskin, she preferred Venice to Rome because its worshippers seemed more serious and less absorbed in the cult of the Virgin Mary, and she celebrated the memory of Fra Paolo Sarpi and, in Florence, of Savonarola as "Protestant" critics within the Roman Catholic Church. Despite her love for Italy, her commentaries are underpinned—although sometimes half-heartedly so—by a sense of "Northern" superiority, the latter, in emulation of Ruskin, always firmly associated with gothic architecture: "The feeling is not the awe that is produced by the great and sombre Gothic domes of Milan and the North," she says, confronted with St. Mark's, and on an earlier visit to Winchester, she affirms, somewhat ambiguously, that "one is almost chilled by the grand stateliness and simpleness of an English cathedral" if "used to the human interest given by the touch of homely tawdriness that is always evident in foreign cathedrals, the artificial flowers, the humble tallow dips burning before a shrine."[46] Alice Jones never separated art and ethics as Walter Pater did, although she imitated his approach in other ways, and she probably found his paganism palatable only because it was "touched with the feeling, the restraint [and] the purity"[47] of Christianity, as her colleague E. C. Cayley pointed out in a review of *Marius the Epicurean*. For similar reasons, she preferred—visiting her favourite works in the Uffizi—the austerity of "pre-Raphaellite [sic] Madonnas and Annunciations"[48] to Botticelli's *The Birth of Venus*.

Alice Jones's writing, although exceptionally fine, was not the only such contribution to *The Week*. As a whole, this periodical offered in its essays and book reviews a significant alternative to the materialist evaluation of art by Canada's businessmen and its typological interpretation by the clergy. *The Week* reviewed, for instance, Pater's *Imaginary Portraits* and *Plato and Platonism* (both co-published by Williamson in Toronto), printed lengthy evaluative obituaries for both Pater and Ruskin, and a critique, by Arnold Haultain, of Pater's *Appreciations, with an Essay on Style*. It reprinted the Reverend J. G. Wood's essay on "The Dulness of Museums" from *Nineteenth Century*, provided sketches on "Portrait Painting" (by the renowned Canadian portraitist John W. L. Forster), "The Value of a Picture," "An Appreciation of Modern French Art," and "The Fine Arts and their Relation to Each Other," besides offering comprehensive overviews of Italian Renaissance art and literature. Travel sketches such as "L.L.'s" "Letter from Italy" or "C.A.M."'s "An Artist Abroad" habitually included knowledgeable comments on the art history and aesthetic impact of the sights seen. Fascinated with Turner, "C.A.M." compares the painter's work with Coleridge's, suggesting that "the former lived high above the human level, among flashing brilliancy and shimmering nebulous light, while the latter soared in a rarefied atmosphere of theosophic haziness,"[49] and describing, in close detail, not so much Turner's paintings in London and Glasgow galleries, as his own emotional response to them. In combining scientific exactitude with spirituality, Turner's paintings overcame the limitations of realism, whose alleged superficiality *The Week*'s critics chastised as much in pieces on Dutch genre painting as in domestic works displayed at the 1886 Ontario Society's Exhibit. Appalled, like Ruskin, by the onslaught of modernity, another contributor deplored the excavation work in the Coliseum which bared a subterranean sewerage and storage system and deprived the building of its thick coat of luxuriant plants: here, too, an ideal seemed to have given way to realism. After expressing initial disappointment with Rome, "a labyrinth of dirty, noisesome lanes and alleys," the author continued: "But we are looking at Rome from an aldermanic point of view. Surely *its* streets, of all streets, should be looked at with the eyes of an artist. Surely, once within its sacred walls we should forget civic reform, and be satisfied with thoroughfares that are insanitary because they are picturesque; and irregular though they may be—steep, perhaps, or narrow—full of endless, purposeless twistings and twinings—we should see in them only a succession of paintable 'bits', wonderful in colour, and as forceful in their clearly defined light and shade as Regnault drew them, or an Italian sun can make them."[50] In stark contrast to the muscular Christianity of a William H. Withrow, some contributors to *The Week* tempered their observations with fashionable *fin-de-siècle* world-weariness: "From the Boboli Gardens must we take our farewell view of Florence. There is something very fascinating about these deserted grounds. In summer, when a motley crowd dances upon *les tapis verts*, and shrieks in the sombre alleys, it seems like desecration. No! one must linger in them at twilight, when all is still, or visit them on a winter's afternoon while the mists still flit about their paths and groves like the ghosts of past joys. These gardens, and many others besides, seem like the graves of so many delightful pleasures—dead forever. To-day nervous excitement supplants a quiet enjoyment. *Le Monde s'est fait vieux,* alas!"[51] Other contributors, however, had little use for the romanticizing nostalgia of the more effete Ruskinites. *The Week*'s editor, Goldwin Smith, ironically observed in his narrative of a visit to his former home, *A Trip to England*: "It is easy to understand that to the soul of the Ruskinite the sight [of the English manufacturing districts] must be torture, though the Ruskinite wears the cloth, uses the hardware, and, when he travels, is drawn by engines made here over rails produced by these forges"[52] and a similarly reserved tone appears in Ruskin's obituary in *The Week*.

Despite various objections to Ruskin's utopian excesses and, as Alice Jones pointed out, to his oppressive teaching methods, *The Week* was clearly permeated by his ideas. Inspired by his interpretation of Turner's atmospheric art in *Modern Painters*, Jones sketches the tints and shapes of a winter sunset over Florence, not as the static properties of a completed artifact, but as a process and transitory moment: "On Christmas Eve we climbed the steep curves that wind up the slopes of San Miniato, and, just as the red flush was creeping over the mountains, reached the terrace before the church, and stood looking down on the domes and spires of the city, and on the hills that enclose it. A blue vapour hung over the town, through which the great dome of the cathedral rose majestic, and the turretted tower of the Palazzo Vecchio soared."[53]

The travel motif, central in Ruskin, informs the structure of all of Jones's sketches as well; her wanderings through the city imply a journey through history toward aesthetic and moral revelation. Just as Ruskin invites his reader in "The Vestibule," the final chapter of the first volume of *The Stones of Venice*, to follow him "on an autumnal morning, through the dark gates of Padua" toward the city of Venice, so Jones emerges from the narrow medieval darkness of the Via dei Servi to be confronted with the vastness of Brunelleschi's dome: "its great curve deeply red in the lurid light that shone through weird storm clouds, breaking after a day of rain."[54] Less dramatic but equally fulfilling is a moment of spiritual tranquillity in Venice, "in this sleepy atmosphere and during long lazy hours in the soft swing and silence of a gondola."[55] Leisurely relaxation and close attention to selected detail replace the dogged comprehensiveness of conventional tours and guidebooks; in a hallucinatory sequence and in long meandering sentences, Jones recalls the portraits of Venetian doges seen in a picture gallery and the epiphanic moments of history represented by them. As in Walter Pater's *Renaissance*, charismatic individuals epitomize in their life's achievements important eras in the development of mankind, their dreamlike procession once again an allegory of man's journey through life:

One sits in front of Florians in the end of the long spring afternoon . . . and dreamily in that dreamy air one seems to see that stage of the piazza filled with its long pageant of Venice's history. All the morning, in the neighbouring Palace of the Doges, one has followed that history, and the grim, keen-faced Doges, who on those walls are so curiously intermixed with the most sacred figures, here step out of their frames and come to play their part like Irving's Louis XI or Charles I. When one sees in the Sala del Maggior Consiglio, in the midst of the seventy-two portraits of the Doges, that black space inscribed with the traitor's name of Marino Faliero, or reads of the death of Francesco Foscari, who, after dooming his own son to torture and death, breathed his last at the sound of the great bell which announced the election of his successor, one longs to see their lives and deaths touched by Shakespeare's magic.[56]

Obviously a voracious reader, Jones both welcomes the guidance of congenial authors (Shakespeare, George Eliot, W. D. Howells, Robert Browning, Thomas Adolphus Trollope, Mrs. Oliphant to mention only a few) and deplores their effect on her spontaneity. Modern in her awareness of the growing impossibility of authentic experience, Jones approaches St. Mark's with trepidation: "why try to write of what Ruskin, Lord Lindsay and Symonds have described over and over again? Why should one try to add to what is perhaps some of the finest prose writings in the English language— Ruskin's description of St. Mark's?"[57] Pleased that her visits to Florence and Venice are not the first and with her "sight-seeing conscience" consequently at ease, Jones delights in revisiting her favourite spots and pictures, but she also anxiously anticipates disappointment with a sight gloriously preserved in her memory: "I had half dreaded the sight of St. Mark's, for fear that in this second visit there might be some disillusionment to disturb the place that it had held in my memory. But I need not have feared. That complex and fantastic beauty of the real can hold its own even against the idealized recollection. When I saw once more the glittering façade shining across the piazza, it momentarily crossed my mind that I had thought it larger, but the same satisfied sense of beauty and perfection which that sight had given before quickly returned."[58]

But while Alice Jones watched and recorded her own responses carefully, she avoided direct contact with the "natives" as much as her materialist or religious compatriots; unless they could be comfortably accommodated as a picturesque element, the people seemed disturbing, even loathsome intruders in their own home. Jones's colleague "L.L." did welcome Italians as "agreeable travelling companions" but only because they could be stereotyped as amiable children, "affectionate . . . with pretty genial manners."[59] And "G." contemplated, from a safe distance, the artist's models lounging on the Spanish steps, "each procurable for about four francs a day."[60]

In contrast to Grace Denison and Kathleen Coleman, Alice Jones rarely spoke to Florentines, Venetians, or Romans; or, if she did, she neglected to write about the experience. She treasured her knowledge of Robert Browning's residence in Venice believing it to provide a moral authority among a fickle people ready to sell the beauty of their past for ugly modernity. Her only descriptions of natives occur in sometimes exquisitely crafted scenes in churches, markets, and cafés. In a particularly accomplished sketch of the Florence Baptistery, Florentines contribute to the touchingly naive atmosphere, as would figures in a painting:

> It might be difficult, though I confess that I have never tried, to pass through that Piazza del Duomo without pausing for a fresh glance at some one of its beauties, the creamy-tinted bas-reliefs of Giotto's campanile, or the wonderful details of the bronze gates of the baptistery, which Michel Angelo compared to the gates of Paradise, and which it took Ghiberti forty years of toil to finish. Whenever I stroll into that baptistery, I become fascinated by the spectacle of the making of Christians of new-born Florentines. Here, ever since the walls of the great Duomo rose opposite, and this first cathedral became the baptistery, every Florentine baby, high or low, has been brought for baptism, and here, on a short, dark winter afternoon that had already become too shadowy in the dark church to afford one more than a glimpse of the mosaics up above, we loitered to watch one group after another approach the font, and one stiff swaddled little bundle after another held up to the sleepy-looking priest, who, after putting the salt in their mouths and pouring the water over their heads, dried and powdered them in such a grandmotherly fashion. Some groups were quite festive, with young girls to carry the long tapers, and a smart white silk coverlet to throw over the baby. But one consisted of one gaunt, bare-headed woman, and the little newly-made Christian, which she grasped with one hand, while she held the lighted candle with the other. The child kept up a shrill, feeble wail, as though foreseeing that the world would not welcome it over-rapturously. The lighted candles threw the figures of priest and acolyte into strong relief as they paused, in the middle of one ceremony, for an animated argument. We counted four separate parties before we turned away."[61]

While Denison and Coleman sought to educate Canadians through social reform, Alice Jones probably felt that such a concern would have interfered with, perhaps even eliminated, her pursuit of art. Yet she too felt that she had a pedagogic duty to fulfil toward her compatriots. Alert to the educational influence of great art not only on herself but also on her young nation, Alice Jones inquired why English and Canadian churches had not made greater use of fresco painting to teach the congregation, an interest she shared with painters like Reid and Bourassa. *The Week* in general was concerned with the tardy development of the arts and their patronage in Canada, particularly English Canada, and the novelist John Talon-Lesperance for one held out the Desjardins collection in Quebec City as a glowing model.[62] *The Week* clearly perceived its national task in shaping the tastes of its readers so that their necessarily practical preoccupations might be complemented by the "sweetness and light" granted by the arts only.

6

Metaphors of Travel

1. THE MOTHER-AND-CHILD REUNION

Conservative Canadian men regarded independently travelling females
with such hostility partly because these women questioned the masculine
self-image, that of the sinewy champion of the frail and helpless. Eagerly
supportive of the Cult of Manliness, Canadian imperialists viewed their
frontier nation as a playground where the best qualities of British manhood
could be pitted against both a hostile climate and political and social
anarchy.[1] Susanna Moodie sadly but proudly waved her husband goodbye
as he limped toward Toronto to join the troops against William Lyon
Mackenzie's rebels, and in Ralph Connor's *Corporal Cameron of the
North West Mounted Police* (1912), a young Mounted Police officer,
inspired by his duty to "keep . . . intact the Pax Britannica amid the
wild turmoil of pioneer days,"[2] fearlessly disciplines a dangerous criminal
in a gambling den. Gentlemen in the service of the young Queen Victoria,
her colonial subjects became nineteenth-century knights, even crusaders,
ready to rush from the corners of her Empire to defend the Camelot of the
British monarchical system against the onslaught of republicanism.[3] Thus,
their self-image contained two components not always fused in happy
harmony: vigorous youths preparing the land for a glorious future, they
were also the children of Mother England, and while the former granted
them exemplary strength, the latter implied dependence. Central to
imperialist thinking, the parent-child metaphor, paradoxical *mélange* of
the Romantic divine child, solitary and self-sufficient, and the colonial

sibling, obedient and imitative, captures much of Victorian Canada's national predicament and deserves to be studied in one of its richest sources, travel writing about Europe.

The prospect of travelling to Britain or France was the promise of a homecoming for most nineteenth-century Canadians, but especially for United Empire Loyalists. Certain that their journeys would be the realization of ancestral memories carefully nurtured in conversation, letters, and mementoes, they did not fear the unfamiliar. "That dream that had delighted me in my boyhood, and which followed me through the changing cycles of my life, had at length found a consummation,"[4] wrote Caniff Haight, a Toronto druggist and bookseller, upon his arrival in London in 1895. An act of filial affection, travel to England was also a patriotic duty toward the centre of the Empire. A messianic imperialism informs the Reverend Moses Harvey's advice that Canadians visit the homeland as often as possible in order to keep sentimental attachment as alive as military liaison. Harvey rhapsodized in his 1871 "Notes of a Trip to the Old Land": "In the hearts of each generation of colonists there would, in this way, grow up that reverential attachment that most resembles the love of child for parent—that tender regard that would lead them to rush to her aid in the hour of need, from earth's farthest extremities."[5] French Canadians, in contrast, approached France with a mixture of passionate love and deep resentment. Thus, Sylva Clapin— librarian, journalist, and schoolteacher—assured his readers in 1880 that he felt no compunction about leaving London for France because "L'enfant ne s'élance-t-il pas tout droit dans les bras de sa mère?"[6] One Edmond Lambert, however, who celebrated the word "France" as "le plus beau nom, le plus doux, le plus digne, le seul qui soit jalousé, envié, béni, adoré"[7] in his *Voyage d'un Canadien-Français en France* (1898) was promptly reprimanded by a reviewer in the *Revue canadienne* for his tearful lyricism.[8] Exaggerated praise was felt to indicate a lack of pride, likely to create the false impression that French Canadians longed to return to the tutelage of a nation which had shamefully forsaken them on the Plains of Abraham. France, here, was seen as the guilty but still loved partner in a divorce or as an unreliable parent who must not be flattered with extravagant demonstrations of lasting affection, but whose attentions were nevertheless an essential part of French-Canadian identity. It is probably no coincidence that a daguerrotype offered by the Montreal citizen Alfred Chalifoux to the Empress Eugénie on the occasion of Captain Belvèze's visit to Canada depicts the connections between France and its former colony in the guise of four decidedly grim looking children representing, respectively, Saint-Jean-Baptiste, an Indian chief, Jacques Cartier, and a miniature Napoleon III.[9]

As Canadians began to explore their motherlands' cities and country-sides, they discovered—as most tourists do—that mental image and reality did not coincide, a discovery disillusioning enough for the ordinary traveller, but deeply painful for the colonist whose sense of national and personal selfhood depended on a firmly defined image of the mother country. In travellers' expectations, Britain and France were affectionate parents, ready to clasp their overseas children warmly in their arms. At the same time, they were formidable models to whom the colonist looked for guidance in every sphere of his life. Without regular contact with Britain, the source of civilization, Canada would—so Moses Harvey feared—remain steeped in barbarism: "the more frequently her colonial children can visit the Old Land to study there the best models, the more likely are they to advance steadily in all that dignifies and refines a people, and gives stability and freedom to a nation."[10] But instead of a ready-made family eager to introduce him to the mysteries of a traditional civilization, the Canadian traveller encountered strangers, inhabitants of anonymous, industrialized cities, not in the least impressed by his arrival. "An oppressive sense of loneliness seemed to weight me down in the midst of the surging tide of millions of people. My very identity seemed to be lost"[11] complained Caniff Haight. For those whose trip to England was in the nature of a religious quest, the journey of a pilgrim to the holy grail of Imperialism, the disappointment in the reality was even greater. For James Elgin Wetherell, a high-school principal from Ontario, the journey assumed the special framework of a literary pilgrimage to the "Land of Burns," the "Land of Scott," and the "Land of Tennyson." But his comments on Glasgow are at odds with the generally controlled, mellow mood of this "summer trip to Britain:" "A Visitor of Glasgow from across the sea . . . must be prepared to have his sensibilities continually shocked by horrible street brawls and harrowing scenes of poverty and sin."[12] In an attempt to soften the criticism of England's social system implicit in this description, Wetherell adds: "and that in a land where religion and education and philanthropy have reached high-water mark."[13] But his horror at the failures of industrial progress in an otherwise idealized England is unmistakable.

The metaphor of Canada, the child, alludes to the innocence and potential fragility of the young nation, but conversely it also points towards a youthful vigour now lost by the old countries. In describing Canada's qualities to prospective immigrants, propagandists often spoke of their country as a utopian version of Britain and France where the errors committed by the mother countries had not yet been repeated, and, it was hoped, never would be. Addressing the Congrès catholique in Paris, the Curé François-Xavier Antoine Labelle rejected allegations that, being young, Quebec was subject to illusions concerning its resources and perserverance. On the contrary, he thundered, his was a virile race, hardened by adversity and united "comme une grande famille pour la conservation de notre foi et de notre nationalité."[14] The French Revolution's slogan "liberté, égalité, fraternité" applied equally well to Quebec, he claimed, except that there liberty did not mean licence, equality implied protection of the weak by the strong, and brotherhood was not a blasphemous union against authority, but, on the contrary, "la fraternité d'enfants dévoués sous la conduite d'une même mère, qui est l'Eglise."[15] Labelle clearly emphasized the Church, and not the State, as French Canada's emotional centre, although he also, if only *pro forma*, acknowledged the protection of the British Empire.

The rhetoric of the child-metaphor became unmistakably ambiguous at world expositions, where Canada's displays emphasized its natural resources and agricultural capabilities and documented its educational facilities. But besides suggesting that it was a younger, better version of the mother country, Canada also wanted to attract prospective immigrants and investors, and proof of progress invariably required evidence of technology and industrialization. Andrew Spedon, a journalist visiting the 1867 *Exposition universelle* in Paris, voiced his concern with an overly pastoral image when he wrote:

> I was wonderstruck with [the Canadian display's] peculiarly barbarous-like exterior and felt curious to know to what uncivilized tribe of Indians or Northern Asiatics it belonged; on either sides of the portals stood two wooden pillars, about twelve feet in height, in the form of trees, and having the bark on, surmounted by garlands of leaves, &c. Between these portals were a sort of framework, around which were placed stuffed animals, belonging apparently to Arctic climates. Among them I observed some frightful-looking specimens of white owls, having heads like lynxes and eyes as large as tea-cups—also, other eccentric-looking fowls, besides bats, beetles, and butterflies, —and a few specimens of fire-flies, horse-gnats, mosquitoes, &c., preserved in glass bottles!

Spedon concluded: "Canada was altogether mis-represented; and like an affrighted child seemed crouching behind the forest shadows of the savage age."[16]

Torn between technological progress and nostalgic idealism as national criteria, travelling Canadians could not adopt a consistent point of view. Some, like Célina Bardy, a member of the Quebec *haute bourgeoisie*, responded with a mixture of anger and amusement at the sensation her sophisticated attire caused among the audience at the Paris Opéra;[17] a very few others borrowed an aggressively *ingénu* attitude from American travellers. Although never as self-confident in their studied naiveté as Mark Twain's *Innocents Abroad*, the occasional Canadian expressed his criticism of European refinement and his faith in Canadian moral health through a persona affecting childlike candour. Deliberate ingenuity seemed an effective self-defence among a people who insisted on thinking of the inhabitants of their former colony as pre-historic cannibals, even though men like Benjamin Sulte, a prominent French-Canadian journalist and historian, had energetically refuted the stereotype. In an 1873 series of articles entitled "Le Canada en Europe" quoting extensively from the contemporary French and British press, Sulte complained bitterly about French Canadians' reputation as "une race de nains, à la peau noirâtre . . . une classe de crétins,—tandis qu'à leurs yeux [i.e., des journalistes] les Anglais, les Ecossais, les Irlandais qui nous entourent sont des hommes d'une taille superbe, au teint clair et animé, jouissant d'une santé de fer de Hull, et par-dessus tout intelligents en diable."[18] Since even repeated explanations and corrections seemed to have little effect, some French-Canadian travellers cynically donned the cloak of the stereotype they were expected to inhabit, anticipating with grim satisfaction Parisians' predictable judgements, a strategy once again successfully pursued in the 1960s and later when Quebec performers confronted Paris audiences with brazen displays of *joual* theatre and song. "J'étais au Louvre," says the writer Pamphile LeMay in an 1885 travel sketch,

je regardais une statue de marbre—une grande fille très peu enveloppée dans ses voiles de déesse, au teint gâté par l'âge, d'une tenue digne, pour une payenne. . . . Après quelques minutes, je dis à mes compagnons en extase:—Oui, c'est bien elle! . . . la huronne de Lorette.' Alors il se fait un grand mouvement autour de la statue, tous les yeux me cherchent chargés de foudre, et un savant dans la géographie du Canada s'écrie en me montrant à la foule:—Un sauvage du Canada! Je venais de profaner la Vénus de Milo.[19]

Similarly, Hector Fabre, journalist and Canadian commissioner in Paris from 1882 onwards, gently mocked his compatriots' exaggerated hopes for a warm welcome in the capital: "Peut-être, se dit-on, que le Paris moderne, le Paris de Napoléon III et de M. Haussman [sic] restera indifférent et froid. Mais la vieille France, la France de Racine et de Corneille, tressaillera. La nouvelle de l'arrivée d'un Canadien au Havre se répandra rapidement dans tous les châteaux de la Bretagne et de la Normandie. Les vénérables douairières diront aux marquis, leurs fils, de m'inviter à chasser le cerf sur leurs terres. On me préparera des fêtes; on songera à me retenir au milieu de cette jeunesse française qui a dégénéré, et à laquelle j'infuserais un sang nouveau.'' The tourist's expectations were, of course, frustrated as soon as he encountered an officious customs officer who, to the proud assertion that the recently arrived came from Lower Canada, responded: "Je n'y vois pas d'inconvénients, pourvu toutefois que vous n'ayez pas de momie dans votre malle.''[20]

While Victorian Canadians were occasionally willing to identify with Americans in asserting their new-world youthfulness and health, they also used the child metaphor to distinguish themselves from their neighbours to the south. Such distinctions became especially aggressive in opinions expressed about the New Woman, who often confirmed her newly won liberation by travelling more or less independently on routes previously reserved to women in the safe custody of fathers, brothers, or husbands. In contrast, Queen Victoria's sober immersion in marriage and motherhood and her long widowhood were praised as a colonial woman's model. On the walls of his Nova Scotia cottage, the Loyalist William Croscup prominently displayed a ''homey and familial [scene] . . . in the Crimson Drawing Room at Windsor Castle showing Victoria seated with Louis Philippe on a sofa, while Prince Albert stands before him with his three children, Victoria, Albert, and Alice, who are being presented. . . . Enshrined above the mantelpiece, the scene becomes an icon of the joys of family life under the British Crown.''[21]

Few of the many sermons preached or pamphlets and books published across Canada on the occasion of Victoria's Golden and Diamond Jubilees neglected to celebrate her wifely and maternal qualities; both Kathleen Coleman and Adolphe-Basile Routhier, reporting from the 1897 festivities in London, placed special emphasis on the Queen's exemplary family life and the care she had taken to include children from city and countryside in the celebrations.[22] For Routhier, Victoria's traditional views of marriage and family were important enough—or so he declared—to outweigh his emotional attachment to France, a nation apparently bent on destroying its moral core by facilitating divorce.[23] More sincere perhaps were declarations of filial loyalty toward the Empresses Eugénie and Carlotta, both casualties of Napoleon III's ambition to confirm France's role as world power. Self-styled chivalrous defender of the Empress of the Mexicans, Narcisse-Henri-Edouard Faucher de Saint-Maurice, an author and journalist from Quebec, joined a hapless expedition to Mexico to support Maximilian's tottering régime.[24] And in 1882, Joseph Marmette, an historical novelist, sadly contemplated Eugénie's portrait, a latter-day Niobe, ''la grande infortune de ce temps, en face de celle qui fut impératrice, épouse et mère, et qui, jetée violemment sur la terre de l'exile, a tout perdu, beauté, trône et famille, et, brisée par la douleur, descend lentement la longue spirale de sa désolation.''[25] In an age when historical painting still largely relied on allegory, visions of France, the unfortunate mother, were often incarnated in vivid images: Faucher de Saint-Maurice, for example, shocked at the news of France's defeat by the Prussians, suffered hallucinations of a distraught woman striding across battlefields.[26] Appalled at the godlessness of modern Paris, Routhier contrasted an imagined picture of Marie-Antoinette, devoted mother, accompanying her children to the *Conciergerie*, with Gustave Doré's *Songe de la femme de Pilate*, in which Pilate's wife, awakened from a nightmare prophesizing her husband's crime, appeared to represent France, preparing to rouse herself from her present inertia.[27]

Despite their efforts to dissociate themselves from republicans in general and from the "Emancipated American Female" in particular, Canadians frequently suffered identity crises abroad because Europeans confused them with Americans. Here, the child-metaphor became once again a means of self-defence. It now served to designate Canadians as the obedient offspring of Britain, while the Americans were an unruly and anarchist brood. "What is important to us is the Queen and the Royal Family;" affirmed Richard Thomas Lancefield, librarian of the Hamilton public library and founder of the *Canadian Bookseller*, in his *Victoria, Sixty Years a Queen: A Sketch of Her Life and Times* (1897), "to us, and to the men of Australasia, of India, of Africa. High above all parties here or there rises before the eyes of English-speaking men the vision of the Hereditary Monarchy. Who would make a pilgrimage to Britain to find there, not the Queen or one of her blood, but some political tool sitting for his term of office in the presidential chair of the British Republic?''[28] Thomas C. Watkins describes the American passengers on his boat as a cheerful, infantile species who clamber about the ship with the agility of monkeys: "With the natural curiosity which is inherent in the American character, they rush to and from end to end of the ship, they survey her from topmost to the spardeck, then they plunge down into her interior, examine the saloon, the ladies' cabins, the state-rooms; ask any number of questions of men and officers, who are all busy getting ready to sail and have no time to reply, and converse with numerous friends who came to see them off.''[29] Watkins professes to be similarly amused by an Independence Day parade organized by the Americans on board ship, during which they cheered the president and, out of politeness toward the Canadian passengers, Queen Victoria as well. Safely encased in the stereotype of energetic but amiable children, Americans seemed not quite so overwhelming to travelling Canadians; revealingly, few narratives, either in English or French, are without a set comic scene involving Yankee tourists. Such scenes were, needless to say, perused differently by American readers, among whom the Canadian James De Mille's *The Dodge Club; or, Italy in 1859* (New York, 1869) was a great success because it transformed the pose of aggressive non-sophistication into an assertive democratic state-ment. The American novelist William Dean Howells even turned the child-metaphor against Canadians when, irritated by their demonstrations of affection for the Crown, he wrote: "its overweening loyalty place[s] a great country like Canada in a very silly attitude, the attitude of an overgrown, unmanly boy, clinging to the maternal skirts, and though spoilt and wilful, without any character of his own."[30]

Ironically, English and French Canadians—united in their satire of American tourists—also used the child-metaphor to criticize one another. The Abbé François Pelletier sarcastically described a Protestant congrega-tion on board as if they were a horde of screaming children: "9h—Ré-union au salon. Ma foi, les protestants sont en verve. . . . Toute la bande crie à la fois.—Sont ils tous de la même secte?"[31] Gatherings on board ship, especially Sunday Services, were the first occasion for Victorian travellers to sort out national and social differences and to declare allegiances. For Canadians, it was only the first episode in an often contradictory series of self-definitions accompanying the quest for both their colonial heritage and their nationhood. Northrop Frye, writing in the Conclusion to the *Literary History of Canada*, formulated it thus:

It is not much wonder if Canada developed with the bewilderment of a neglected child, preoccupied with trying to define its own identity, alternately bumptious and diffident about its own achievements. Adolescent dreams of glory haunt the Canadian consciousness (and unconsciousness), some naive and some sophisticated. In the naive area are the predictions that the twentieth century belongs to Canada, that our cities will become much bigger than they ought to be, or like Edmonton and Vancouver, "gateways" to somewhere else, recon-structed Northwest passages. The more sophisticated usually take the form of a Messianic complex about Canadian culture, for Canadian culture, no less than Alberta, has always been 'next year country.' The myth of the hero brought up in the forest retreat, awaiting the moment when his giant strength will be fully grown and he can emerge into the world, informs a good deal of Canadian criticism down to our own time.[32]

2. THE JOURNEY TO JERUSALEM

The sentimentalism suffusing some descriptions of the imperial mother-and-child reunion frequently attained religious intensity. A journey to Britain or France was a holy pilgrimage to the source of a colonist's identity: "I would have every colonist look to Old England as the Hindoo to his Ganges, as the Mahometan to his Mecca, as the Jew to his Zion, as the devotee to the shrine of his favourite saint,"[33] affirmed Moses Harvey, as did Edmond Lambert, who opened his effusive travel notes on France with "C'est un culte qui ressemble à [la] religion profonde."[34] Despite the strong associations between imperialism and religion, however, travelling Canadians—many reared in an ascetic spirit—were aware of the contradictions between the glitter of imperial pageantry and the transience of human life, although patriotism often urged them to focus on a culture other than their own for the comparison. From the Arc de Triomphe, Egerton Ryerson looked down upon a splendid worldly panorama; but he concluded, "In fifty years the mass of this vast multitude will be numbered amongst a bygone generation; and these stately works of art shall perish. What a worm am I amongst such a multitude! yet I am destined to immortality; have but a few years to live in a probationary state, but an eternity to exist!"[35]

Influenced by the wayfaring metaphor common to both Roman Catholic and Protestant thought, travellers of both denominations likened their journeys to the soul's pilgrimage through life and to its temporary exile from everlasting union with God. The crossing especially, exacerbated perhaps by the miseries of seasickness, gave ample opportunity for such contemplations. "I always think a noble vessel, her white sails spread like the wings of an albatross, and filled with the breeze, is a beautiful type of the soul of the Christian on its heavenward journey,"[36] wrote Maria Elise Lauder, who had studied theology at Oberlin University, and the narratives of ministers and priests like Henri Cimon or Hugh Johnston are filled with similar interpretations. To some, even the other passengers appeared in an allegorical light, representing types in the struggle of truth against evil rather than individual human beings. The Abbé Léon Provancher, an amateur botanist, pitted himself against a Darwinist aboard ship, classifying him as if he were a rare insect ("trapu, carré des épaules, de taille moyenne, le crâne en partie veuf d'une pilosité rousse qui ne s'étalait plus qu'à la nuque et aux tempes") and assuring him that he, Provancher, traced his origins to "Adam, qui sortit pur et parfait des mains du Créateur";[37] his compatriot J.-C.-K. Laflamme observed an arrogant young American at the dinner table, concluding a farcical description of the man's eating habits ("Hier il mangeait des asperges, et à chacune d'elles, il paraissait dire: Mon Dieu . . . que c'est une grande condescendance de ma part de vous croquer même du bout des dents; moi je suis sans reproche, mais les autres, quel tas de petites [sic] gens!") with "Le pharisien de l'Evangile est enfoncé par le type."[38]

The most logical destination in such a spiritual journey was Jerusalem. Devout (and wealthy) Canadian parents sent or accompanied their sons to Palestine as the crowning conclusion to a *grand tour*, and the brothers De Mille only reluctantly cancelled their plans to visit the Holy Land after a prolonged stay in Rome. William Henry Parker and Thomas Stinson Jarvis both explored the holy sites with which they were probably more familiar from Bible, hymns, engravings, and panoramas than with large parts of their own country. James Douglas from Quebec, who then intended to enter the Presbyterian ministry but later became an eminent professor of chemistry and a mining expert, travelled to Palestine with his entire family in 1854. There they "were included in the first group of Christians to be admitted to the sacred enclosures at Jerusalem where stands the Mosque of Omar on the site of the Jewish temple."[39] Priests and ministers like the Abbé Dupuis, Provancher, Cimon, and Johnston arrived to replenish their faith and bring home to their flock traditional metaphors and parables enriched by experience. Some, like Provancher, even took it upon themselves to organize and conduct tours to the Holy Land.

Travel to Palestine was facilitated during and after the Crimean War: in 1854, James Douglas benefitted from an agreement only recently formulated between the Ottoman Empire and western European governments concerning access to the holy sites. Thomas Stinson Jarvis, visiting the English Cemetery with the graves of "those brave fellows . . . that fell wounded in the Crimea, and lingered in the hospital at Scutari till they died,"[40] invested the spot with the romance of lives sacrificed in the fulfilment of a holy duty, and his words are meant as homage to "the poetry of a soldier's life and the fine essence of martial glory"[41] which made his just completed journey to the Holy Land possible. Jarvis travelled as a private citizen, but for the remainder of the century European potentates, increasingly aware that the days of their reigns were numbered, tried to demonstrate the legitimacy of their regimes with ostentatious building programmes and official foreign visits, some of them self-consciously modelled on the crusades and crusaders' churches. In 1856, the Ottomans granted France "the Church of St. Anne, the most magnificent surviving crusader church in the city,"[42] and the birth of the Prince Imperial in the same year—assuring, Napoleon III undoubtedly thought, the continuity of the Second Empire—was celebrated with a public dinner given by the French Consulate. At Miramar near Trieste, Napoleon's protégé, the ill-fated Emperor Maximilian of Mexico, built an exact replica of the Church of the Holy Sepulchre as his private chapel. Kaiser Wilhelm II, arriving with a grand entourage in 1898, inaugurated the new Church of the Redeemer, its campanile—designed by the Emperor himself—overtowering all other buildings in the Old City of Jerusalem. And the Princes of Wales, the future Edward VII and George V, appeared with renowned historians and photographers to help them understand Jerusalem's complex traditions and compile a lasting record of their experience. Since western nations were using the city to demonstrate their goodwill, Jerusalem seemed the ideal location for "A Permanent International Tribunal or Supreme Authority. Recognized and supported by the combined powers of the whole world; that the nations may thus be left without excuse for warfare thenceforth,"[43] as Henry Wentworth Monk of Ottawa argued in a letter to the British Prime Minister, quoting pertinent passages from the Bible to indicate that his idea had been preordained by God. An eccentric fruit-farmer born in Carleton County, Monk acquired some fame when the Pre-Raphaelite painter William Holman Hunt, fascinated with his "knowledge of the history, and his enthusiasm for the progressive thought stored in the Bible," took him under his wing during a visit to Jerusalem, where Monk had travelled "to become familiar with the features of the land of Promise." Monk continued to lobby for his idea "among Popes, Czars, Emperors, Kings, Presidents of Republics, Ministers of State, heads of Churches, and those native and foreign, and newspaper editors,"[44] before he died in Ottawa in 1896. The National Gallery there holds Holman Hunt's fine portrait of him which captures the charisma Monk must have exerted on his contemporaries, although he was generally considered insane.

His vision was, however, more humane than that embodied in a model of the holy sites exhibited at the 1867 Paris Exhibition. If, as Claude Lévi-Strauss has argued, the miniature reflects the delusions of power, this particular specimen amply supported his theory. The London Society for Promoting Christianity among the Jews displayed a model of the Church of the Holy Sepulchre, "the roofs and sections . . . all removable, so that the altars, shrines, and convents may be seen stretching over and underneath each other," and a contributor to *Harper's* sharply exposed political competitiveness masquerading as spiritual integrity: "In order to see the footholds of some of these—all are distinguished by various colours—it is necessary to remove stratum after stratum of the stronger countries, and find others that have burrowed far into subterranean vaults. Every one of these little shrines has cost a bloody war."[45]

After the opening of the Suez Canal and Britain's acquisition of Egypt, travel to the Near East became even more of a demonstration of British power. His own Christian fervour gratified by such an opportunity, Thomas Cook fully exploited these new avenues for his expanding business, his enterprise having been sanctioned by royal patronage when the future Edward VII enlisted his services. Hugh Johnston was impressed: "Even such personages as the Crown Prince of Austria, the Emperor of Brazil, Lord Dufferin, and Gladstone, have travelled under [Cook] in preference to an independent tour."[46] Cook's Tours turned the painful, hazardous pilgrimage of old into an homage to the modern age, "tents . . . placed in a circle, and . . . the saloon, a spacious tent that serves for parlour, *salle à manger*, and general gathering-place [in the centre of the encampment]."[47] Large meals consisting of "tea and coffee, eggs and omelet, cutlets and hot chicken" for breakfast and "soup, lamb, chicken, vegetables, pudding, pastry, nuts, dates, figs, and oranges" for dinner made the traveller forget that he was "out upon the Syrian wilds."[48] Cook's employees folded tents and stored baggage with the speed and discretion of the staff at grand hotels, amenities which may have temporarily eclipsed, even in the Reverend Johnston's mind, the virtues of a Spartan upbringing. They may also have briefly dimmed the spiritual goal of his journey. Indeed, considering these preliminaries, Johnston's first enthusiastic comments on Jerusalem sound rehearsed: "Jerusalem is the city of cities—the centre of the strongest affections and holiest memories—the true capital of the Christian World! The very sight of it thrills the soul with such feelings as no other spot inspires! It is linked with the grandest, and most sacred events in the history of mankind!"[49]

A different response came from the Abbé Léon Provancher whose work as an amateur scientist influenced all of his perceptions.[50] Born in Bécancour, Lower Canada, in 1820 and baptised by François Le Jamtel, a priest who had escaped to Canada during the French Revolution, Provancher was ordained in 1844, before beginning a productive career as an author and editor of scientific, historical, and religious publications, among them *Essai sur les insectes et les maladies qui affectent le blé* (1857), *Traité élémentaire de botanique* (1858), *Flore canadienne* (1862), *Le Verger canadien* (1862), *Les Oiseaux du Canada* (1874), *L'Echo du Calvaire* (1883), *Histoire du Canada* (1884), along with the periodicals *Le Naturaliste canadien* (founded in 1869 and continued after Provancher's death by his pupil, the Abbé Victor Alphonse Huard), and *La Semaine religieuse du Québec* (founded in 1888 and also continued by Huard), and two travel books, *De Québec à Jérusalem: Journal d'un Pèlerinage canadien en Terre-Sainte en passant à travers l'Angleterre, la France, l'Egypte, la Judée, la Samarie, la Galilée, la Syrie et l'Italie* (1884) and

Une Excursion aux climats tropicaux: Voyage aux Iles-au-Vent, St-Kitts, Névis, Antique, Montserrat, La Dominique, La Guadaloupe, Ste-Lucie, La Barbade, Trinidad (1890).

An irascible man, Provancher repeatedly embarrassed clerical authorities with his tempestuous outbursts in the daily press, directed—"sous prétexte que [le *Courrier du Canada*] a confondu un iguane avec un poisson"—"contre l'ignorance de tout le peuple canadien, contre l'abbé Labelle et la politique etc.,"[51] as the diarist of Quebec's Petit Séminaire noted with some dismay on 13 September 1888. Denied his annual government grant of $400 for the publication of *Le Naturaliste canadien* in 1891, Provancher became so vituperative that his religious superiors forbade him to send further letters to the editor of any publication in the province. But despite his eccentricity, Provancher was clearly admired for his knowledge and energy. "Le Père Provancher avait bien des travers," conceded the seminairy's diarist in 1894, "mais sa tête était richement meublée,"[52] a compliment which had earlier found expression in a number of public honours; Laval University conferred an honorary doctorate on him, and the Royal Society of Canada received him into its membership.

Provancher's voyages to Jerusalem were a natural extension of his worldview, determined as he was to reconcile the ideas of Divine Providence and modern science, spiritual pilgrimage and efficient travel, age-old Christian messianism and nineteenth-century French-Canadian nationalism. Thus, Provancher not only both enlisted and imitated Cook's services for several pilgrimages to Europe, but he also insisted (after a number of other projects, such as the founding of a Canadian guest-house, an agricultural settlement in Palestine, and a periodical devoted to the Holy Land, and the purchase of the eighth Station of the Cross had failed) that a painting by Joseph-Adolphe Rho, an artist from Saint-Hyacinthe, be installed in the chapel—situated two miles outside of Jerusalem—commemorating the baptism of Christ by St. John the Baptist. After endless diplomatic difficulties, Provancher's sheer tenacity brought him success, and "Saint Jean-Baptiste baptisant Notre Seigneur" henceforth proclaimed French Canada's messianic role as did the chapel dedicated to the same saint in Sacré-Coeur in Paris. Rho also painted a tableau depicting Provancher's 1884 pilgrimage to the River Jordan in the company of several distinguished fellow countrymen in order to demonstrate that travel to Palestine was now almost a national enterprise, no longer an individual excursion as it had been when the Abbé Léon Gingras visited the Holy Land in the 1840s.

In contrast to Hugh Johnston's emotional effusions on his first sight of Jerusalem, Provancher approached the city with the methodical thoroughness of the scientist. He first recorded precise geographical, geological, and meteorological data ("Jérusalem est située à environ 75 lieues de la Méditerranée, au milieu de la chaîne des montagnes de la Judée qui court de l'Est à L'Ouest. Le plateau sur lequel elle repose est à 2610 pieds au-dessus de la Méditerranée, et cette altitude lui assure, malgré sa latitude, une température bien supportable en toute saison de l'année"),[53] before presenting an equally thorough overview of the city's history. Next comes information on the population, with a breakdown of the religious denominations represented and particularly detailed comments on Islam and Protestantism. As he wanders through the city and its environs, the Abbé rehearses at length biblical episodes associated with the sites visited, effectively dramatizing such events as Christ's appearance before Pilate for his readers, to whom he clearly wishes to give a refresher course in the historical foundations of their faith.

Like most travellers to Jerusalem, however, he found its impact to be purely associative, and he was unable to reconcile its spiritual spell with its physical decay: "Otez à la ville sainte le prestige des événements à jamais mémorables dont elle a été le théâtre, et vous en faites la ville la plus maussade qu'on puisse voir."[54] Centuries of pilgrimages had, moreover, created a flourishing trade in relics, and Protestant sensibilities were especially offended by the inauthenticity contaminating the symbols of their faith: "After viewing all the doubtful sights in and about the Holy City," complained Jarvis, "the mind turned with an intense longing to something about which no imposition seemed possible."[55] Archeology offered solace since excavations were being conducted with the same scientific briskness in nineteenth-century Jerusalem as they were in Rome and Pompeii, and James Douglas senior ventured into "extensive ancient quarries . . . from which the stone used for Solomon's temple had been procured," an adventure exposing him and his family to "the risk of being seen, and perhaps fired upon, by Turkish sentries."[56] Another escape from the disappointments of Jerusalem ("one by one the dreams of childhood have the gloss of imagination taken from them, and each sight dispels part of the pleasant early delusion that somewhere on earth there is a likeness to Paradise,"[57] Jarvis wrote sadly) was poetry, and Jarvis for one deliberately ignored the real city as often as he possibly could, trying instead to recapture the magic its name had possessed before he saw it: "in that moment of farewell the old city seemed all at once unfamiliar to our eyes . . . it was Jerusalem passing again into the idea. Even before losing sight of it, it took the form of the mind's fancy before ever gazing on it."[58] Yet whereas medieval mapmakers had distorted their drawings of the world to place Jerusalem at the centre, many now asserted that the New Jerusalem was to be found elsewhere, whether in Rome, as Provancher would have it, or in the glass-and-steel palaces of the great exhibitions, as those with a fervent belief in the mission of industry and technology suggested.

The rejection (or at least the very conditional acceptance) of Jerusalem as a spiritual centre was also exacerbated by anti-semitic sentiments. To a mind trained to perceive reality allegorically, the dirty, narrow streets of Jerusalem seemed a reflection of the population's cultural decadence, a view some travellers expressed with equal virulence about Rome, as Nérée Gingras's diary showed. Even during the journey, travellers vented their displeasure at Jewish passengers, perceiving them—as did J.-C.-K. Laflamme—as incarnations of Judas Iscariot or as greedy Fagins, as did Hugh Johnston. Despite Jarvis's protestations to the contrary, his attitude toward the Jewish population had clearly been shaped by his biblical instruction; like his views of Jerusalem, his ideas of the Jews wavered unresolved between metaphor and reality: "The Pharisees, with their long clothes, tall black hats, and long lightish curls hanging effeminately over their sickly, dirty faces were always particularly odious to me; and it was not on account of any biblical prejudice that made these men disgusting, for I had revolted from them before knowing they were the old sect of Pharisees."[59] Not even British missionary and philanthropic activity had taught them to mend their ways, complained Hugh Johnston, "for although Sir Moses Montefiore, of London, has built rows of home-like cottages for their accommodation in the suburbs, yet they prefer their execrable lane-like streets and wretched hovels within the walls."[60] Such views, combined with the bitter anti-semitism current among Canadian ultramontanists (in Rome, Judge Routhier imagined that the Tiber, repelled, hurried more quickly through the ghetto than through other quarters,[61] and Jules-Paul Tardivel commended the pope for keeping a close eye on the Jews),[62] consolidated prejudices which were to have severe consequences for Canada's growing awareness of its multiculturalism.

7

Views of European Cities

If travellers retained a paradoxical image of Jerusalem, so too did they consider Europe's great cities contradictory mixtures of glory and decay. Encouraged by the advent of gaslight, steam-power, and photography, some like the Reverend James Douglas in 1867 concluded that "the Millenium . . . is to be a Reign of Peace on Earth; Not the End, But the Summer Time of the World" and that the modern cities of the western world, ennobled by the blessings of technology and Christian brotherhood, were to be so many incarnations of the New Jerusalem.[1] Similarly, a contributor to the *Revue canadienne*, comparing "les grands travaux des modernes . . . à ceux des anciens," chose biblical imagery to express his pride in the achievements of his century: "Comme un roi superbe, [l'homme] parcourt sur ses chars enflammés, précédé, comme autrefois Möise, le jour, par une colonne de fumée, la nuit, par une colonne de feu . . . et, comme le Leviathan de l'Ecriture, le voilà qui, déjà, plonge au sein des mers qu'il a couvertes de ses navires."[2]

This Canadian dismissed the works of pagan antiquity as pitiful as compared to Christian modernity. The Reverend Moses Harvey was somewhat more cautious in his conclusions. Confronted with the remains of Pompeii, he asked himself, "Human Progress—Is It Real?" In the ruins of ancient cities lay the imprints (or "daguerrotypes," as Harvey phrased it) of civilizations so sophisticated that "the highest praise we can bestow upon our modern civilization is that it reproduces the splendour of those old nationalities, and perhaps rivals the long-buried glories of the past."[3] Moreover, the achievements of modern cities were dimmed by pollution, social misery, insurrection, and unbrotherly rivalry among competing nations, with Paris—in ruins from the recent events of the Siege and the Commune—as shocking evidence. Did human history then develop in repetitive cycles, and was man an incorrigible brute as Darwin's *The Descent of Man* (published in 1871, the year of the Franco-Prussian War) seemed to suggest? A contributor to *The Saturday Reader* had an apocalyptic vision of London, its "factories and workshops" silent and "the innumerable railways, once burdened daily with the weight of countless tons of human and mercantile traffic . . . buried and forsaken": "Towns and cities must as inevitably go through birth, youth, rise, and decay, as does man."[4] Not so, claimed Harvey, who—in a concept he shared with such Canadian scientists as Sir John William Dawson, principal of McGill College—combined Darwinist theory with the traditional teachings of Christianity.[5] Thanks to "young, bright-eyed" science and to the physical and moral health of the northern race, he thought of mankind as developing in "an ascending spiral curve" toward perfection, by "courageously assail[ing] the worn out and bad."[6] The most violent battlegrounds of progress and decay, cities were still the nerve-centres of civilization, nourishing the country with material and spiritual provisions: "all forms of human corruption are, in this centre of human activity, encircled by splendours and contrasted with purities and kindly charities, and sweet domestic affections."[7] Although he was clearly aware of the violent complexities of modern urban life, Harvey contemplated the city as an allegory rather than as a phenomenon. Other religious Canadian travellers shared his approach, choosing both metaphysical and geographical vantage-points from which to survey the city, categorizing humanity as Scripture had taught them to and frequenting churches and tabernacles for fortification.

Some travellers, however, forswore such aloof pinnacles, defiantly or enthusiastically plunging into the unpredictable stream of urban life instead. "Loiterers" or *flâneurs*, many of them journalists gathering colourful material for the *feuilletons* of their papers, became an ubiquitious feature in the streets of Europe's great cities during the nineteenth century. The installation of broad pavements and gaslight, of sidewalk cafés and covered arcades, not to mention improvements in general sanitation, created the prerequisites for such ambling. Writing *flâneurs* provided their readers—as Kathleen Coleman did—with synopses of the more sensational novelties in fashion and entertainment: moreover, they isolated and described individuals from the steady stream of passers-by, classifying them according to the principles of the new science of phrenology. A "botanist on asphalt," the *flâneur* made pronouncements on the character, profession, and milieu of strangers observed, based on their appearance only;[8] heir to the Enlightenment's faith in the City as Virtue,[9] the *flâneur* strolled confidently about, replacing the theologian's trust in Scripture with an equally fervent faith in empiricism. The appropriate literary forms for such a "quickened, multiplied conscious-ness," as Walter Pater was to call it, were multifaceted fragments rather than lengthy narratives embodying a centralist worldview.

Quebec authors like Napoléon Aubin, Hector Berthelot, Hector Fabre, Napoléon Legendre, and Arthur Buies embraced the ideal of the stroller wandering through the streets of Quebec or Montreal, observing their fellow-citizens at their daily tasks, in the market-place, at a funeral, in their salons. The Swiss-born Aubin used the word *flâneur* (adopted in Parisian French only in 1835 when it appeared in Balzac's letters)[10] as early as 1837, when he subtitled his paper *Fantasque* "journal rédigé par un flâneur." Quebec loiterers delighted in shocking the bourgeois with flippant *aperçus*, their work as gently subversive as that of their Parisian colleagues who had to watch their step carefully under Louis Philippe's régime. Hector Fabre drew up a humorous list of "des articles du code du flâneur de la rue Notre Dame," evicting all such respectable citizens as "père[s] de famille, propriétaire[s] ou conseiller[s] municipal" from the club and disqualifying all those guilty of carrying an umbrella "par simple précaution" or making a "serious" purchase at five o'clock in the afternoon.[11] Even these few quotations make it clear that the *flâneur* and his *chroniques*, as his work was often entitled, formed an important antidote to the staid respectability of a Judge Routhier and other conservatives. Napoléon Aubin for one openly declared his independence: "Je n'obéis ni ne commande à personne, je vais où je veux, je fais ce qui me plaît, je vis comme je peux et je meurs quand il faut."[12] In love with city-life and its sophistication, Quebec *flâneurs* undermined the rural myth propagated by French-Canada's conservatives, although they were clearly often an ostracized minority. As Buies explained it in the preface to his *Chroniques canadiennes*: "La causerie est le genre le plus difficile et le plus rare en Canada; on n'y a pas d'aptitudes. Il faut être un oisif, un propre à rien, un déclassé, pour y donner ses loisirs."[13] The pressures appear to have been too much for Buies, who ended his life in the services of the Curé Labelle, composing works on the settlement of rural areas in Quebec. Yet the liberal tradition was strong enough to prepare the ground for such recent urban novels as Michel Tremblay's *Chroniques du Plateau Mont-Royal*, appropriately set in Montreal's Rue Fabre and echoing even in its title the tradition of Quebec's liberal journalism.

The mere fact that Fabre—however humorously—offers his description of the Montreal *flâneur* in a series of prescriptions ("Les passants s'arrêtent un peu partout: au coin de la Rue St. Jean-Baptiste, aux quatre coins de la rue St. Gabriel; les flâneurs ne s'arrêtent qu'au coin de la Place des Armes, côté Lyman, au coin de la rue St. Lambert, et au coin de la rue St. Vincent''),[14] expresses a confidence as great as that of a conservative surveying the city from *his* particular perspective—the moreso since Montreal and Quebec were thoroughly familiar hunting-grounds. Neither attitude fully responded to the threatening opacity of great cities, their anonymity and chaos. Once confronted with a foreign metropolis, the tourist—conservative *or* liberal—often had to turn his presumed competence into a defensive fantasy, propped up by his guidebook's detailed instructions. Arthur Buies felt deeply alienated by ''Paris le désert''; and Grace Denison, an accomplished ''loiterer,'' painfully recognized the fragility of her particular fantasy—that of the social reformer at large protected by her goodwill—when she almost perished on an impromptu outing through the slums of Cologne.

Contemporary authors bore witness to the fearful impenetrability of modern cities. Edgar Allan Poe's stories, especially ''The Man in the Crowd,'' and Baudelaire's poems depicted the stroller as disintegrating into the crowd; Eugène Sue—influenced by James Fenimore Cooper—declared Paris a savage jungle of crime and poverty in his immensely successful *Les Mystères de Paris* (1842-43); Victor Hugo's Inspector Jabert hunted his victims into the Paris sewers, and Charles Dickens spoke of London as a prehistoric waste of mud in the famous opening pages of *Bleak House* (1852-53). In all of these, the carefree elegant *flâneur* has become a detective obsessively determined to capture an elusive criminal and thereby to create an equally elusive social and moral order.[15]

Sue, Dickens, and Hugo were widely read in Victorian Canada, providing readers with an imaginative frame of reference for the very amorphousness of the modern city.[16] Several publications echo the title of Sue's *Mystères*: Henri-Emile Chevalier, Hector Berthelot, and Auguste Fortier all wrote novels entitled *Les Mystères de Montréal*, published in 1855, 1880, and 1893 respectively. Charlotte Führer's *The Mysteries of Montreal: Memoirs of a Midwife* (1881), a sensationalist, semi-fictional account of Montreal's seamier side, and Arthur Campbell's suspense novel *The Mystery of Martha Warne: A Tale of Montreal* (1888) imitate both Sue and Dickens in passages such as these:

> St. Urbain Street is in no way remarkable except that it is always very dirty. As every street in the city is in a more or less wretched condition about the first of April, this street at that season of the year loses its sole claim to distinction. This night it fully sustained its reputation. Water was running down the middle of the street in a furious manner, two or three different streams of it, sometimes coalescing, sometimes

dividing into many more. The sidewalk was not in a much better condition. It was paved with brick, and was very uneven; the slush was mixed with ashes which had been put out to prevent people from slipping when it was icy, and in the darkness it was not always possible to tell whether a black spot ahead was a piece of brick pavement, a heap of ashes or a pool of water.[17]

Historicism and the rural ethos prevented serious nineteenth-century writers in both English and French from depicting metropolitan life in their work. Post-Confederation poetry is notoriously devoid of realist depictions of city life, and John Hare's *Anthologie de la poésie québécoise du XIXe siècle* (1979) lists only one poem with an urban scene, Eustache Prudhomme's "Un Soir dans la cité" (1886). Historical novels and romances provided nostalgic, antiquarian views of cities, above all, Quebec City. Popular fiction, however, such as the publications cited above, anticipated modern urban novels like Gabrielle Roy's *Bonheur d'occasion* (1945); likewise, nineteenth-century travel descriptions of London, Paris and Rome gauge Canadians' imaginative responses to large cities when few other contemporary texts provide such information.

H.   "A Picturesque London Scene," *The Dominion Illustrated.*

1. LONDON

On their pilgrimages to the homeland, most English-Canadians considered London the most important goal of their journey. Seat of the government and Queen Victoria's capital, it symbolized more than any other part of Britain the heart of the Empire, the maternal centre of a large colonial family. Judging from contemporary Canadian periodicals, there was an almost limitless interest in all phases of London's history, its ancient lineage gratifying to the colonial who was seeking to confirm his cultural roots. In the 1870s for instance, the *New Dominion Monthly* published sketches on "Norman London," "Saxon London," "London in the Olden Time, British and Roman," and "The Tower of London as a Prison," in which the archeological strata of the city were unearthed along with the different phases of its past. "We have all of us . . . heard that the star of empire moves westward," asserts the author. "We know that all things gravitate to a centre. . . . It will not, therefore, surprise us . . . to know that the most populous, most wealthy and most maritime city on the face of the earth is the capital of two small islands on the extreme verge of the Atlantic Ocean,"[18] before introducing London as a compact encyclopedia of western culture. Yet, although the city conjured up memories of national splendour—memories revived in the dazzling display of royal pageantry—its ever-growing size, anonymity, and social problems alienated visitors who had come to confirm their faith in Britain. Even the author of the *New Dominion Monthly* series was taken aback by London's amorphous hugeness when he witnessed the crowds attending the celebrations at the end of the Crimean War: "The great charge at Balaklava was nothing to it; but when the vast crowd had melted away and we were left to walk the streets all night, the silence and desolation of the vast city was something appalling. . . . London asleep was like a dead man looking at you."[19] The sinister aspects of London life were explored in such publications as "the Porter letters, describing . . . the slums and social problems of the metropolis of the world"[20] in the *Toronto News* in 1887. Still, the myth of the imperial centre was powerful enough to send Canadians away with heightened expectations. Once in London, many struggled to keep their ideal alive, sometimes arriving at an uneasy truce with their disillusioned colonial sentiment.

Caniff Haight, a Picton druggist and bookseller, who had made himself a name with his first book, *Country Life in Canada Fifty Years Ago*, published his memories of travel in Britain in *Here and There in the Homeland: England, Scotland and Ireland, as Seen by a Canadian* (1895), a work successful enough to be re-issued in 1904 as *A United Empire Loyalist in Great Britain*. Descendant of one of the Pilgrim

Fathers, of a Quaker Family of Duchess County, New York, and of United Empire Loyalists, Haight expressed a patriotic sentiment for Britain so sincere and possessed a historical knowledge so redoubtable that he was commissioned to transcribe Loyalist papers held in the vaults of the Smithsonian Museum, in addition to publishing two further books, *Before the Coming of the Loyalists* (1897) and *Coming of the Loyalists* (1899).[21] Naturally, Haight eagerly anticipated his arrival in London, but he was rudely awakened from his mythic dream when he found himself in an unwelcoming city: "An oppressive sense of loneliness seemed to weigh me down in the midst of the surging tide of the millions of people. My very identity seemed to be lost in the magnitude of numbers, and I felt like taking up the plaint of the Ancient Mariner—'Water, water everywhere, / Nor any drop to drink.' "[22]

Haight's comparison of London to an ocean also pervades the remainder of his book; even after weeks of sightseeing, London has not imprinted an indelible pattern on his mind. It continues to be amorphous like water, and even its most prominent landmarks—like St. Paul's Cathedral—are almost submerged in "the surging tide of restless humanity that whirls and breaks around it."[23] He travels through London's streets and lanes as if he were the captain of an exploratory vessel; in doing so he passes by houses "as thickly encrusted as an old ship is with barnacles."[24] Haight's metaphor does imply a long and venerable history, but it also replaces the ancient idea of the state as a ship firmly ruled even in the stormiest weather, with an alarming sense of decay and stagnation. Ironically, the very fluidity of London life enhances that sense of alienation: unpredictable, the city is always new, never a familiar friend, certainly never a warm and welcoming mother. A visitor to London feels like a seafarer without a compass, suspecting that the real treasures lie "in countless depths, hidden away as it were, and must be sought after."[25]

Moreover, with Queen Victoria spending much of her long widowhood away from London, the city did not seem as emphatically the heart of the Empire as it might have otherwise. Haight had to travel to Windsor to experience a moment of loyal rapture, and here the ocean metaphor finally takes on positive connotations with a "swaying sea" of enthusiastic subjects, all saluting the monarch as if she were a brilliant beacon in a troubled sea: "It would be impossible for Canadian blood to witness such an ovation without imbibing its spirit; impossible . . . to look over the swaying sea of men and women waving hats and clapping hands without cutting circles in British air with a Canadian 'tile'—utterly impossible."[26]

For Victoria's jubilees in 1887 and 1897, London briefly became the glamorous centre of the Empire once more, and Canadian delegates were called upon to evoke the splendour of the celebrations for their compatriots at home. But here too disillusionments and inconsistencies crop up, although more obliquely. Kathleen Coleman, sent to London by her paper to describe the festivities of the Queen's Diamond Jubilee (and invited by Wilfrid Laurier, generally considered one of the "stars" of the occasion, to accompany him to a ceremony in Buckingham Palace), conjured up a fairy-tale mood in her first letter to Toronto, a mood she sustains, at least superficially, for the remainder of her descriptions. London, bathed in "the soft blue mists of June,"[27] emerges like a dream from a romantic poem, a New Jerusalem with church spires gleaming in the early morning sunshine and the dome of St. Paul's illuminated at night "like a vision, mystic, wonderful."[28] References to religious symbols punctuate the letters, firmly anchoring the dazzling sights described in Britain's mission before the world. Kipling's name is evoked as the troops file past, "their cuirasses glittering, the tall white plumes on their helmets waving in unison, so perfect was the marching of their horses . . . Kipling, Kipling! One felt like shouting the man's name, and calling for three cheers for him. His verse kept time to every movement of the troops."[29] Important landmarks in the city are surrounded by an aura of historical and literary associations: "What would Dr. Johnson say if he saw his beloved old thoroughfare arraying itself in crowns and gewgaws of shivering lights?"[30] The journalist animates her letters by allegorizing buildings, streets, ships, underlining the moral values represented by them, but also bringing lifeless things like the Bank of England close to her readers as if they were dear old friends: "Nothing . . . could be more girlishly girly than the conduct of the Old Lady of Threadneedle Street. To see a venerable female, whom one has always respected, come out in a low-cut gown and diamond necklace is a shock to the feelings, but when it comes to an old, old lady, whose stability, financial standing, and undoubted respectability have been the talk of the world, when it comes to her coming out with all her diamonds and rubies ahung about her old neck, and strange and startling fiery horns standing up behind her old ears, one's feelings become shocked almost beyond expression."[31] Coleman wanted her readers to see, feel, and smell the ambiance of the Jubilee pageantry. Her third letter, "The Via Triumphalis," records the hammering, singing, and shouting during the night before the grand procession, the sounds echoing through the intricate and mysterious maze of London. The procession announces itself with a distant roll of drums and the stirring sounds of "Rule Britannia" sweeping through the crowds: Kit creates an exhilarating sense of space, movement, and anticipation.

Kit wrote in an age when journalism subsumed the roles which radio and television play today, and her reporting fulfilled a more complex social role than contemporary journalism does. Her writing acquired literary qualities whenever it came to drawing imaginary scenes recreating for her readers, as well as it could be done in words, the scenes she had been commissioned to experience for all of them. Years later, a contributor to the *Canadian Magazine* wistfully remembered Kit's description of the Jubilee; now, in 1917, the world was far from its glitter and the only lights permitted in London were the searchlights "feeling after some raider of the air which seeks to pour down death on the crowds below."[32]

Yet although Coleman celebrated the Victorian Age at its most ostentatious and powerful, she was not insensitive to its ironies, inconsistencies, and injustices. Her reports are subtly counterpointed with reminders of social misery, the threat of war, and the ultimate hollowness of imperialist demonstrations. Her love of Dickens had taught her to sketch sentimental but still poignant cameos like the following, observed as a coda to the "Lights o' London": "one poor window displayed a common old oil-lamp, draped about with red paper. Two penny dip-candles spluttered on either side of it. From a broken pane above, a penny Jack hung limply, and inside, pinned on the opposite wall, one could see a brave picture of the Queen, set about—by what poor hands, God knows!—with a wreath of tawdry paper roses. The room seemed empty, but a sewing machine with some white work on it, and a pair of little crutches leaning against the wall, under the Queen's picture, brought a passionate sense of the pain and grief of the poor."[33]

A similar contrast between splendour and fearful reality informs Coleman's descriptions of the grand *toilettes* observed on the way to Ascot, in the procession, and at a fancy dress ball given by the Duchess of Devonshire. As the editor of a woman's page, she was required to present the occasional item on fashion, and her employer promptly reminded her of her duties when she had not attended to them for some time. *To London for the Jubilee* contains numerous sketches of elegant women's clothes, presented with a thorough knowledge of fabrics and sewing techniques and in a specialized fashion vocabulary: "The young Duchess of Marlborough wore a pink foulard, and three little frills edged with lace over white satin. The sash was black. A charming toque of black and white chiffon, with pink roses, topped up this gay costume, and the Duchess looked very well, very English, and very, very young."[34] Considering Kit's own notoriously unkempt appearance (a disgruntled reader who had seen her at a horseshow described her as a "tall, gaunt, passé woman, nearer to fifty than forty, gowned shabbily in an old black silk that smelled of ammonia . . . and wearing a hat—a dusty, old chip hat, laden with ancient feathers, which matched your air of shabby gentility; old black kid gloves, printers'-inked at the fingertips, and large feet, encased in merely passable shoes; a face like a mask, powdered heavily, impassive, hard,

1. Fred C. Martin.

2. Thomas C. Watkins.

3. "Egerton Ryerson," painting by Théophile Hamel.

4. Ethel Davies.

5. Napoléon Bourassa.

6. Moses Harvey.

7. Ovide Brunet.

8. Thomas-Étienne Hamel.

9. J.-C.-M. Laflamme.

10. Louis Fréchette.

12. Gertrude Fleming's father-in-law, husband, and son. No photograph of Gertrude Fleming herself has been found.

11. Charles Herbert Mackintosh.

13. Kathleen Coleman.

14. Alice Jones.

15. Narcisse Henri Edouard Faucher de St.-Maurice.

16. Hector Fabre.

17. Léon Provancher.

18. "Henry Wentworth Monk," by William Holman Hunt.

19. Canniff Haight.

20. William Withrow.

21. Reverend Hugh Johnston.

22. Octave Crémazie.

23. Adolphe-Basile Routhier.

24. Jules-Paul Tardivel.

25. François Xavier Antoine Labelle.

26. "Trafalgar Square," painted on the wall of the "Croscup Room," Granville Ferry, Nova Scotia.

27. "Lion of Waterloo."

28. "James Croil and Party."

DESCRIPTION OF HOLDER.
Height *5 fet 10 inches*
Color of Eyes *Grey*
Color of Hair *Grey*
Complexion *Fair*
Nose *turned up*
General Appearance *good.*
Age
Signature of Holder
M. E. Hamel
Attested by

These are to certify that *the Most Reverend Thomas Étienne Hamel, of Laval University, city and district of Quebec, in the Province of Quebec,* the holder hereof, whose Description is given in the margin, is a

British Subject; and that these presents are granted to enable *him* to travel in foreign parts.

Given at Quebec this *thirtieth* day of *June* in the year of our Lord one thousand eight hundred and ninety *three.* and of Her Majesty's Reign the fifty *seventh.*

(*Six words erased are null and void*)

By Command

Secretary of the Province of Quebec.

Justice of the Peace.

Administrator.

29. Thomas-Étienne Hamel's passport.

30. Thomas Langton's journal, with his sketches of tourists reading *Baedeker.*

31. "Neopolitan Youths," by Wilhelm von Gloeden.

32. Daguerrotype by Thomas Coffin Doane, presented to the Empress Eugénie by Montreal citizen Alfred Chalifoux.

33. "Demolitions for the Rue de Rennes, St.-Germain-des-Prés on Right," *L'illustration.*

34. "Curiosity-Foreigners visiting the Ruins of Paris," *Canadian Illustrated News.*

35. and 36. The Tiber
embankments before and
after their modernization.

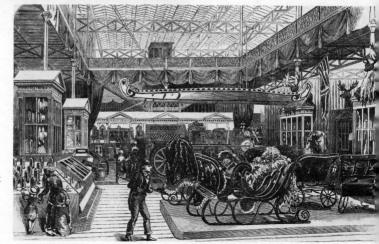

37. The Canadian Court
at the 1851 World
Exposition, *Illustrated
London News.*

38. The Canadian Trophy at the 1855 Exposition Universelle.

39. Kabyle Women at the Paris Exhibition, 1889, *Dominion Illustrated.*

40. "Col. Rhodes and Guide, Caribou Hunting Series" is an example of the photographs exhibited at World Expositions, giving Europeans an idea of Canadian life.

cruel''),[35] such passages sound insincere, and although they give all the required information, they are static and lifeless. As a result, the splendidly arrayed duchesses seem like so many mannequins, parading the gorgeous garments of a vacant society.

Coleman's fashion notes assume an additional irony, when, surveying the Royal Fleet in Portsmouth, she gives equal attention to the military equipment of the men-of-war anchored there (''Each carries four 67-ton 13 in. guns, firing a 1,250 pound shell. The 67-tonners, white and formidable, are placed in pairs at each end of the ship, on pear-shaped towers, plated with 17-inch steel'').[36] She stages, moreover, an imaginary battle between the fleet and Mother Nature: ''Nature, offended at the exploitation of man's little power, palpitated with fury. She sounded her heart-beats, and flung fiery glances down at the great Titans, who sat silent, with drooping flags and lowered crests. It was a sublime moment,''[37] and beneath the enthusiastic jingoism Coleman was expected to deliver runs an undertone of alarm at the possible consequences of imperialist arrogance. Later, after she had covered the Cuban War, Kit was to develop strongly anti-military feelings, although she had to compromise once again during the Boer War, when nothing but enthusiasm for the British cause would do.

Judge Adolphe-Basile Routhier, also in town to witness the Jubilee, explored the idea of the British Empire with equal subtleness, this time from the perspective of a French-Canadian nationalist who had learnt in his long public career to express his views diplomatically. Whereas his chapter on London in *A Travers l'Europe: impressions et paysages* (1881-83) compared the city to a Dantesque Inferno and to Rome in its last days of decadence, *La Reine Victoria et son jubilé* (1898), still retaining the analogy with ancient Rome by comparing the grand Jubilee pageant with the Caesars' triumphal processions, juxtaposes the cruel display of captives in Roman times with Victoria's maternal concern for the humblest of her subjects: ''La Fête impériale et coloniale prenait le caractère d'une fête de famille.''[38] Repeatedly, Routhier alludes to the events of the Franco-Prussian War to underline the Queen's respectful concern for all of her colonial children (unlike the Prussians who, he complains, insisted on humiliating Parisians by marching through the Arc de Triomphe and along the Champs-Elysées) to highlight the advantages of a legitimate monarchy over revolution and republicanism, and—one assumes—to justify, obliquely, a French Canadian's enthusiasm for the Jubilee. Thus, Routhier tries to imagine for his readers what Victoria saw from her carriage and what nostalgic thoughts might have passed through her head. Most of them, he fancies, had to do with France, with Louis-Philippe, and with Napoleon III's exile and death. Whereas in *A Travers l'Europe*

Routhier had somewhat contemptuously affirmed that Britain was a better taskmaster than France because she was at least Christian, if not Catholic, the occasion now required that he wax enthusiastic: "Mais, grâce à Dieu, l'avenir de la dynastie royale d'Angleterre a de meilleurs gages de stabilité. Elle est fondée sur la légitimité dynastique et sur la légitimité conjugale."[39]

The jubilee provided a temporary frame of reference for Coleman and Routhier. Ordinarily, however, London's vastness seemed a wilderness, a jungle, an irrational, dangerous growth, especially to those visitors who approached it after a stay in Edinburgh. A New Athens distinguished by "a combination of the sternly beautiful of both art and nature,"[40] Edinburgh appeared clearly and rationally structured and the Georgian architecture of its buildings and crescents admirable, with appropriate landmarks like Edinburgh Castle, the Walter Scott Memorial, and Holyrood House signalling significant moments in its history. An overview of the city's design and its place in the surrounding landscape could be easily gained by climbing up to the Castle or any other elevation, and *Baedeker's* advised tourists to commence any visit to Edinburgh in just this way. By contrast, no view from a tower or monument in London guaranteed a panoramic overview; on the contrary, the observer could expect to be even more impressed with London's luxuriant chaos of buildings and thoroughfares. Andrew Spedon, fresh from sentimental days in Edinburgh, complained: "the vision is almost paralyzed with the sight; everywhere around, even into the immensity of distance, is to be seen the dense and complicated labyrinth of buildings, interspersed with hundreds of lofty spires, turrets, and massive piles."[41] Spedon may well have been prejudiced against London, for the Scottish capital was his birthplace (*"the most hallowed spot on earth"*),[42] but his impressions are confirmed by Maria Elise Lauder, a woman of German descent, in her *Evergreen Leaves; or "Toofie" in Europe*. Lauder's travellers long for a fog-and smokeless day, "the blue of our own Canada,"[43] so that London may appear to them "all bright and glittering in the smokeless air" as it did to Wordsworth early one morning on Westminster Bridge. One useful substitute for a central point of observation, for some, was the double-decker bus, whose motion turned the absence of a centre into a virtue and whose ubiquitousness allowed eager tourists to make quick escapes and easy transitions.

Fog and grime, unattractive brick buildings and labyrinthine streets, the squalor and crime of the slums all seemed to belong to a primitive civilization, with St. Paul's "in the hoary dinginess of years . . . like some huge pyramid rear[ing] its lofty and venerable head."[44] Spedon's choice of the words "rear" and "head," which may point toward a sphinx, still almost contradicts the implications of "lofty" and "venera-ble": like Dickens in the famous opening paragraphs of *Bleak House*, he seems to think of a pre-historic era when "the waters had but newly retired from the face of the earth"[45] and of a dinosaur rather than monumental architecture. *Baedeker's* increased the traveller's apprehensions about London's safety; despite assurances in 1892, that much progress had been made in the City's lighting system and street design, it warned urgently against "the artifices of pick-pockets and the wiles of impostors."[46] The tourist was to shun the advice of strangers, to ask for help from one of London's 17,500 policemen, a postman, a commissionaire, or a shop-keeper instead, and to apply special caution in "crossing a crowded thoroughfare, and in entering or alighting from a train or omnibus."[47] In general, *Baedeker's* emphasis was on indoor sightseeing, offering an impressive thirty pages of information on the National Gallery and almost as many on Westminster Abbey and the British Museum, but only two on the ports and docks along the Thames.

The average tourist, however, was ill-equipped to appreciate endless galleries of paintings. Andrew Spedon, undaunted, simply listed the prices of the more expensive works: "Among some of the most costly pictures, I noticed Murillo's Holy Family, which cost $15,000; Raising of Lazarus, $20,000; Raffaelle's St. Catherine, $25,000; Ecce Homo and Mercury Instructing Cupid, $52,000; St. Paul's Veronese's Family of Darius, $70,000, besides others of similar character and cost."[48] A contributor to the *New Dominion Monthly*, conveying his impressions of the National Gallery, felt unsure whether a good Protestant was safer inside a museum than in the streets of London: popery and offensive realism tainted many of the pictures and sculptures. "One painting represents St. John, the Evangelist, raised to Heaven. He is being drawn up by the wrists, and the expression on his face is one of great bodily discomfort, as well as it may be,"[49] sneered this Canadian. He was equally displeased with the museum's collection of Turners, casual works, he felt, which did not "tell well for his industry."[50] Rare exceptions from such philistinism were Canadian painters themselves, to whom London's vast collections of art were holy shrines: "The first thing which strikes us is a kind of mellowed glory and the quiet peace," wrote Robert Harris to his family in Charlottetown, "The sounds of the city are shut out and on a summer afternoon, there is a kind of dreamy feeling in everything produced, perhaps, by the quietness and solitude."[51]

Most Canadian visitors were forever in search of a sanctuary sheltering them, if only temporarily, from "the bustle, noise, stench and smoke of the city."[52] When he was not roaming through galleries or at work in his studio, Robert Harris often quietly sat in a church, deep in reverie, till the church warden chased him out. His colleague Emily Carr, homesick for the west coast forest, found refuge in London's parks.[53] Many other visitors, appalled at Londoners' readiness to desecrate the Sabbath, determinedly attended one church service after the other. Andrew Spedon visited both Spurgeon's Tabernacle and Dr. Cumming's sermons, offering knowledgeable analyses of both preachers' appearances and performance. Spurgeon disappointed him with his "pale, inexpressive appearance" and a "head . . . not of the highest phrenological order."[54] Still, he was enchanted with the plain directness of the minister's argument, whereas he found John Cumming's appearance and performance, although intellectually more impressive ("fore-head expansive and prominent, especially in the region of the reflective faculties"), too philosophical to appeal to the general public. John Cumming was a minister of the Scottish Kirk, but underlying Spedon's subtle criticism is an attack on the elitism of the High Church, an attack rather more forcefully presented by another frequenter of London preachers, the Reverend Hugh Johnston, when he assessed Canon Liddon's preaching in St. Paul's in 1881.[55]

To Protestant English-Canadians, London's famous churches were both peaceful islands and welcome reminders of national glory, although some Ruskinites pointed out Westminster Abbey's architectural superiority to St. Paul's.[56] French Canadians, however, trained to distrust classicism as the symbol of rationalist chill, made sharp distinctions between these two buildings; the city seemed even more of a thicket to them, with Catholic chapels tucked away in side-streets and almost submerged in a hostile region. One particularly complex response came from Jules-Paul Tardivel in the late 1880s. Greeted by bright September sunshine, "tout comme à Québec,"[57] he felt instantly at home in the city: after all, London was his mother's birthplace. Tardivel's father, a Frenchman who had emigrated to the United States in 1848, had married an Englishwoman; this triple heritage of France, Britain, and America was to determine Tardivel's allegiances and thinking to the end of his career.[58] Descendant of a fervently Roman-Catholic family, Tardivel was sent to the classical college of St. Hyacinthe in Quebec where he performed exceptionally well. From the beginning, his schooling was marked by militant Catholicism. He witnessed nineteen of his school-mates enlist with the papal *zouaves*; prize compositions were designed to follow developments in Pius IX's papacy; classical writers were banned in favour of theological and patriotic works. Tardivel's talent soon attracted the attention of major Quebec newspapers such as *La Minerve* and *Le Canadien*; from 1881, he published his own paper, the long-lived and influential ultramontanist organ, *La Vérité*. When he travelled through Europe in the late 1880s, he sent regular letters to *La Vérité* describing his experiences; in 1890, these were published in a book dedicated to young French-Canadians as *Notes de Voyage en France, Italie, Espagne, Irlande, Angleterre, Belgique et Hollande*, together with numerous portraits of clergymen visited and famous sights seen. Despite the characteristic apologia at the beginning of the work declaring it a casual enterprise, Tardivel clearly designed the *Notes* as a didactic compendium. He himself borrowed the occasional statistics from popular guidebooks, but he advised his readers to avoid *Baedeker* and the others because he rightly suspected a pro-Protestant attitude behind their selections and descriptions.

Tardivel's special family background made him a somewhat atypical French-Canadian traveller: he felt sentimentally attracted to London when he should ideologically shun it; later, on his arrival in Paris, he felt like a stranger, so much so that he spent much of the following letter explaining and justifying his response. It was not family sentiment which makes him feel this way, he assured his readers, but Quebec's North-American way of life. Faith and language were French, but constant contact with the English affected daily life: Tardivel even used the word "entamer," that is, "to break the armour or breast-plate" to describe the process of infiltration. If Tardivel's explanation—presented as a quotation of an analysis offered by someone else—appears somewhat unconvincing, one's suspicions are even further aroused later on when he claims the absence of beggars in Paris as proof that here the spirit of Christian charity had survived better than in haughty and egotistical London, where the poor were hidden in workhouses.

Against this personal background, Tardivel's wanderings in London assume their special, ambiguous meaning. On the one hand, he was enchanted by its "belles grandes rues, larges, propres, bien pavées, pleine de lumière"[59] and by the Thames, which—although smaller than the St. Lawrence—was still a real river, not a dirty canal, as he had been led to believe. On the other hand, however, he sought out sanctuaries of Roman Catholicism by attending mass in Maiden Lane, dining with the Jesuits in Farm Street, and visiting "L'Eglise catholique de l'Oratoire." The two most visible architectural symbols of Britain's—and his own—divided past were St. Paul's Cathedral and Westminster Abbey, the first a cold, bare temple of Protestantism filled with the tombstones and memorial busts of the worldly, the second a church which—although now also in the hands of the Protestants—still housed the graves of Edward the Confessor and Mary Stuart. Implied in the juxtaposition of these two churches was also an equation of classicist art with Protestant individualism and of Gothic architecture with Catholic humility, a contrast restated by most French-Canadian visitors to London and one extended to include national characteristics in such comments as the lawyer and journalist Edmond's Paré's in 1887: "A Londres, l'architecture est sévère comme les moeurs; cette sévérité va jusqu'à la lourdeur et quelquefois jusqu'au mauvais gôut."[60] Another traveller—the redoubtable Judge Routhier— agreed, suggesting that the borrowings from Gothic art in St. Paul's—notably the nave—were in poor taste, because they had been stolen from Catholic practice.[61]

Although exhilarated by the sounds of the famous "London roar," Tardivel appears to have avoided extensive wanderings through the city; he too declared himself defeated by its size, using water and jungle imagery to evoke its intricacy. Thus, he claims to have found, by accident, the snaking subterranean "rivers" of the subway. He has heard of Whitechapel and the docks—both then made attractively notorious by a series of as yet unresolved murders—but he preferred to spend the afternoon in his hotel room, poring over letters and newspapers from home, with genuine London drizzle obscuring the window-panes: "C'est là que j'ai reconnu le Londres de Dickens," he says half miserably, half triumphantly, before concluding his sketch with a lengthy invective against liberalism.[62]

Although churches and tabernacles sometimes seemed the only refuge from modern London, the industrial age *had* spawned a building in which industry and religion declared themselves inseparable partners and in which chaos gave way to classification and order. Just as visitors no longer needed to climb St. Paul's because Burford's panorama at Leicester Square offered them a painted bird's-eye view of London, regularly updated to include the latest buildings,[63] so too could tourists travel to Sydenham to admire the greenhouse architecture of Paxton's Crystal Palace, designed in the shape of a basilica, with its encyclopedic collections of everything man's ingenuity had dreamed up in the course of his history. There were no smelly lanes here, but admirably arranged courts such as the Industrial Court, the Manufacturing Court, the Egyptian, Greek, Roman, Byzantine and Medieval Courts. The weary tourist, relatively safe from pickpockets and hooligans, could even hire a wheelchair to be pushed about the galleries at his leisure.[64] Unlike the museums in the city, the Crystal Palace was surrounded by gardens and sporting-fields, simulating a utopian setting where city sophistication and country simplicity lived in perfect harmony. New inventions were displayed not as destroyers, but as enhancers of aesthetic beauty. Kathleen Coleman, for instance, enchanted her readers with descriptions of an electrical exhibition turning Victorian drawing-rooms into Aladdin's caves: "Allen and Mannooch show a suite of rooms, a Jacobean dining-room, and an exquisite French boudoir and bedroom. The boudoir is draped with blue velvet on the lower part of the walls, and the ceiling is transparent, painted with clouds, the electric light shining through it, giving the idea that it is filled with moonlight.''[65] Exoticism—so useful a disguise of utilitarianism—was also a comfortable way of dealing with strange human beings. Whereas the tourist had been warned that the average London slum-dweller could be more savage than an aborigine, no such fears need detain the *flâneur* in the Crystal Palace. Here representatives of various cultures, engaged in harmlessly entertaining activities, were put on display, such as a pair of ''Japanese Jugglers . . . wonderful little boys turning summersaults with swords in their mouths, or balancing themselves on top of pyramids.''[66] Andrew Spedon even suffered a bout of homesickness when a game of lacrosse was put on by some Indians from Caughnawaga, but he quickly regained his white man's composure when the players ''became wonderfully excited, even to a phrenzied ecstasy of joyous feelings''[67] at his appearance: he lived up to the sensation he had caused by offering to deliver their mail in Canada.

Some Canadians, muscular Christians all, braved the dangers of modern London to obey their mission. Andrew Spedon spent long hours with an Irishman and his accomplice—both determined to relieve the Canadian of his money and watch—in the backroom of a tavern, using the occasion to hold forth on the dangers of alcoholism. His compatriot Lydia Leavitt, on the last leg of a tour around the world, solicited the protection of a policeman before she ventured into the slums, venting her wrath at ''some well-meaning ladies [who] were holding a *service* in a lodging house, but to me it seemed worse than mockery. . . . Tell these poor starving children of the crucifixion, and how it will affect them, for are *they* not crucified every day by cold and hunger?''[68] Leavitt echoed Dickens's anger at ''telescopic philanthropy,'' and his novels were, indeed, the imaginative model for most visitors to London. Appropriated by tourists in general— some, like Tardivel, were positively disappointed when they were met by crisp, sunny autumn skies instead of drizzle and fog *à la Bleak House*—Dickens also provided an important inspiration for those authors with a social conscience. Such visitors not only used his books as guides to picturesque quarters and quaint types (a genre pursued in publications like William R. Hughes's *A Week's Tramp in Dickens-Land* [1891] and Alfred Rimmer's *About England with Dickens* [1899]), but also accepted his philosophy, a step other Canadian readers would have found too dangerously close to socialism. The Reverend John Godden of Durham, Quebec, for instance, scolded the novelist in his *Notes and Reminiscences of a Journey to England* (1873): ''let us hope that while amusing a certain class of society, and labouring to rise above the pressure of adversity, and for the meat which perisheth, he did not forget to work for that which endureth unto everlasting life,''[69] probably expressing the

sentiment of his more conservative compatriots. Kathleen Coleman—who
had borrowed her pseudonym from Kit Nubbins in *The Old Curiosity
Shop*, much as Agnes Scott, writing for the *Ottawa Free Press*, signed
herself ''The Marchioness''—anticipated such objections in 1892 when
she sent a series of letters to the *Toronto Mail* describing (often in close
imitation of the novelist's style) a pilgrimage through Dickens's London;
her last letter especially is a passionate reply to his detractors:

> Many may say that what has been written of him in these columns is
> purely sentimental ''gush.'' It may strike some people that way, but
> assuredly every word came from the heart, and from one's love of the
> man in and through his works. It has been advanced that Dickens did
> more harm than good by his writings: that his frequent choice of
> scenes of low and sordid crime—of coarse and vulgar life are revolting
> to good taste, that such reading lowers the tone of the mind and blunts
> the perceptions of young readers (I knew one lady myself who would
> not permit her daughters to read Dickens ''because he never wrote
> about high class society''). Again, others cavil at the tone he employed
> in connection with religious subjects, such as Mrs. Jellyby and
> Borrioboola Gha, or Mr. Stiggins collecting to send out flannels to
> infant negroes, or on Mr. Chadband's treatment to Jo, or Mrs.
> Pardiggle's district visiting. It has been alleged also that Dickens
> described and ridiculed religion in every possible manner, that his use
> of slang was injurious to the young person, that he was without
> humour . . . and that his pathos was mere bathos. I am not
> pretending to defend Charles Dickens. He wants no defence. His
> books are monuments that will last till that anti-Christ of a New
> Zealander comes here with his sketch-book, and, did Dickens need
> anyone to defend his name and memory as a writer, half the most
> brilliant writers in the world would well and ably execute the task, but,
> having wandered lovingly with him in spirit, through Dickensland here
> in London, knowing that there is no romantic aspect about his
> wonderfully graphic pictures, knowing too that his true and natural
> realism is as far above that of Zola and the French school as the blue
> sky is above foggy London, I cannot help winding up these papers by a
> few words in his praise who has taught us so much. Taught us to look
> around and see the misery and distress lying at our doors; taught us
> the beauty of compassion and kindliness for the lonely and miserable;
> taught us to be less selfish and brutal and cowardly; to be braver and
> better and more healthy in mind and soul than we were before. Under
> his delineations vice is always hateful, and very often loathsome. It is
> the manner in which subjects are treated, not the selection of them,

that constitutes the difference between good or hurtful literature.[70]

Even before Coleman undertook her pilgrimage through Dickens's London, her letters richly echoed the master's presence in the public imagination. She counselled a lovelorn young woman, by referring her to Emily's fate in *David Copperfield*: "I am so sorry for you, yet what can I do to help! Be careful of Mr. Peggotty, my dear. You will not find many like him nowadays. You must not mind Steerforth. You really mustn't,"[71] or she noted with delight that the public's sense of justice had been sharpened by Dickens's exposure of child labour; thus, a jury's decision to send a battered child back to his master because "a sound box on the ear livened a boy up," elicited angry comment from the evening papers, "and, of course, the name of Oliver was introduced."[72]

Never one to dwell on sights without incorporating a dramatic presentation of the people associated with them, Coleman investigated Dickensian landmarks in London through their present-day inhabitants: she wandered through the slums, inspected a rats' meat shop, interviewed the friends of a murdered woman. She watched a mother pawn her child's clothes for a bottle of gin, observed the "miserable, shrewd-faced children,"[73] already doomed to continue their parents' abject existence. As often, she focuses on the deterioration of the women as a particularly evil symptom of social corruption, borrowing Dickens' image of women as either pure or depraved madonnas to do so: "She came out, the wretched, shivering baby crying with cold and want, and with the few half-pence she got for the child's things, she went into the public house and called for drink."[74]

Coleman pays close attention to Dickensian detail—the ravaged faces, rags, smells, and foul language—but she also recreates his evocation of sprawling, fog-ridden London in an almost hallucinatory scene imagined at midnight, on one of London's bridges. A procession of Dickensian characters throngs through her mind, haunting and comforting her at the same time: "Little Dorritt wandering lonely and cold through the ghastly streets. Nancy hurrying away with Rose Maylie's handkerchief pressed against her bursting heart—going to her death! Lost little Em'ly with Mr. Peggotty vainly searching for her. Lost Martha flying down the riverside in despair. All the homeless and lost of London seem to crowd by and look over the bridge and point at you with reproachful fingers."[75] Yet the scene concludes with a conciliatory vision. Reviving, like Dickens, the ancient metaphor of the city as body politic, Coleman asserts her belief in humanity or, more precisely, in the goodwill of the British nation, for "glancing across the lights of London you see the tall towers of Westminster rising against the dull red glow."[76] Thus, the journalist—

once again in keeping with her double (even duplicitous) function as social critic and spokesman of an official organ— frames her Dickensian sketches with a loyalist flourish, enhanced by a ritual visit to the writer's grave in Westminster Abbey. The vision of the Empire, troubled as its reflections had become, still provided a comforting frame.

2. PARIS

Even after a wearying boat- and train-ride, travellers arriving in Paris were almost unanimous: the splendour of the French capital eclipsed anything London had to offer: "London is a man in soiled clothes, Paris a dandy with beaver, cane and kids; London is a working day with smoke and dirt, in Paris it is ever Sunday,"[77] noted the journalist John McKinnon from Summerside, Prince Edward Island, and even the Reverend Hugh Johnston, always fully convinced of Anglo-Saxon superiority, grudgingly acknowledged "their superiority to us, in delicacy and refinement of taste."[78] Andrew Spedon, after experiencing the "immense poverty, wretchedness and profligacy"[79] of London, rapturously declared Paris "THE CITY OF THE WORLD . . . THE ELYSIUM OF TERRESTRIAL GLORY,"[80] while a contributor to *Belford's Monthly Magazine* celebrated the gaslit Rue de Rivoli as a scene from "the enchanted cities of the *Arabian Nights*."[81]

Most agreed that Baron Haussmann's plans had been successful in creating a clean, beautiful city and that Napoleon III had inscribed his name on Paris "indelibly and honourably."[82] Like citizens of other new nations, Canadians were interested in practical and prestigious city design. Haussmann's often controversial plans for the grand boulevards, parks, and public buildings included the installation of gaslight and of a complex water supply and sewage system. Industrialization and overpopulation had, earlier in the century, brought squalor to the crowded medieval quarters of Paris; Haussmann's plans called for improved sanitation of such areas not only to provide better living conditions for the populace, but also to abolish likely breeding-grounds for revolutions such as had occurred in 1830 and 1848. The straight, symmetrical new thoroughfares were both aesthetically pleasing and militarily strategic; troops could now be moved swiftly into those districts most prone to insurrection.[83] Although the planners of Ottawa had, for both practical and ideological reasons, not followed the example of modern Paris (or Washington, for that matter),[84] Canadian city-designers were still sufficiently impressed with Haussmann's accomplishment to imitate him elsewhere. C. Pelham Mulvaney, then retired from his work as a priest of the Church of England and a teacher of classics at Bishop's College and immersed in the study of Canadian history, lauded Toronto's "metropolitan design" in 1882: "Toronto's main highway, flanked by the most brilliant shops and the stateliest public buildings, runs east and west from frontier to ocean,"[85] and he praised the new Post Office, "faced with cut stone and elaborately ornamented in the Italian renaissance style as modified of late years by Baron Nausmann [*sic*] of Paris."[86] Some, like William H. Withrow, complained that such cities fostered monotonous sterility, but he too—having ascended in a balloon tethered to the Place des Tuileries—marvelled at the "noble vista of the Champs Elysées, the far-winding Seine, the grand environment of the city and glory of the setting sun."[87]

Visiting French Canadians, by contrast, were both indignant at and heartbroken about the demolition of the medieval quarters. To Judge Routhier, the boulevards seemed like gigantic wounds inflicted on an ancient organism. Wandering through Paris on a Sunday morning, he observed workers on the new Boulevard St. Germain, engaged in the double blasphemy of demolishing old buildings and working on a Sunday. To Routhier, their activities echoed the frenzy and fruitlessness of the Inferno: "une foule d'ouvriers en blouse démolissaient, déblayaient, charroyaient, et rebatissaient. Je cheminais au milieu des ruines. . . . La rue était encombrée, et l'air retentissait de mille bruits et de clameurs, mêlées de blasphèmes."[88] Many Parisian streets lost their old names, especially those which recalled pre-Revolutionary, that is to say, monarchical and Roman-Catholic France, the era fondly preserved in French Canada's ancestral memory. The more Paris changed; the more it lost its value as a symbol of ethnic pride. The Abbé Ovide Brunet, writing to his superior E.-A. Taschereau in 1862, melancholically described Haussmann's demolitions as a destruction of "le berceau de Paris,"[89] as a violent removal of the old city's heart. Such feelings only exacerbated the alienation some French-Canadian travellers experienced upon arrival when they—like their English compatriots— failed to be welcomed by the friendly crowds they had somehow expected to assemble at the railway station. Arthur Buies plunged into deep anxiety when Paris—"un nom qui donne le vertige"[90]—greeted him with complete indifference. Like Caniff Haight in London, Buies felt submerged in an endless sea of strangers, "toujours renouvelées . . . confuses, tourmenteés, sombres, avides, inquiètes."[91] Penniless, Buies saw himself mocked by the elegance and opulence surrounding him, and only after a sleepless night spent poring over an article he intended to submit to a Paris newpaper did he convince himself that Paris would accept him too: "je me levai à la hâte, brûlant de voir Paris dans sa fièvreuse activité; je ne le redoutais plus: au contraire, il me tardait d'aspirer son souffle puissant, de saisir le sein toujours gonflé où s'alimentent le génie défaillant, l'espérance lasse d'attendre.''[92]

The pain of a chilly reception may have been especially acute for those French-Canadian visitors who, following the current stereotype, classified the British as cold and remote and the French as cordial and gregarious. Most English-Canadian travellers in contrast simply maintained a censorious attitude toward the superficial frivolity believed to be characteristic of the French. Both Hugh Johnston and William H. Withrow were appalled at the general nonchalance in marital matters and at the strong public support for divorce. They felt—as Routhier had done in London—that Paris resembled Rome in the last days of its decline, and the Reverend Alexander MacDonald, later to become bishop of Victoria, British Columbia, confessed in 1900 that he would "rather live in London with its dullness and fog, than live in Paris with its gaiety and sunshine. . . . The Parisian, who is irreligious, parades his irreligion and seems to glory in his shame.''[93] Even during church services, Parisians could be relied upon to behave like irresponsible children. Johnston occasionally amused himself by attending a Roman Catholic service as if it were a theatrical performance, relishing the pomp of High Mass in the Madeleine, where singing, bell-ringing and kneeling were, he felt, needed to keep an infantile congregation occupied.

Whereas Johnston had systematically explored London's major sights, devoting much time to commenting on the city's famous preachers, his background forbade him to give more than passing attention to the French capital. Pastor of "the old historic St. James Street Methodist Church, of Montreal''[94] at the time of his journey to Europe and the Holy Land in 1880, he had accepted his congregation's offer to finance his trip in order to revive his flagging health. Originally a schoolteacher, with a first-class teacher's certificate and the position of headmaster to his credit before he was eighteen, Johnston prepared himself for the Methodist ministry at Victoria College and afterward served congregations in Windsor, Hamilton, Montreal, Toronto, Washington, as well as replacing, in 1897, the Reverend W. H. Milburn as acting chaplain to the United States Senate. Johnston's *Toward the Sunrise: Being Sketches of Travel in Europe and the East* (1881), first published in the *Christian Guardian* and successful enough to go through at least three editions, describes his travels through England, France, Italy, Palestine, and Egypt, with major parts of the book devoted to London and Jerusalem. *Toward the Sunrise* probably drew additional readers because it also contained a eulogy for William Morley Punshon, the famous Methodist preacher, who accompanied Johnston on the journey and died suddenly on the way. Punshon was also the subject of an acclaimed biography, a genre Johnston considered, together with rousing sermons, particularly important in public instruction. Thus, besides writing about Punshon, he composed a biography of Senator John MacDonald, published several lectures and sermons, and contributed a chapter to A. B. Hyde's *The Story of Methodism throughout the World* (1894). In 1886, he exhorted his Toronto congregation with a sermon entitled "Shall we or Shall We Not?" in which he condemned the vices of drinking, gambling, dancing and theatregoing, closely associating the latter with the French actress Sarah Bernhardt's tour through Canada: "How is it that actors and actresses can set at defiance all the laws of morality, can live in scandalous and admitted wickedness, and lose not one iota of popularity"[95] he inquired angrily, charging that the cost of such performances was enough to finance several smaller churches for an entire year. Johnston's prejudice against French levity may well have been fuelled five years earlier when his stroll through the Louvre elicited an emphatic "we maintain that three-fourths of the Venuses and Aphrodites of the Louvre and Luxembourg, are intolerable and indecent, for they are not goddesses, not women or maidens, but nude female figures."[96]

In twenty short pages taking up part of one chapter only, Johnston describes Paris by night, reflects on Victor Hugo, the French language, Napoleon III's boulevards, the Place de la Concorde, the guillotine, the Arc de Triomphe, Napoleon I, the Tuileries, the Commune, French art, the Luxembourg Gardens, the Madeleine, Notre Dame and its history, the Morgue, the Sainte Chapelle, the Panthéon, the Dôme des Invalides, the Musée de Cluny, the Sorbonne, the Bourse, Place Vendôme, Père Lachaise, the Gobelins, and Versailles, and he concludes with remarks on life in Paris and on a Sabbath spent in the French capital. Predictably, many of Johnston's comments are cursory and abrupt, presented in the random order of casual remarks negligently scattered about a negligible city.

Much as French-Canadian visitors, especially priests, often shared their Protestant colleagues' horror with the worldliness of Paris, many still diligently sought to discover the remains of pre-Revolutionary France and to build their continued faith in the old mother country on its foundation. Like architecture, city design acquired national meaning and visitors read the patterns of streets, the location of buildings and monuments, and their names as if they were precious hieroglyphics of a lost age or else threatening harbingers of a new era. The Curé Labelle, for instance, largely responsible for the messianic settlement of *les pays d'en haut* and one of the most energetic and charismatic characters to emerge from the nineteenth-century French-Canadian clergy, visited Paris to promote emigration to Quebec. Here he embarked on a search for "la rue Canada," a humble, industrious street, as he noted with satisfaction, where Paris lost its habitual guise as a spoilt princess. Façades were irregular as they had been before Haussmann and as they still were in Quebec: "je me serais cru dans la haute-ville de Québec, ou à Montréal dans la rue Notre-Dame, avant que le commerce ne l'êut élargie."[97] In a tavern on Rue Canada, Labelle—at six feet and three hundred pounds a man not easily ignored—lectured a guest on the true nature of the French colony before departing contentedly, "heureux d'avoir découvert le Canada en plein Paris, comme autrefois Jacques-Cartier en plein océan."[98] An almost bohemian appearance in his threadbare and often dirty *soutane*, his permanently dishevelled hair, and his happy indulgence in drinking, smoking, and spitting, Labelle must have left a lasting impression on anyone who met him.

The most extensive reading of Paris as ultramontanist allegory occurs in Adolphe-Basile Routhier's *A Travers l'Europe*, its vision so seductive in its cohesiveness that it was to entice numerous other Canadian tourists. Now perhaps best remembered as the author of Canada's national anthem, Routhier was the incarnation of nineteenth-century Quebec conservatism: as judge of the Superior Court of Quebec, he created a storm in 1876, when he ruled in the infamous case of the contested Charlevois election that the clergy had not only the right but also the moral duty to influence their parishioners' vote. Although the ruling was reversed on appeal, Routhier remained one of Canada's foremost lawyers. Educated at Laval University, he had been called to the bar in 1861 and had taken up practice in Kamouraska. An ever-increasing number of honours were bestowed on him: from 1897 to 1906, he served as judge of the Vice-Admiralty Court of Quebec and, from 1904 onward, as chief justice of the Superior Court. He was a charter member and, in 1915-16, president of the Royal Society of Canada, and he was knighted by George V at the latter's coronation in 1911. Although he was twice defeated in his attempts to win a seat in the House of Commons for the county of Kamouraska, he was offered the lieutenant-governorship for the North-West Territories, a post which he declined.[99]

A skilful orator, Routhier was frequently invited to speak on occasions of national importance, such as the centenary of Christopher Columbus's arrival in America, but also on controversial matters, such as the suffragette movement. A man—if one is to judge by the piercing look in his eyes—not easily meddled with, he acted as a passionate defender of the *status quo*, becoming a symbol of suffocating conservatism to such liberals as Louis Fréchette and Louis-Antoine Dessaulles. Routhier clashed with his opponents in polemical exchanges, the most famous being his quarrel with Fréchette over Routhier's *Les Causeries du Dimanche* (1871), a collection of essays on religion, politics, and literature, and a short dramatic sketch entitled "La Sentinelle du Vatican", which will be of note again in the chapter on Rome. Routhier had composed these pieces—as well as a series of "pastels littéraires" published under the appropriate pseudonym of Jean Piquefort—to protest against liberalism of any description. Reviews of Routhier's many publications (including patriotic works such as *De Québec à Victoria* and *Québec et Lévis à l'aurore du XXe siècle*, and *Le Centurion* and *Paulina*, both historical novels about the time of early Christianity) repeatedly turned into battlegrounds, with progressive journalists like Jules Fournier holding the self-assured judge responsible for Quebec's tardy intellectual development. Praised by *L'Evénement* as "un ouvrage où la philosophie chrétienne se mêle ses hautes leçons à une agréable et spirituelle narration,"[100] Routhier's *A Travers l'Europe*, perhaps more than any other *récit de voyage*, established the travel-book as an important ideological tool in French-Canadian culture.

Half of the first volume of *A Travers l'Europe* is devoted to a description of Routhier's eight-month stay in Paris, a description mirroring, in subject-matter and style, the issues and polarities that occupied all of his thinking. Unlike Johnston's rambling tourist chapter on Paris, Routhier's description is carefully composed, eliminating all information that would disturb his design. By establishing a series of oppositions, proceeding from large to increasingly detailed contexts, Routhier reads Paris as an allegory of the Church Militant engaged in a battle with nineteenth-century materialism and liberalism.

The first eight chapters are devoted to Parisian churches, the rest—introduced by a chapter on palaces and museums—to the secular side of the city: "Après les églises, les palais. N'est-ce pas dans l'ordre? L'église est supérieure au palais, tant par sa destination que par l'incomparable dignité de celui qu'elle loge et qu'elle honore."[101] Within this over-arching opposition of church and state are contained more specific dualities, symbolized by individual buildings. Routhier invites his reader to climb the St. Jacques Tower, a sixteenth-century belfry and ancient gathering-point for pilgrims bound for the holy shrine of Santiago di Compostela, to gain an overview of Paris with him. In choosing this sacred vantage point, Routhier declares his philosophy, just as the creators of city panoramas declared theirs in selecting, as Barker did, the top of the Albion steam engine from which to view active, industrialized London or the roof of the Tuileries, as did Pierre Prévost, to give Parisians access to a view hitherto reserved for the privileged.[102] From his tower, Routhier perceives a Paris dominated by the Panthéon and the Arc de Triomphe, symbols of the two opposite forces which have shaped French history: "Ces deux géants de pierre, se dressant presque en face l'un de l'autre aux deux extrêmités de

Paris, semblent être l'expression de deux Frances, la France Guerrière et la France Chrétienne, et ils rappellent deux gloires bien différentes: Napoléon et Sainte Geneviève, la guerre et la religion, l'épée et la croix.''[103]

Routhier's glance travels gradually from buildings associated with the triumph and the defeat of wordliness—le Dôme des Invalides, le Palais Bourbon, l'Académie française, le Palais Luxembourg, le Quartier Latin—toward the symbol of Paris's Christian origins, the Panthéon, burial-place of Sainte Geneviève: ''n'était-il pas convenable que sa patronne fût placée sur cette montagne audessus de tout ce monde de professeurs et d'étudiants qui s'agite et pérore à ses pieds?''[104] Even Routhier's descriptions of secular buildings and quarters are punctuated with brief references to churches—St. Clothilde, St-Germain-des-Près, St. Sulpice—components of a religious subplot to remind the reader that Routhier's glance, preoccupied as it may momentarily be with buildings housing power and learning, moves toward a spiritual anchor-point. At the Panthéon, his glance changes direction, ''un demi-tour à droite,''[105] to survey—after the world of aristocracy and scholarship on the left bank—that of bourgeois wealth and pleasure on the right. The Exchange and the Opera embody these pursuits, but the warning finger of the column on Place Vendôme toward the west reminds the observer of Parisians' fickleness in days of adversity: ''Qu'il est triste de se rappeler qu'en 1871 il s'est trouvé des Français, assez peu soucieux de la gloire de leur patrie pour abattre et briser ce glorieux trophée!''[106] Routhier concludes his bird's-eye view of Paris by looking down at the buildings of the Ile de la Cité spread out at his feet and by focusing—as he had done with the Panthéon—on a religious monument, the Sainte Chapelle, survivor of revolutions and wars, to remind Parisians of their Christian origins: ''le mât-de-hune de cet admirable vaisseau [that is, l'Ile de la Cité] est la Sainte Chapelle, bijou d'architecture gothique, dont la flèche découpée à jour, audacieuse, aérienne, s'élance vers le ciel avec l'ardeur des saints du moyen-âge, et avec la foi du grand roi qui l'a bâtie, Saint Louis,''[107]

Repeatedly, Routhier uses buildings, monuments, and streets as stage-settings for imagined scenes from the past, the better to manipulate his audience into sharing his interpretation. Particularly well calculated is his sketch of Marie-Antoinette's departure for the Conciergerie, a scene in which setting, dialogue, and metaphor are used to create the image of a royalist world in eclipse: ''Je voyais le jeune Dauphin marchant au côté de sa mère et poussant de ses petits pieds devant lui les feuilles sèches qui jonchaient déjà les allées—ce qui faisait dire au roi: 'Les feuilles tombent de bonne heure cette années! . . . C'est de cette dernière station douloureuse [that is, la Tour du Temple] que le fils du Saint Louis devait être conduit à l'échafaud quelques mois après!''[108]

Exploring the intellectual and artistic world of Paris, Routhier encountered—or was determined to encounter—the same contrast between blasphemy and traditional faith he had noted in its streets. After explicating Notre Dame's architecture for his readers as if it were a sacred book chiseled in stone, he then deplored the moderns' tendency toward sensuous realism in his examination of the collections in the Louvre. He attended lectures by evolutionists and disciples of Feuerbach and juxtaposed them with descriptions of an evening spent with the Christian workers of Paris and a sermon delivered by Père Hyacinthe, a fervent preacher, whom even the *New Dominion Monthly* called a "Catholic Protestant" and a Roman-Catholic counterpart to Charles Spurgeon. Routhier visited the theatre and compared George Sand's scandalous work with Henri de Bornier's historical drama *La Fille de Roland*, "qui m'a semblé un réveil de la poésie catholique en France, et qui m'a convaincu de l'immortelle vitalité de l'art dans ce beau pays."[109] Surviving the violent contrasts of Paris required manliness and maturity, suggested Routhier. For a young, impressionable person, especially a woman, the temptations of the city might prove too strong: the very asphalt exhaled the poisonous odour of a gangrenous society, as Louis Veuillot had earlier suggested in *Les Odeurs de Paris*, and few French Canadians, reared in the robust physical and spiritual climate of their homeland, were sufficiently prepared to resist impious Paris and find "le Paris . . . qui croit, souffre et espère!"[110]

If visitors to London explored the city with Charles Dickens's novels in hand, they roamed through Paris guided by Victor Hugo's colourful evocations of medieval life in the French capital in *Notre-Dame de Paris*. Yet, although visitors like Routhier admired Hugo's craft and shared his love for the Middle Ages and its architecture, they also frowned upon his republican politics and his pantheism. Thus, Routhier's bird's-eye view of Paris and his long chapter on Notre-Dame are clearly modelled on Hugo's "Notre-Dame" and "Paris à vol d'oiseau" in the third book of *Notre-Dame de Paris*, but the judge significantly modified Hugo's vision to assert his own opinions and to criticize the French author's at the same time. Whereas Hugo evoked the image of an exuberant organism depending for its energy on the dialectic interaction between the sacred and the profane, Routhier created a static vision with Church and State confronting each other, unreconciled. Although it became almost impossible for visitors to Paris to escape the spell of Hugo's novels (in 1877, the painter Robert Harris searched "for a bit of fifteenth-century gable mentioned in *The Hunchback of Notre Dame*"),[111] some French-

Canadian travellers ostentatiously avoided any association with the writer. As Hugo was entombed in the Panthéon on 29 April 1885, the Abbés Labelle and Proulx refused to join the crowds, visiting Louis Veuillot's grave in the Montparnasse Cemetery instead. In his eulogy of Veuillot, Labelle looked upon the two writers as representatives of Janus-faced Paris: "Ce sont deux génies, égaux peut-être par les dons de la nature, par la fécondité de l'esprit, mais dont l'un a habité des hauteurs sublimes, tandis que l'autre, malheureusement trop souvent, s'est égaré dans les bas-fonds obscurs et tortueux du matérialisme."[112]

Hugo's works, questionable as their philosophy may have been to some Canadian tourists, still provided a welcome vision of an intact, medieval society, a vision precious not only because it provided nostalgic memories of a world largely destroyed by Haussmann's demolitions, but also because it helped to repress the shocking implications of the Franco-Prussian War and the Commune in 1870-71, a catastrophe which continued to occupy Canadians' minds for the rest of the century: as late as 1897, *La Presse* of Montreal ran a serial on the events. News of the outbreak of war between Prussia and France had been received with great alarm in Quebec, where the confrontation was soon considered an almost mythic battle of Homeric proportions between the Latin, Catholic race and its Germanic, Protestant adversary.[113] A subscription was started to help the victims, and a demonstration was organized, which proceeded from the Place Frontenac through the streets of Quebec to the Lower Town, "où elle se dispersa en entonnant le dernier couplet de la Marseillaise et aux cris de Vive la France! Vive l'armée!"[114] Faucher de Saint-Maurice, praying with his compatriots for the salvation of France in the chapel of Saint Césaire, had a terrifying vision of a dishevelled mother country, echoing Ernest Meissonier's painting "The Siege of Paris" and Honoré Daumier's lithograph "Horrified by the Inheritance," published in *Le Charivari* on 11 January 1871: "Elle avait les yeux en pleurs, les cheveux épars: elle était drapée dans une ample tunique tricolore, maculée, trouée, déchiquetée: elle marchait seule à grands pas, avec des gestes désespérés, dans une immense plaine couverte de ruines et de débris fumants."[115]

The Quebec poet and bookseller Octave Crémazie, living in exile in Paris because of financial difficulties, experienced the Siege at first hand, recording the events in a journal to be forwarded to his family once the mails were moving again. Unlike the Brothers Goncourt, who survived the Siege without major disturbances in their luxurious lives and who wrote of it with the detachment of voyeurs, Crémazie suffered through a bitterly cold winter with food rationed and dear. On 3 November, he paid four francs for a pound of donkey-meat, rabbit cost twenty-five francs, and fresh butter sold for the same fabulous sum. As the Siege continued and his resources shrank, he lived on dog- and rat-meat, while cats had been promoted to "un mets d'aristo."[116] Crows were available aplenty because the many corpses littering the battlefields attracted scavengers, a fact Crémazie and other starving Parisians desperately tried to put out of their minds: "La sauce, les épices qui assaisonnent cette ratatouille endiablée, le pain impossible, noir, du vieil acajou et lourd comme du plomb, que nous avons mangés dans ces derniers temps, tous cela m'a donné une gastrite de première qualité,"[117] he complained on 18 February. Inhabitants of the left bank fled from the constant shelling to other parts of Paris, carrying their few belongings with them, "C'est un spectacle navrant de voir, par cette température sibérienne, tous ces pauvres petits enfants, grelottant de faim et de froid, trainés par leurs parents, qui vont demander un abri de maison en maison."[118] Gay, vivacious Paris had suddenly turned into a ravaged desert, an abrupt fall which Crémazie—like other conservative French Canadians—associated with France's weakening Christian ethics and faith. "Je croyais à la France chevaleresque de nos péres," he wrote melancholically during the Commune, but instead he found himself among "une agglomération d'hommes sans principes, sans moeurs, sans foi et sans dignité."[119] Many conservatives shared Crémazie's conviction that God had justly punished France for its past sins, and the love and support they loudly expressed for the mother country once again resembled a child's compassion for his wayward mother.[120]

The young Adolphe-Basile Routhier, then only thirty-one, used the occasion to don Louis Veuillot's judgemental pose, condemning France's decadence along with its debased literature: "La France est châtiée par Dieu et elle l'a bien mérité. . . . C'est la Providence qui a voulu que la France ne fût pas prête. La Prusse n'a été entre ses mains qu'un instrument aveugle et sans mérite, comme le fut autrefois Nabuchodonosor. . . . Depuis 1789 et la grande révolution satanique, la France a choisi pour mère une marâtre, qui s'appelle la Liberté, et cette infâme l'a pervertie. Voltaire et Victor Hugo ont remplacé Dieu."[121] As so often in Routhier's career, his providential interpretation of history opened the floodgates for a polemic between conservatives and liberals, a bitter argument laying bare the basic forces struggling to dominate Quebec's intellectual life. Hector Fabre—now often ranked, together with Arthur Buies, as one of French Canada's finest nineteenth-century journalists— challenged Routhier in *L'Evénement*, asking him ironically how Providence could punish France and reward Prussia at the same time: "L'histoire n'est pas un recueil de pénitences à l'usage des peuples . . . la défaite de la France s'explique par des causes humaines."[122] Routhier did not, of course, relent, and for several weeks the *Courrier du Canada* and *L'Evénement* printed an increasingly vicious dialogue between the two men, terminated only by a satirical sketch depicting Fabre as the hypocritical Basile in Beaumarchais's *Le Mariage de Figaro*.

From the beginning of the War, French-Canadians suspected their English compatriots of rejoicing in the news of France's downfall. Indeed, to many English Canadians the Prussian victory seemed a confirmation of the results of the Battle of Waterloo. William H. Withrow, never one to mince words, benevolently observed the presence of Prussian troops in Alsace-Lorraine, convinced that their racial superiority over the French marked them for victory.[123] Similar prejudice informed Hugh Johnston's emotional outburst at the sight of the charred ruins of the Tuileries and the Hôtel de Ville: "these rioters and destroyers, with murder in their heart, and the torch of the incendiary in their hand, [laid] waste the marble city."[124]

But shocking as the events of the War had been—and the *Maritime Monthly*, along with other Canadian periodicals, published a compassionate report on the aftermath of the Siege and Commune, describing melancholy funeral processions "wending their . . . way to the cemetery of Père la Chaise, bearing the victims, who had died from their wounds, or who had sunk under the privations of the Siege"[125]— some tourists were tickled by its sensationalist aspects, even found it a welcome occasion for souvenir-hunting. Thomas Cook, sensing an especially profitable market for his agency, conducted tourists to Paris to view the ruins; John McKinnon entertained his readers with tales of how starving Parisians ate the animals in the zoo, adding with a sarcastic nod to Darwin, that "Monkeys were spared from a suspicion that men and women might be feasting on their ancestors."[126] One Canadian was only with difficulty dissuaded from carrying an unexploded shell away with him, and Parisian urchins conducted a thriving business with Prussian spiked helmets and shell-fragments. Panoramas of the Siege of Paris kept the event alive for years in Paris (where Fred C. Martin and Nérée Gingras were much impressed with the picture's realism), elsewhere in Europe, particularly Germany (Grace Denison pondered the commercial aspects of modern warfare when a German veteran showed her the panorama in Dresden), and even in North America. Philippe Philippoteaux's "The Siege of Paris" was exhibited in the 'Rotunda at Union Square' in New York, and Louis Braun's panorama of the Battle of Sedan travelled to Cincinnati in 1886 and, later, to Toronto, where it was exhibited at the corner of Front and York streets.[127] Forerunners of wartime news coverage, these panoramas also became important means of alternative interpretation: not only were French and German painters bound to differ in their analysis of the events, but also there was strife among the German states as to which deserved prominent representation. Louis Braun's panorama for instance so unduly focused on the Bavarians' contribution that Berlin insisted on the preparation of another version extolling the Prussians' involvement.

One author quick to discern the satirical aspects of modern news coverage was, once again, James De Mille, who exploited the events of the Franco-Prussian War in his 1873 novel *A Comedy of Terrors*, which culminates in a flight from Paris by balloon in the manner of Gambetta. Oblivious to the frantic preparations for the Siege, a Mrs. Lovell from Montreal travels along the Champs-Elysées, assuring her daughter that

> the people . . . have nothing whatever to do with these preparations. It's all the Emperor. He does it for the effect. He has some deep-laid plan. He's always contriving something or other to excite the Parisians. The Parisians need some excitement. Now the Emperor

I.　"The Civil War in Paris," *Canadian Illustrated News.*

sees that they are tired to death of *fêtes* and shows and splendours, so
he is defacing the statues, putting up barricades, and chopping down
the trees to create a grand sensation.[128]

Once convinced that indeed there will be a battle, Mrs. Lovell is delighted;
she already thinks of the event as if it were a colourful panorama and
assumes that her status as tourist will protect her from any unpleasantness:

> The Prussians in France? . . . How very nice that would be if it were
> really so. Why, we would have a chance to see a battle, who knows?
> Why . . . the greatest desire of my life has always been to see a
> battle. I think I'd go miles to see one. Yes, miles. Why, if I really
> thought the Prussians were here, I think I'd try to find out in what
> direction they were coming, and engage rooms there to see the battle.
> That's the way Byron did at the battle of Waterloo, and he wrote such
> a lovely poem.[129]

"There is probably no city in the world," noted *Baedeker's Handbook
for Travellers* in 1900, "which ever underwent such gigantic transforma-
tions in its external appearance as the French metropolis during the reign
of Napoleon III, and few cities have ever experienced so appalling a series
of disasters as those which befell Paris in 1870-71."[130] Living through
periods of glamour and modernity as well as devastation and anarchy,
Paris seemed a powerful embodiment of the city as Babylon to many
Victorian visitors, but it was also the strongest challenge to those predicting
its ultimate downfall. Restoration during the Third Republic and
successful International Exhibitions in 1878, 1889, and 1900 proclaimed
France's survival and renewed cultural leadership. The Communards with
whom Thiers' government had dealt so severely also persisted. In 1882,
Robert Harris witnessed a funeral at which the famous Communarde
Louise Michel, released under general amnesty in 1880 from life
imprisonment on Noumea Island in the Pacific, delivered the eulogy.[131]
And Sacré-Coeur, built on Montmartre by public subscription to
commemorate the Franco-Prussian War, presided over an increasingly
lively community of artists ready to continue Edouard Manet's and
Gustave Courbet's legacy in launching Paris into modernity.

3. ROME

With some selective editing, London and Paris could, despite their
vastness, still be grasped in a unifying vision. In contrast, a lifetime, let

alone one short visit, seemed too little to explore the historical associations of Rome, its ruins, and its art-treasures. A city without a natural centre, Rome defied determined sightseers, who found themselves wandering aimlessly through Rome's dark lanes and sun-lit piazzas and happening upon famous sites they had not bargained for instead of accomplishing their daily ration of monuments and ruins. Tardivel declared himself defeated in 1889, suspending his letters to *La Vérité* for two weeks because he felt paralysed by "le sentiment de mon incapacité absolue, radicale, d'écrire sur Rome d'une manière tant soit peu convenable,"[132] and the otherwise so articulate Abbé J.-B. Proulx complained that his pen "comme un cheval rétif, s'arrête et s'arc-boute devant une course trop longue."[133] Many travel books deteriorate, once they reach Rome, into mere enumerations of buildings visited and works of art seen, much as the National Gallery in London—so warmly recommended by *Baedeker*—left the average tourist unappreciative, searching for words, and bone-weary. Indeed, the metaphors most often used for Rome were those of the museum and the encyclopedia, both aptly capturing the intimidating presence of endless objects requiring an antiquarian's knowledge of, and passion for, the past. Gertrude Fleming was not the only one to capitulate before a city apparently preoccupied with archeology.

Perhaps best prepared for a visit to Rome were college graduates, whose studies had thoroughly immersed them in the city's great past. Alumni of Acadia College, James De Mille and his brother Elisha conducted their *grand tour* of England and the Continent in 1850-51 and went about their sightseeing in Rome with the dogged determination of students cramming for a final exam. Even the very first day was filled with touring, studying Italian, and conscientiously keeping a journal, a programme which the brothers appear to have diligently pursued for the remainder of their stay.[134] Visitors, however, rarely admired classical culture without reservation. In his novels *The Martyr of the Catacombs: A Tale of Ancient Rome* (1865) and *Helena's Household: A Tale of Rome in the First Century* (1867), De Mille clearly perceived Christianity as morally superior to classical culture, and Adolphe-Basile Routhier, in enumerating the authors who had taught him to appreciate Rome, dismissed Horace as "le vieux scélérat."[135] Indeed, the value of classical studies was hotly debated in Quebec, and Jules-Paul Tardivel's college, St. Hyacinthe, rejected the study of "pagan" authors altogether. Its grand vicar, the Abbé Joseph Sabin Raymond, recommended that classical history be pursued—and cautiously at that—as a harbinger of Christianity, and not as a revelation "de la grandeur sociale et morale des nations anciennes et du prétendu héroisme de leurs hommes célèbres."[136] Latin was the language of the Church, and for that reason only it was worth studying. Suspicion of the values embodied in classicism and its successors, the Renaissance and the baroque, pervaded many Canadians' responses to the city. The sensuousness of statuary and paintings in St. Peter's and the Vatican galleries scandalized many more than Abbé Léon Provancher, who complained in 1884: "Il arrive malheureusement souvent que les artistes . . . ne s'inspirent pas assez du véritable sentiment religieux qui doit diriger leur pinceau ou leur ciseau, et nous mettent sous les yeux . . . des personnages de l'Olympe dans une absence de vêtements que des regards de mortels ne pourraient pas toujours considérer sans courir les risques de ternir la pureté de leur âme."[137]

Christian monuments had risen from heathen temples, but displeasure with Rome's continuingly ostentatious paganism drove tourists literally underground: the catacombs became favourite haunts during the nineteenth century for this and other reasons. In a series of letters to the *Canadian Methodist Magazine*, later gathered in *A Canadian in Europe: Being Sketches of Travel in France, Italy, Switzerland, Germany, Holland and Belgium, Great Britain and Ireland* (1881), William H. Withrow reflected on the Rome of early Christianity for his readers, many already familiar with his study of the same subject (*The Catacombs of Rome and their Testimony Relative to Primitive Christianity* [1874], a work richly illustrated with samples of grafitti and primitive artwork) published several years before he had even set foot in Italy to enthusiastic reviews in England including compliments from Gladstone. The book went through three editions, being possibly "the only book we suppose ever published in the colonies of which the same can be said,"[138] as the *Cyclopedia of Canadian Biography: Being Chiefly Men of the Time* (1886) commented admiringly. Never one to waste time, Withrow was renowned for accomplishing much of his copious reading while on horseback as a circuit rider serving Methodist communities in Ontario. Of United Empire Loyalist stock, he was educated at Toronto Academy, Victoria College, and the University of Toronto and ordained at Hamilton in 1864, subsequently serving communities in Waterford, Montreal, Hamilton, Toronto, and Niagara. Like Adolphe-Basile Routhier, Withrow wrote and spoke on a vast number of subjects, and he received many honours acknowledging his contributions to the Dominion's cultural life: he was elected a Fellow of the Royal Society of Canada in 1883, sat on the Senate and Board of Regents of Victoria University, on the Senate of the Wesleyan Theological College, Montreal, and of the University of Toronto, besides filling many other posts related to religion and education. He fervently believed in Canada's success as a nation, provided it pursued the path of Christian morality, and tried to teach his compatriots the appropriate virtues in historical works like *The History of Canada* (1880), *Our Own Country Canada* (1899),

J.   "Catacombs," from William Withrow,
      A Canadian in Europe.

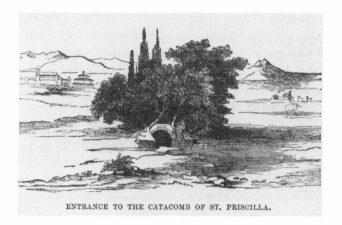

ENTRANCE TO THE CATACOMB OF ST. PRISCILLA.

Men Worth Knowing; or, Heroes of Christian Chivalry (1882), and
Missionary Heroes (1882), and in didactic novels illustrating the life stories
of exemplary Methodists, such as *The King's Messenger; or, Lawrence
Temple's Probation* (1879) and *Barbara Heck: A Story of the Founding of
Upper Canada* (1882). Besides his activities as a historian, teacher,
publisher, and preacher, however, Withrow also had a strong interest in art
and architecture, having worked with William Hay, a Scottish architect
and disciple of Pugin who lived in Toronto from 1850 to 1860,[139] before
entering the ministry. A novel published in 1880, *Valeria: the Martyr of
the Catacombs; a Tale of Early Christian Life in Rome*, fictionalized
material from *The Catacombs of Rome*, and—like its predecessor—
became a much-praised bestseller in Canada, England, and (in a pirated
edition) in the United States.[140]

Withrow's interest in the catacombs is not only symptomatic of a general
fascination in the nineteenth century with these subterranean burial-places
of early Christianity (Victor Hugo called them the "vaults of the world" in
Les Misérables), but also points to their specific significance for both
English and French-Canadians, a significance which deserves to be
discussed at some length because it is one of the most illuminating
examples of ideological conflict between the two revealed, obliquely,
through the art and architecture of another country.

Scarcely known during the Middle Ages, the catacombs were only
actively investigated from the sixteenth century onwards when interest in
Christian antiquity was revived under the impact of the Reformation.
Reformers and counter-reformers alike used the inscriptions, frescoes, and
graffitti to support their positions, either to prove that a significant break
had occurred from the teachings of the early church or to suggest that—on
the contrary—Christian dogma had developed in an uninterrupted
continuum. A theory of *disciplina arcani*, "hidden teachings," was
developed to explain the absence, in the inscriptions and illustrations, of
elements needed to formulate a coherent doctrine.[141] Nineteenth-century
theologians, both Roman-Catholic and Protestant, exploited the "mes-
sage" of the catacombs for similarly contradictory purposes because they
felt that their faith had entered an era of crisis comparable to that of the
Reformation.

English- and French-Canadians echoed the religious concerns of their
mother countries and discussed them with the passion of messianists.
Canadian responses to the early church reflect the battles of ultramontanists
and Protestants at home; moreover, they were assertions that the purity of
early Christianity had been revived in the colonies. In keeping with the
spirit of the nineteenth century, explorations were now conducted
systematically, scientifically. Under the patronage of Pius IX, Giuseppe

Marchi and Giovanni Battista de Rossi studied old church calendars and documents and maps, their precision made possible by the fact that most of the graves and inscriptions were as yet undisturbed. The marble slabs marking many of the tombs were scanned for information on persons and places and the martyrs' legends reread for any historical information they might contain. The material thus located was sufficient to reconstruct, with some certainty, the original state of the catacombs and to provide nineteenth-century travellers with the kind of useful antiquarian knowledge a typical Victorian tourist craved. Armed with Anna Jameson's *Sacred and Legendary Art* (1852-61), he invaded the gothic gloom, Christian memories, and historical associations of the catacombs. Both sensational and instructive, they were a Victorian tourist's heaven.

Besides providing his readers with a host of facts about art history, William Withrow refers to the catacombs as visible proof that the Roman Catholic church had sinned against its humble origins and sealed its corruption with the dogma of papal infallibility: "Could the simple bishops of the primitive ages behold the more than regal state and oriental pomp in which, surrounded by armed halberdiers, amid the blare of martial music and thunder of the guns of St. Angelo, their successor of to-day rides in his golden chariot from his stately palace to the majestic fane of St. Peter—the grandest temple in the world—they would find it difficult to perceive therein any resemblance to their own humble and often persecuted estate, or to the pure and spiritual religion of the meek and lowly Nazarene."[142] Withrow's books, used as guidebooks by fellow-Methodists like Hugh Johnston and William Morley Punshon,[143] but—considering their large publication figures—possibly also by Canadian, American, and British tourists at large, consolidated anti-papal sentiment during an era when ultramontanism became increasingly militant. It is, therefore, somewhat surprising to learn that Withrow not only compiled the materials for *The Catacombs of Rome* with the generous help of "the Archbishop of the Catholic Church of Toronto, the very Rev. Dr. Lynch," but also received "a grateful letter from a priest of the Roman Catholic Church saying that he had used *The Catacombs of Rome* as his printed guide in a visit to that impressive refuge and burial place of the early Christians."[144]

Contrasted with the sophisticated artwork of the tombs along the Appian Way, the clumsy etchings of the catacombs were the first signs—or so Withrow thought—of a manly religion about to dethrone effeminate heathenism, a view also firmly held by French-Canadian visitors to the catacombs. Not accidentally did Quebec parishes adopt the names of the saints of the catacombs; ten called themselves Sainte-Cécile, four Sainte-Agnès, and four Sainte-Philomène to remind themselves that they were "chrétiens assiégés dans un monde hostile"[145] and that their situation echoed that of the early Christians engulfed by pagan Rome. Similarly, Adolphe-Basile Routhier's novels *Le Centurion* (1908) and *Paulina: roman des temps apostoliques* (1918), although not specifically concerned with the catacombs, still speak about the early Church, duplicating—in their anti-realist starkness—the virtues of that era of Christianity. To French Canadians, however, the catacombs proved the uninterrupted heritage of the Church, certainly not its corruption: thus, Tardivel thundered: "Je ne sais pas comment un protestant de bonne foi peut visiter les catacombes sans se convertir aussitôt; car il a sous les yeux la preuve matérielle que l'Eglise n'a pas changé."[146]

Still, tourists could not spend all of their visit prowling about in subterranean corridors. There *was* modern Rome, chosen capital of the new Italian nation in 1870, and the changes were radical enough to demand a response. Long sheltered from modernity by the repressive regimes of Leo XII and Gregory XVI, Rome had retained its idyllic character as a country town much longer than any of the other great European cities; herds of sheep and goats continued to gather in its squares all through the century. Some changes were introduced when Pius IX, welcomed at his election as a liberal Pope, introduced gaslight and supported the building of a railway (condemned by his predecessor as "une chemin d'enfer"), including the Ponte S. Paolo, a metal bridge completing the direct connection between Rome and its seaport, Civitavecchia, improvements which—together with administrative reforms in the tariff system and criminal code and with a recognition of science signalled in the founding of an Agricultural Institute—boded well for Italy's civic growth. Although his pontificate did not fulfil the high hopes associated with the early months of his reign, Pio Nono initiated developments to be continued by his adversaries.[147]

Rome was systematically groomed for its new function as the national capital. Tenement houses were constructed to accommodate the expected influx of new inhabitants, with the population rising from 200,000 in 1870 to double that number in 1900. With an eye to Haussmann's work in Paris, city planners developed a series of districts radiating from central squares, with the Termini railway station, the modern traveller's entry into the city, as a starting point. Memorable events of Italy's recent past were celebrated in the names of streets and squares and the tradition of ancient Rome was re-asserted, as the Capitol, city centre in the days of the emperors, was slowly to assume that function once more.[148]

Even excavation works assumed a brisk purposefulness in the service of the modern state. The Coliseum, much damaged by use as a quarry and so overgrown with lush vegetation that a herbarium of four hundred

K.   "Excavations in the Forum, Rome," *Canadian Illustrated News.*

specimens could be assembled from it, was cleaned in 1874, and the subterranean passages beneath the arena were exposed; similarly, the kitchen gardens surrounding the temple of Minerva Medica were removed as inappropriate. The new Italy explored and displayed its treasures with a certain scientific detachment, a quality believed to be worthy of a recently created nation, and tourists, especially from England and America, arrived in ever-increasing numbers to admire its accomplishments.

English-Canadian Protestants shared with the English and Americans a vivid interest in the unification of Italy, even if they never offered practical support to the movement.[149] Canadian periodicals wrote enthusiastically about Giuseppe Garibaldi and Vittorio Emmanuele, the wise and modest representatives of a modern state.[150] Alice Jones, in a long complimentary article on the Italian royal family, even declared the House of Savoy honorary Britons, when she commended it for descending "from a fugitive Saxon prince" and for retaining "in its more Southern home many characteristics of the sturdier Teutonic race. . . . I daresay it would surprise many an English person to learn that the present King of Italy is a descendant of the Stuarts, the first of thehouse who took the title of King."[151] The Montreal writer Arthur Campbell sought out Vittorio Emmanuele's tomb in the Pantheon, honouring "the remains of the first King of Italy, the liberator, the *ver galant'uomo*, the incarnation of modern Italian history,"[152] and Chester Glass, a Toronto barrister, cherished memories of Garibaldi, "that glorious little chap,"[153] on a visit in 1881, while, the following year, the painter Robert Harris attended a "Funeral Solemnity" for Garibaldi in Paris presided over by Victor Hugo's grandson and crowned by the singing of the Marseillaise and the Italian national anthem, forceful "like the Voice of Niagàra."[154] Rome's efforts to become a modern capital like Paris and Berlin were benevolently and unsentimentally noted by Charles R. W. Biggar, an eminent Toronto lawyer, when he revisited the city in the 1890s: "Young Italy is a giant in the pride of manhood, and New Rome the capital of 'New Italy' is (to my thinking) one of the most progressive, cosmopolitan, clear, well-governed, and beyond all doubt or comparison, the most interesting among the capitals of Europe."[155] Excesses in property speculation which had left some of Rome's noblest and wealthiest families bankrupt were only the growing pains of any large city and a phenomenon he had also observed in his native Toronto.

Panegyrics honouring Garibaldi and Vittorio Emmanuele were generally complemented by a condemnation of the papacy, an institution believed to be responsible for keeping Italians—and French Canadians— in medieval ignorance and for hindering the development of a true nation. The *Canadian Spectator* especially provided its readers with endless articles on the history of the papacy, complemented with analyses of ultramontanism in Canada ("a political power . . . antagonistic to Canadian nationality")[156] and reviews of apostate literature such as *Spiritual Struggles of a Roman Catholic*, a book authored by one N. Beaudry of French-Canadian descent and dealing with an explosive matter, as the bloody riots surrounding the apostate Alessandro Gavazzi's visit to Quebec and Montreal in 1853 had proven, when ten onlookers were killed and dozens wounded. Alice Jones articulated a hostility widely shared by her Protestant compatriots when she sarcastically reported on the drastic measures effected by the Vatican to alleviate the Pope's poverty: refusing to accept the annual endowment granted by the government, he now had to charge admission to the museums of the Vatican and reduce the papal army: "This awe-inspiring body will henceforth consist only of two generals, two colonels, two majors, four captains and a hundred men; although every man of the *guarda nobile* will now have a horse to ride on, instead of, as before, being obliged to share the use of his with a comrade."[157] Generally, the ascent of the new Italian nation was— often in misinterpretation of actual fact—believed to indicate an emergence of Protestant spirit, a utopian event for which even Canadian school-children had been prepared for some time: in 1850, the Hamilton Grammar School offered a copy of Robert Baird's *Protestantism in Italy* to one of its best students.[158] William Withrow never tired of castigating the superstition and ignorance perpetrated by the papacy, affirming that "In this land, long groaning under pagan, and then under Papal persecution, the Gospel has now free untrammelled course. Under the shadow of the Vatican is the propaganda of the Bible Society, and on one of the best streets of Rome rises the handsome façade of a Methodist church. To use the figure of Bunyan, Giants Pope and Pagan may both munch with their toothless gums, but they cannot come at the pilgrims to harm them."[159]

Startled and horrified by modern Rome, French-Canadian Catholics took refuge in the works of Louis Veuillot, whose books *Le Parfum de Rome* (1862) and *Les Odeurs de Paris* (1867) provided a metaphor which was to influence the idea of Rome in most French-Canadian travel books for the remainder of the century: the true Rome, that is, Christian Rome dominated by the Vatican, was permeated with the violet scent of holiness. Since Italian unification, however, the pope's earthly powers had been virtually eliminated; he had become "the prisoner of the Vatican," his former summer palace, the Quirinale, now occupied by Umberto I, son of Italy's first king, Vittorio Emmanuele I. Thus, the perfume of Rome was in danger of being overpowered by the stench of revolution, the body odour of an unruly laity. The *Abeille du Séminaire de Québec*, reporting on the lying-in-state and funeral of Vittorio Emmanuele in 1878, declared that the services of a professional embalmer were required to prevent the dead King from overwhelming his cortège with his smell;[160] Judge Routhier, contemplating the excavation works in the Coliseum, perceived an analogy between the stagnant waters filling the newly exposed canals and the offensiveness of republican Italy.[161] For some, the fragrance of saintliness had literally gone underground; Henri Cimon, writing in *Impressions de voyage*, insisted that the bones of the saints of the catacombs exhaled the violet perfume of sanctity.[162] Such visitors were determined to retain an idealized vision of what Rome had been and ought to be again, a vision radically eliminating any evidence of the modern city. Several travellers borrowed their metaphors from Monsignore Gerbet, the bishop of Perpignan, who perceived in the very physical situation and appearance of Rome a reflection of its holy destiny:

> Placez [la ville de Rome] au sommet d'un rocher, cette position de citadelle convient-elle à la capitale du pacifique empire de la foi et de la charité? Dans le fond d'une vallée, son horizon serait trop rétréci pour une ville dont l'horizon moral doit embrasser le monde. Au milieu d'une vaste plaine, entrecoupée de prés fleuris, de vergers, de bosquets, l'austère et majestueuse cité aurait une ceinture trop riante. Vous figurez-vous enfin Rome port de mer, évidemment cette

situation serait trop turbulente et trop criarde pour elle. Il ne lui faut ni la montagne, ni la plaine, ni la mer séparément, mais une combinaison de ces trois points de vue lui sied parfaitement.[163]

Rome truly seemed the New Jerusalem, a view affirmed by the Abbé Léon Provancher on his return from his pilgrimage to Palestine: "On va pleurer à Jérusalem; on vient se consoler à Rome."[164]

The most determined reader of Rome as typological metaphor was, once again, Adolphe-Basile Routhier. As his vantage point, he ostentatiously chose the Gianicolo, "cette colline où fut crucifié saint Pierre, près du couvent où vint mourir le Tasse;" naturally, Routhier omits to mention that this hill had also become firmly associated in Romans' mind with Giuseppe Garibaldi who had defended the city from this strategically critical point against the French troops in 1848, an event to be commemorated with the erection of the general's statue in 1895. Defiantly ignoring all evidence of the New Italy, Routhier points out the sacred triangle formed by the basilicas of Saint Peter, Saint Paul, and Saint John, each symbolizing a different aspect of the holy trinity: "Pierre a les clefs, il est le Chef, il est le Père! Paul est le Docteur, la Science, la Parole, comme Jésus est le verbe! Jean est l'Amour, la Charité, symbole de l'Esprit-Saint."[165] A smaller triangle, formed by the churches and gravesites of Saint Helena, Saint Monica, and Saint Cecilia, is suitably contained within the all-encompassing one, and Routhier pays homage to the new dogma of the Immaculate Conception by pointing out Santa Maria Maggiore on the Esquilino as an additional landmark. The whole battle-plan of the Church Militant appears to be spread out at his feet: "ce sont les généraux de la grande armée du Christ, dont les tentes s'élèvent à l'avant-garde sur les trois faces de ce camp militaire qui s'appelle Rome."[166] As in his descriptions of Paris, Routhier draws sharply dualist images of the Eternal City, juxtaposing—in the manner of St. Augustine— wordly and divine governments. Cut off from its heart, the Vatican, the city of Rome languishes like a moribund organism, an idea which the judge also developed in a dramatic sketch performed at numerous Quebec colleges and schools; in *Une Page d'histoire: la sentinelle du Vatican* (1871), a papal *zouave* engages in a belligerent conversation with a presumed Garibaldian who later reveals himself as a superior testing his soldier's steadfastness: the mighty heart of catholicism must be protected until it can safely resume its life-giving function once more.[167]

A visit to the Holy Father, Pius IX or Leo XIII, was usually the climax of a French Canadian's visit to Rome. Here too memories of the *zouaves*' loyalty were occasionally evoked, when the pope encouraged his visitors to hold themselves in readiness for any future defence of the Vatican.

Through the intervention of the famous Cardinal Antonelli, Routhier was admitted to several audiences, events that made him more than ever determined to shun the king and his entourage. "En entendant le camérier," he tells of his first encounter with Pius IX:

> qui lisait nos noms, il me regarda et dit: *Judex justus, fortis et sapiens.* Je lui serrai la main et la baisai une seconde fois pour lui témoigner que je comprenais son conseil. Il allait passer outre, lorsque le camérier ajouta: "de Québec." Alors Pie IX s'arrêta, et se retournant vers moi, il m'adressa ces paroles, avec un sourire ému: "de Québec"! Un Canadien! Oh! les bons Canadiens, je garde leur souvenir. Ce sont eux qui m'on envoyé de si loin des soldats pour me défendre. Dites à mes bons zouaves que je les aime toujours."[168]

Whereas the Vatican was a relatively safe enclave with the papacy sheltered from profane intruders, Tardivel encountered a monument in the Campo Verano, with which the pope's cause—or so Tardivel felt—had been unforgivably sullied. Below the names of the papal *zouaves* killed in 1867, an epitaph denounced the Italian revolutionaries as "parricides"; in 1871, the Italian government added a marble slab declaring the entire monument a historical curiosity, preserved by "Roma redenta" for its citizens as a lesson in the eccentricities of theocratic governments. Tardivel, enraged, commented:

> Je n'ai pu lire cette inscription lâche et menteuse sans éprouver un mouvement de légitime colère. Etrangers, ces braves de tous pays qui sont accourus à Rome, à la voix de leur père, défendre, contre un ennemi sacrilège, le patrimoine de l'Eglise universelle! Si j'eusse eu, à côté de moi, trois ou quatre amis, comme Barnard, Prendergast, Guilbault et Couture [papal *zouaves*], et que nous eussions une pince, je leur aurais certainement proposé d'enlever cette inscription détestable.[169]

Even those Canadian travellers who were supportive of the new regime were occasionally disillusioned with the New Italy, especially toward the end of the century. Arthur Campbell observed the new quarters of the city with a melancholy eye. Uniform tenement blocks had replaced old buildings and crooked streets along the Tiber, but the expected influx of new inhabitants had not always taken place; some of the new constructions remained empty or half-finished, others were invaded by the homeless of Rome and deteriorated rapidly. Campbell, who had read Emile Zola's acerbic novel *Rome* (1896) from his trilogy *Les Trois Villes: Lourdes,*

Rome, Paris, agreed with the French writer that these tenements, decrepit before they were even finished, symbolized the dimming of Italy's national dream. Looking down from the dome of St. Peter's as Zola's hero had done, he perceived the basilica as "a ghost from the Middle Ages," sitting among the ruined remains of two civlizations, the ancient and the modern. Goethe's dream—inspired by Rome—of world culture and Mrs. Browning's enthusiasm for free Italy expressed in "From Casa Guidi Windows" lay defeated before the ugliness of modernity. Campbell concluded with a *fin-de-siècle* weariness reminiscent of the writers of *The Week* discussed earlier: "such a bright dream it had been, that liberty was going to cure all ills; and now, when all was accomplished, where was the gain? The thought sickened me—were all dreams of men to end so?"[170]

Despite his disillusionment, however, Campbell did better justice to the city than some of the determined Victorian travellers who had preceded him. Loathing prescribed itineraries, Campbell almost passively submitted to the allure of Rome and its environs, and his descriptions, contrary to the structured essays of William Withrow and Adolphe-Basile Routhier, resemble Henry James's leisurely walks and drives through ever-changing scenes described in his Italian sketches.[171] Escaping from "friends afflicted with the church mania," Campbell—accompanied by "the delightful Mrs. B."—drives at breakneck speed along the Via Venti Settembre and through the Porta Pia, out into the Campagna. Far from appearing a suitably austere setting for a spiritual metropolis, the campagna presents itself "stretching away from miles and miles ahead of us . . . green with the fresh greenness of spring; and the air was laden with the fragrance of innumerable hyacinths. . . . Mrs. B and I commenced to pick them; and when the cabby saw us doing it he followed our example; and we soon returned to the carriage with three armfulls."[172] The catacombs, warmly recommended to antiquarian-minded visitors, seemed "dismal holes" to him, and his description of a visit thoroughly mocks earlier, rapturous accounts:

> I spent a morning in them—four hours—and came out a new man; to get back anywhere above ground was in itself a joy. You go down a ladder into a well, a Dominican monk leading the way. Arrived at the bottom, you find yourself in a dark, damp, underground labyrinth of small passages, brown, grimy and gritty, with a suggestiveness of rheumatism about them. The monk lights tapers, giving one to you and keeping one himself; and you go prowling about, in and out, for hours through these dismal places. The sides of every passage are honeycombed with holes, wherein they once buried the dead. Most of the bones are gone; being those of early Christians, they were

accounted holy, and were carried away by the cart-load to sanctify other places with their presence. Twenty-six cart-loads, it is said, were taken to the Pantheon and put under the floor. Many are left, however. The monk holds a taper up, and you read a quaint Latin inscription over a cavity, stating that so-and-so, with his wife and children, lie underneath. The monk thrusts in his hand and brings out a bone—an arm or leg of one of the family—and gives it to you to examine. Then you go on groping along . . . when I once more drank in the fresh air and the sunshine, I felt that the heroism of the early martyrs was explained—people who spent much of their time in such holes must have found any escape a relief, even if they came out only to face the lions.[173]

Campbell's equally iconoclastic colleague Sara Jeannette Duncan satirized the catacomb mania even more strongly in her novel *A Voyage of Consolation* (1898), in which she ridicules the contemporary fascination with primitive Christian painting, and holds Christian righteousness up to light: " 'Can you tell them apart? . . . the Christians and the Pagans?' " asks one inquisitive visitor of the guide. " 'Yes,' replied that holy man, 'by the measurements of the jaw-bone. The Christians, you see, were always lecturing the other fellows, so their jaw-bones grew to an awful size. Some of 'em are simply parliamentary.' "[174]

More even than in London and Paris, visiting Canadians remained aloof from the population in Rome, having been advised by their guide-books that the Italians were a fickle, childish people who irresponsibly wasted their lives with song and dance and that the tourist did well to treat his porters, guides, and cab-drivers with a firm hand. Thus, Italians were considered either a bothersome distraction from one's sightseeing or else a picturesque addition to it. The models lounging on the steps of Trinità dei Monti seemed a perfect illustration of Italians' theatricality and lack of substance. There, next to "ferocious-looking men from the Campagna who pose as bandits," sprawled madonnas, cherubs, St. Sebastians, flower girls, matrons, John Baptists and Beelzebubs, all available at approximately four francs a day.[175] Besides being untrustworthy, because natural actors, Italians were suspected of having an innate propensity for thieving and brigandage, a stereotype consolidated by numerous sensational novels and stories. In the activities of Garibaldi and the unification of Italy, the Abbé Léon Provancher perceived a development of banditry on a national scale. Now, not only were harmless travellers robbed of their belongings, but also the entire Church had been deprived of its rightful property. Provancher—who, at the conclusion of *De Québec à Jérusalem* provided a six-page summary of national characteristics outlining the typical Arab,

Italian, Frenchman, and Englishman—thought the Italian deceitful, vain, greedy, and given to emotional excess, although he admitted that in Francis of Assisi and other saints, this volatile passion had also been channelled into an especially fervent faith.[176] Travellers to Italy often came to assert their own moral superiority, separating the land (and its monuments and buildings) and its people into two almost unrelated stereotypes, one idealized, the other wholly negative. For Canada, such stereotypes were to prove a serious problem when Italian immigration began in the 1890s; for a long time, a prejudiced public perceived them as knife-wielders, vagabonds, and organ-grinders, who could be best assimilated into Anglo-Saxon society by swift conversion to Protestantism.[177] It took some time for the lesson of Italian unification, which had brought together states of different historical backgrounds and dialects, to take root in Canada's management of its own ethnic diversity.

8

Canadians at World Expositions

In her charming pastiche, *The Elegant Canadians* (1967), Luella Creighton imagines a startled organizer at the 1867 *Exposition universelle* in Paris as he unwrapped the Canadian exhibits. Besides oil and watercolour paintings, there were other definite signs of civilization: red and white wine as well as liqueurs and cordials; linens, shawls, flannels, lace, embroideries and a lady's straw hat; fine soap; artist's implements and materials; and "delicately constructed [sewing machines], mounted on iron enamelled trays, some with scalloped edges, gilded and painted with roses and shells."[1] All these objects combined with the formidable evidence of rich mineral resources, extensive railroads, canals, and roads, flourishing agriculture, and a solid educational system to project the image of a thriving, sophisticated country. "Shaken, the Frenchman repaired to his two-hour luncheon," fantasizes Luella Creighton, "eating his thin soup with loud sups and striking his thick slices of bread petulantly into his bowl. This exposition, this *trop beau* show, was sapping to the morale."[2]

Andrew Spedon did not agree with Creighton's sullen Frenchman that Canada's 1867 display showed both elegance and efficiency: on the contrary, he found the exhibit "rustic beyond redemption," to borrow Robertson Davies's words, hence unworthy of a young and vigorous nation. The year of Confederation, 1867, may be considered a watershed in the formation of Canada's self-image and in its participation in world fairs: no longer divided into several colonies, the country now had to project a unified image, a strong common purpose. It also had to decide whether it wanted to join the western race for urbanization and industry, present itself as a pastoral alternative to both the old world and to America, or somehow find a synthesis between the two. Commissioners preparing Canada's displays could not escape as easily into eclecticism as the average tourist might because exhibits were, after all, not only arranged to please but also designed to attract investors and immigrants.

If Canadian travellers found their identity tested over and over again by supercilious citizens of the mother countries, the situation was even more severe at expositions, often praised as condensed world tours without the inconveniences of travel. Here, Canadians had to assert themselves in "a true microcosm, a world in miniature,"[3] showing cultures at evolutionary stages which ranged from the barbaric to the highly sophisticated: "At times the entire building seems to me a vast dial analogous to that floral dial of Linnaeus, which told the hour by the closing up of some flowers and the opening of others,"[4] marvelled a contributor to *Harper's*. Andrew Spedon, however, felt deeply humiliated that his country should appear as one of the closed flowers or, in his own metaphor, "like an affrighted child . . . crouching behind the forest shadows of the savage age,"[5] a misrepresentation owing to "the bungling mismanagement of stupid officials."[6]

Although it may often have appeared to Canadian observers that their country alone suffered growing pains, world fairs have always been closely associated with crises of national self-assertion.[7] At the 1851 Great Exhibition, the post-Napoleonic rancour between England and France shifted onto an economic level, with France catching up in industrial progress by 1855 when Paris hosted its first *Exposition universelle*, an occasion which coincided with a military alliance of the two former adversaries during the Crimean War. Following the disastrous Franco-Prussian War, Paris proclaimed its rebirth with the Centennial of the Revolution in 1889, and Germany largely snubbed invitations to participate until 1900 when newspapers, *Massey's Magazine* among them, benevolently observed renewed friendship between the two nations.[8] Irked by England's display of old world power in 1851, the United States demonstrated its faith in republicanism at the 1876 Centennial Fair in Philadelphia, and also asserted the nation's renewed unity after the Civil War. The 1893 Columbian Fair confirmed in its legendary "White City" the belief that the Americas were indeed utopia and the old world obsolete. American observers at the 1867 Paris Fair could still complain about, and feel humiliated by, Europeans' ignorance of their country ("We have been much scandalized by English ignorance of America, but if Americans read more French they would often be astounded at items in the French press. For example, the *Moniteur* lately, in announcing the removal of Wells by Sheridan, said, 'The removal seemed to be as acceptable to the white population as to the Republicans!' ").[9] But no such fears were necessary toward the end of the century, when America had clearly established itself as a power well worth knowing. Canada too had made a strong contribution to the 1851 Fair for political reasons, but far from wanting to assert its independence, the colony—especially as represented by the Montreal business community—sought to demonstrate its loyalty after the embarrassing events of 1849, when the Parliament Buildings had been burnt down, the governor general publicly insulted and a manifesto signed recommending annexation to the United States. The *Anglo-American Magazine* emphatically declared its allegiance to Britain when New Yorkers erected their own Crystal Palace in 1852, an enterprise the magazine considered doomed to expose the Republic's pitiful resources as compared to the "Anglo-Saxon Monarchy['s] . . . ancient vigour and enthusiasm."[10] In 1900, Canada's display in Paris gained additional attraction "through the brilliant achievements of her volunteer soldiers in South Africa," and an observer commented with considerable satisfaction that, coincidentally, the Boer pavilion had been erected "immediately beside the British colonial building,"[11] thus anticipating the outcome of the war. At world fairs too, then, Canada saw herself as one of the Empire's obedient daughters ("situated in the midst of the group of Great Britain and her colonies, where, like Cornelia, surrounded by her children, the great mother of nations could point proudly to her numerous offspring and say, 'These are my jewels' "),[12] a self-image not without some undesirable practical implications.

At the zenith of his power in 1867, Napoleon III was showing Haussmann's Paris off to the world: "The magnificence of the Second Empire is beyond dispute," affirmed *Harper's*. "Paris is the unchallenged queen of cities, and Napoleon III has abundant reason to congratulate himself on the success that has attended his efforts to eclipse the world in making his capital the temporary emporium of all that is useful and lovely in the civilized world."[13] To this uncritical observer, the 1867 Exposition seemed like a cosmic reflection of imperial power, its main building "one circle of dazzling radiance, leading the astronomic mind to hazard comparisons with the belts of Saturn,"[14] and to Andrew Spedon Paris appeared as the "ELYSIUM OF TERRESTRIAL GLORY."[15] In proudly displaying the latest technological achievements of the age, however, world fairs sometimes uncannily projected the future in which such glory would be dimmed. Although Germany's displays in 1851 were scattered among separate areas assigned to the Zollverein, Saxony, the Hanse Towns, Northern Germany, Prussia, Bavaria and Baden-Württemberg, Prussia's predominance was obvious. Even in 1855, the Canadian commissioner Joseph-Charles Taché admired Prussia's display of weaponry.[16] By 1867, the country's military and political ascendancy had become too ostentatious to be ignored: "The Emperor of the French must have recognized what time of day it is in Germany when, on his first promenade through the building, he paused at the 'Temple of Universal Peace,' which Berlin workmen were just completing and saw in it a single block of steel weighing 38,000 kilogrammes, with 180,000 cannon-balls of 500 kilos each, ready for 1000-pound guns,"[17] a formidable display of military power demonstratively repeated five years after the Franco-Prussian War at the Philadelphia Centennial Exhibition where William H. Withrow—a supporter of Prussian supremacy—saw the great Krupp cannon, its "inert steel and iron . . . almost indued [sic] with life and volition."[18] In contrast, the Austro-Hungarian Empire's inevitable decline seemed, to one visitor, inscribed in its bank-notes "where the value is indicated in *ten different languages.*"[19]

The irony that steel weaponry should have been displayed in a "Temple of Universal Peace" points up the paradoxical nature of Victorian world fairs, or even of world fairs in general. Designed to proclaim universal brotherhood and further world peace, a world fair might be promoted as a "Heavenly City" or a "New Jerusalem"[20] or even be compared to the "shrine of the holy temple."[21] Joseph Marmette, a novelist and civil servant employed by the Public Archives of Canada, infused the 1886 Colonial and Indian Exhibition with the qualities of a fabled land, where even agricultural machinery appeared "comme des crustâces monstres ou d'énormes araignées."[22] Exhilarated by his escape from dreary Ottawa, Marmette was inclined to consider the artificial splendour of the exhibition a fairyland, but travelling toward London, he had been horrified at the evidence of ancient and modern feudalism, the very prerequisities for a display of imperial achievement such as the one he was about to attend. The surface glamour of exhibitions often barely covered naked power struggles, racism, and social misery. A fervently democratic observer of the 1867 Fair reprimanded Napoleon III for building an imperial showcase at the expense of the poor, for perpetuating feudal practises, and for stifling the freedom of the press. The exposition, in short, was not as universal as it claimed to be, but a narcissistic self-display of the rulers. All of Paris seemed a violent anachronism: "Alas, that in so sweet a chateau should be skeleton-closets, and beneath the gay saloon dungeons where Reason and Right lie chained,"[23] a paradox mirrored in the outrageous contrasts of *mi-carême* and lent, of carnival's erotic licence and the stern homilies of Père Hyacinthe. In a sense, world expositions captured the contradictions of the Victorian Age; surrogate journeys around the world,[24] they both focus and enrich this study of developments in the Canadian self-image vis-à-vis Europe and, increasingly, the world, and they may serve as a suitable conclusion as well.

On a summer evening in 1851, staff and students of the Petit Séminaire de Québec descended the steep streets to the Lower Town to attend a *laterna magica* presentation with a very topical subject: the Great Exhibition in London.[25] The first picture, anticipated with much suspense, depicted the Crystal Palace, a structure as elegant and perfect as a well-delivered speech—or so the student chronicler of the seminary's newspaper, a young man obviously steeped in the study of classical rhetoric, termed it. Accompanied by gentle piano music, the slides showed a fairyland of silks, crystals, and musical instruments, beautiful and rich enough to tempt Orpheus. The picture of the Canadian exhibit was welcomed with loud applause: despite its humble contents, everyone was proud of its efforts. Earlier that year, the *Abeille du Petit Séminaire*, quoting the *Montreal Gazette*, had furnished a list of the displays, which included, besides sleighs, furs, stuffed mooseheads, a voyageur canoe, Indian artifacts, samples of grains, minerals, and timber, also such "civilized" items as furniture, a piano, leather trunks, stoves, a church bell, jewellery, artificial teeth and G. Perry & Bros.' fire engine which—"sheathed in copper from the newly discovered mines of the Lake Superior Region, and adorned with paintings of Canadian scenery"[26] —was greatly admired for its beauty and efficiency. Canadian women contributed a tapestry to be used for chair-upholstering, a work later presented to Queen Victoria. The "Committee of the Montreal District Industrial Fair" had organized a preview; to the most successful display at London, Lord Elgin promised a reward of one hundred pounds.

The slides in the *laterna magica* presentation suggested a methodical sequence of displays, giving equal attention to each country, no matter how abundant or modest its offerings; the reality, however, was rather more complicated. Whereas the United States occupied two spaces, one of them very large, in the eastern section of the Crystal Palace bordering on the central nave (with additional American displays, including Hiram Walker's celebrated sculpture "Greek Slave"), Canada was part of a large area adjoining the transept which was devoted to the British Colonies.[27] With South African, African, Indian, and Australian displays opening into the central nave and transept or bordering the south wall, visitors could only reach the Canadian display area by way of the other colonies, a circumstance which must have had an effect on observers' perception. The transition from India's exotic displays to Canada's northern implements may have appeared abrupt, and while illustrative of the rich variety among the members of the British Empire, it also showed the irreconcilable tensions within it. Marmette, listening to the workers in the East Indian exhibit next door, found them alien, incomprehensible: "cette déclamation aïgue, entrecoupée de mugissements de basse profonde, me poursuit encore et m'est restée dans l'oreille comme la mélopée la plus étrange qui se puisse entendre."[28] These tensions between the different ethnic and racial groups in the Empire were mirrored by occasional friction between the English and French commissioners of Canada. During the 1855 Paris exposition, for instance, the *Montreal Gazette* accused Joseph-Charles Taché of leaving most of the work to William Logan, while he spent his own time "at the unofficial functions and in preparing an essay describing Canada's historical development and economic potentialities."[29] Conversely, Taché—whose *Esquisse sur le Canada considéré sous le point de vue économiste* and *Catalogue raisonné des produits canadiens exposés à Paris en 1855* were enthusiastically praised by Paris reviewers—noted pointedly, after introducing Paul Kane's paintings at length, that the French-Canadian artists Plamondon, Hamel, and Bourassa too could have exhibited their work, had modesty permitted them to do so, and that another painter, Antoine-Sébastien Falardeau, had even made a name for himself in Florence.[30]

On a different stylistic level, Andrew Spedon's farcical description of the 1867 Canadian display captures the country's confused representation of its identity, angrily characterized twenty-five years later by Thomas Langton as that of a "hobbledehoy-nation," when he had been mistaken for one time too many as American or British.[31] Spedon's eloquent description of his encounter with the Canadian representative is worth quoting at some length:

All on a sudden my attention was arrested by something stirring among the bushes, I started back staring, no doubt, voraciously fearful . . . a person within the alcove poked out his head and stared at me with a sort of dreamy, bewildered aspect. We both stood and stared keenly at each other for several seconds without either of us attempting to budge a muscle, I saw from his physiognomy that he had not the appearance of an Indian, but in some respects resembled a Frenchman. Mustering up sufficient fortitude I very politely bowed, and addressed him with—"*Bon jour, monsieur.*" "Salut, monsieur," he replied; and forthwith came out of his lair—and when he had stretched himself up to his full figure, he presented a somewhat respectable aspect. "*Monsieur, parlez vous Anglais*," said I—O, oui, monsieur," said he, "Well," said I, "I hope you will excuse me the liberty I have taken in intruding upon your private apartment." "*Oh,*" said he, "it is a part of the Exhibition, and you are perfectly welcome, sir, and at liberty to examine all its contents." "To what tribe of Indians does it belong, sir," said I. "*To what;*" said he, somewhat astonished; then shaking his head, he exclaimed—*Je ne vous comprend [sic] pas.*" Thinking that he might understand me better in French I said—"*A quelle tribue [sic] de sauvages appartient-il,*" "*O, Monsieur,*"—he exclaimed, almost petrified with my interrogation—"*Ceci est le grand départment [sic] de la Nouvelle Dominion du Canada.*" "*Is it possible that this is the Canadian Department,*" I exclaimed, staring at him, with bewildered amazement. "*Certainly it is, sir,*" said he—"*Look up there, sir,*" added he, pointing to a sort of *sign-board* above the alcove. I looked up, and there saw the word CANADA in insignificant letters, surrounded by maple leaves, and surmounted by the figure of a "*Beaver*" chewing at a *maple-branch.* "Then," said I, turning to him, "I suppose you are a Canadian," "I am a French Canadian," said he, "and have charge of this Department." On telling him that I belonged to Lower Canada also, he was perfectly delighted; and we entered into a lively conversation, which continued until the signal-bell announced the retiring hour.[32]

Finding the Canadian exhibit at world expositions remained a problem since it was not always clear whether the country continued to define itself as part of the colonies or as a separate country. Spedon's disillusioning encounter with his country's display began with a nightmarish search for its location:

I travelled through among the divisions of the British Colonies; but nowhere could I discover that of Canada. I then asked of parties where the Canadian Department was; but of such a place, or such a country, no person appeared to have ever heard, or to be in the least acquainted with. In fact I began to think that Canada was either *misrepresented*, or designed by some other cognomen, as "THE NEW DOMINI-ON,"—"THE COLONIAL KINGDOM,"—"LAURENTIA," —"NORLAND," . . . But neither of these names could I see, nor yet any other characteristic of Canada. At length after having narrowly scrutinized every division in the vicinity of the British Colonies, I incidentally came to a small, singularly-looking, contracted apartment, having two inlets.[33]

This "apartment," described by another observer as "a sort of tent, such as used by wood cutters in the forest,"[34] was the exhibition space of Upper and Lower Canada. Until Confederation, the existence of several British

North American colonies complicated co-ordination; in 1867, only Newfoundland, Nova Scotia, and Upper and Lower Canada put in an appearance; Prince Edward Island, New Brunswick, and British Columbia were not represented.

Even when Canada began to occupy its own pavilion, its association with Britain was often emphasized in the architectural style chosen. In 1911 for instance, Canada featured a three-quarter size replica of the Canadian Parliament Buildings, erected in emulation of Britain's neogothic Houses of Parliament;[35] earlier, at the 1904 exposition in St. Louis, the Canadian agricultural trophy imitated the Parliamentary Library in Ottawa. In choosing gothic allusions (coincidentally, Canada's space in 1851 had been adjacent to Pugin's famous Medieval Court), organizers underlined the virtues presumably associated with that style: Anglo-Saxon integrity, muscular Christianity, and racial superiority, thus firmly restating the Myth of the North informing other efforts to formulate the Canadian identity as well. Withrow, for instance, frowned upon the works of art submitted by "southern" nations to the Philadelphia Centennial Exhibition, contrasting them unfavourably with the "northern" contributions: "I must record my protest against the sensuous character of many of the foreign paintings, especially of France, Austria, and Spain. In this respect, they are in striking contrast with the almost universal chaste and modest character of the English and American pictures,"[36] a contrast he perceived also in other, more practical displays. Since one of the most popular features of world expositions became the painstaking reproduction of the very medieval city quarters which had just been destroyed to make way for modern cities, Canada aligned itself with a nostalgic, picturesque past. This was true even when a different style was chosen, such as the severely neo-classical architecture characterizing the 1924 British Empire Exhibition at Wembley, when Britain emphatically restated its power by evoking the memory of Greek and Roman grandeur at a time when its political and military supremacy was beginning to fade.

Inseparable from Canada's architectural declarations of allegiance were demonstrations of its agricultural potential, proclaiming its role as the granary of the mother country. At Wembley, a visitor was startled by "a rustic scene which represented the Prince of Wales, life-size, standing beside his horse on his ranch. Both . . . modeled . . . *out of butter*,"[37] and the Canadian Pavilion at the 1937 Paris Exposition simulated a grain elevator, thus confirming a note struck by an observer in Paris in 1855 who felt that "Canada and British Guiana do honor to the mother country . . . by their flour and their starch."[38] In contrast, the United States displayed farming implements, like the McCormick reaper in 1851, as symbols of determined pragmatism and self-sufficiency.[39]

Instructed by his family to seek out "a bushel of beans from Spring Creek in the vast [*sic*] section of P[rince] E[dward] I[sland] exhibits,"[40] Robert Harris had to assume after a fruitless search that said beans were hidden away in "the Canadian trophy . . . a large wooden framework on which are arranged all kinds of things of Canadian growth and manufacture."[41] Standing nearly sixty feet tall, the trophy, one of Canada's most typical exhibitions at nineteenth-century fairs, emphasized the country's natural resources on a gargantuan scale, but to some observers this form of display still suggested the taxidermic lifelessness of a museum of natural history. The humour in Thomas C. Watkins's enthusiastic description of a trophy may have been involuntary:

> It is built chiefly of the different woods of our almost illimitable forests, and ornamented up along the four sides to the top with skins of animals, stuffed skins of birds and quadrupeds. Agricultural implements, mechanics [*sic*] tools, preserved and salt fish, barrels of salt and flour, specimens of ores and coal, handsome quilts, and ladies needlework, hanks of Indian corn, bundles of woolen and flax yarn, metals and minerals. . . . As you ascend the stair at every turn you are met by the glaring eyes of our wild animals, a brown or black bear, wolf or a deer, a fox or racoon, a meditative owl, a vulture, or some other of our raptorial birds peep out from the many nooks, while our domestic fowl sit here and there in quiet corners looking sedately on the great stream of humanity,[42]

but a contributor to the *Canadian Magazine* was as annoyed as Andrew Spedon at the profusion of stuffed animals summoned to represent Edenic freshness and strength; he even suggested that it was time to abandon the sentimental and attract big-game hunters instead.[43] French-Canadian liberals also criticized the trophy for promoting the Agricultural Myth when advances in technology and industry were, they felt, the only way to make Canada a competitive, well-respected nation: Arthur Buies especially sneered at the pitiful samples of grains, as he called them, and at the commissioners' lack of commitment and efficiency.[44]

Canada's self-image as a country whose nature was determined by its agricultural and wildlife resources was, however, complemented by impressive and internationally acclaimed educational displays designed to prove that an intellectually and artistically active community tempered the pragmatism of its daily existence with "sweetness and light." Exhibits echoed Egerton Ryerson's efforts to establish an educational museum. Presided over by "life-size busts of those immortal educators of the race, Shakespeare, Newton, Herschel and Faraday, as well as by those of the

Prince and Princess of Wales,''[45] glass cases at the 1876 Philadelphia Centennial were filled with maps, models of school buildings, experimental apparatus, globes, a sample school library including *braille* textbooks for the blind, gymnastic equipment, and school furniture. While Ryerson had still found it necessary to shop for basic school materials at the 1851 and 1855 fairs, Canada was now itself reputed for its educational resources, and William Withrow proudly reported that duplicates of several items had been ordered by the governments of Japan, Australia, and the United States: "Many of the foreign visitors, who imagined, we suppose, that the Canadians were a sort of hyperborean barbarians, were greatly astonished to find us taking the lead of the world in one of the very highest developments of the best civilization of the age."[46] Still, here too observers like James Douglas, then professor of chemistry at Morrin College, Quebec, and about to take on a post as manager of a copper works at Phoenixville, Pennsylvania, were irked by the gaucherie of Canadian display techniques, with exhibits entombed in "heavy black walnut cases . . . stand[ing] in gaunt, gloomy rows, like coffins on end in an undertaker's shop."[47] The close proximity of the British exhibit invited comparisons, suggested this critic, which ought to sting Canadians—now claiming independence from the mother country—into a better effort.

Most of the displays described so far suffered from the very fact that they consisted of samples, samples moreover often kept at a minimum because of the expense involved in transporting them (several observers felt that Canada would be much better served by permanent museums installed in Britain and France):[48] Canada's vastness, its scenic variety, and active social life remained essentially intangible until better methods of representation could be found. Maps were certainly among the most important symbolic depictions of Canada. Thomas C. Keefer, an eminent engineer and commissioner for the 1878 Paris exposition, used maps to demonstrate Canada's recently gained expansion from sea to sea and its increasingly sophisticated infrastructure, as well as to teach Parisians— whom he found alarmingly ignorant of Canada's location, let alone its character—a basic lesson in geography: "our exhibitors cards were headed by a small sphere printed in colours which was also used as a vignette for our handbook, showing North America divided between Canada, the United States and Mexico, so that the visitors, in examining any Canadian exhibit, would not fail to know from what quarter of the world it came."[49] In this manner, Keefer hoped to combat the belief he encountered among numerous Frenchmen that Canada was a tropical country (as maple sugar was mistaken for sugar cane) or that its inhabitants were identical with the *Canaques*, a rebellious tribe in New Caledonia.

As well as maps, there were paintings and photographs to illustrate

Canada's rich offerings on a more inclusive scale than samples could. While Joseph-Charles Taché still dismissed displays in "printing, photography and engraving" as "far behind" in 1855 and claimed that exhibition officials only allowed them in order "to stimulate and encourage"[50] better production in the future, Keefer lauded the photographic exhibits as the most popular part of Canada's contribution. Photographs elaborated on the impressions created by maps, concentrating on major achievements in engineering and architecture, such as views of Victoria Bridge and the Windsor Hotel or portraits of the men responsible for these achievements and on pictures of Canadians vigorously enjoying the offerings of their northern location in winter sports, hunting, and festive carnival activities. Although other photographers like Alexander Henderson and Henry Sandham contributed to Canada's exhibits, William Notman and his associates were so successful that they obtained the exclusive rights as official photographers of the Philadelphia Centennial Exhibition, a concession which apparently produced four thousand images. Notman's reputation was enhanced by royal patronage: an album containing his photographs of Canadian scenery and of remarkable achievements in engineering was presented to the Prince of Wales when he arrived in Canada in 1862 to open Victoria Bridge; somewhat earlier, the *Art Journal* of London had commended Notman for reinforcing with his work "the ties that bind us to our valuable colony."[51]

Imperial links were also made clear in Notman's specialty, composite pictures containing the portraits of prominent citizens set against an artistically painted backdrop. His famous "Curling in Canada," exhibited at the 1876 Centennial Exhibition in Philadelphia, depicts John A. Macdonald and Lord and Lady Dufferin, among other celebrities, with Montreal and Mount Royal in the background. Photographs strongly emphasized winter as the quintessentially Canadian season, as the time when the country's best "northern" qualities—physical and moral stamina—were put to the test. The catalogue for the 1878 Paris exhibition lists pictures depicting "Ice Shoves, River St. Lawrence; Harvesting Ice on River St. Lawrence; Ice Jam, Montreal; . . . Ice Cone, Montmorenci; . . . Hoar Frost; . . . Ice Forms, Niagara . . . Icebergs," as well as "Canadian Scenes, illustrating Moose and Caribou Hunting, Snow Show Club, Curling, Fancy Dress Skating Carnival." An earlier exhibit, in 1867, featured scenes of "seal-stalking amongst the ice and the caribou stalking in the middle of the wild and romantic country between St. Urbain and Lake St. John."[52] Notman's photographs turned Canada's winters into festive displays and a tourist commodity, thus significantly counterbalancing the drily scientific and pragmatic depiction of the land

and its resources typified by the agricultural trophy.

Yet Notman's photographs were, of course, not necessarily a more truthful depiction of Canada's essence; rather they created yet another stereotype, the "cold but gay pastoral" featured even today in travel agencies' posters. Many of Notman's winter scenes were, for obvious reasons, taken in a studio, with complicated contraptions—later retouched— holding the object's body in place to suggest vigorous activity in the snow. Similarly, Lansdowne's, Stanley's, and Minto's patronage of winter sports often barely concealed their profound boredom with Ottawa's provinciality.[53]

Occasionally, photography was not considered prestigious enough to promote Canada's resources to the world. Notman hired some of the country's best painters—many unemployed because photography now practically monopolized the portrait business—to create artistic backdrops and sketch in the background for his composites. The Canadian Pacific Railway went one step further, sending artists west on the first trains to record the newly opened terrain and commissioning operatic paintings based on the photographic record thus accumulated. CPR officials had definite ideas of what constituted effective publicity: extensive correspondence between William van Horne, vice-president of the Canadian Pacific Railway, and John A. Fraser, a Notman employee who painted landscapes, concerning a rendering of "Mount Stephen Near Leanchoil, Canadian Pacific Railway" to be executed from black-and-white photographs, documents the extent of official patronage and its influence on the final product. Colours, shapes, and mood were all carefully orchestrated to create images of imperial splendour blossoming in the midst of forbidding terrain, images suitable to be displayed at the Colonial and Indian Exhibition of 1886 preceding Queen Victoria's Golden Jubilee.[54]

World fairs forced Canadian art, like all other exhibits, into juxtapositions and comparisons which often proved decisive to its general development. In 1855, Taché pointed out the works of the Nazarenes as worthy of a Canadian's attention, since "this school devotes itself more particularly to the ideal, and . . . disdains the scenes of real life, striving rather to develop symbolical theories."[55] Similarly many of the Canadian painters attracted to Paris following the Philadelphia Centennial were also drawn by the idealized work of the great French academic and fresco painters. John George Bourinot, discussing "Our intellectual Strength and Weakness" in his 1893 presidential address to the Royal Society of Canada, considered America's progress in the arts, as displayed at the Columbian Fair, a model for Canada's future artistic maturity,[56] a maturity attained in the paintings of the Group of Seven, whose work—exhibited at the Wembley Exhibition—attracted foreign praise, even if critics at home felt that Eric Brown, director of the National Art

Gallery, had committed a *faux-pas* in submitting these unforgivably modern canvases. Fruitful as the contact with other national arts was for Canadians, however, it complicated the definition of an unmistakably Canadian style. "A great number of her pictures were painted abroad, instead of being purely Canadian, with the very scent of the soil—the native birthmark— impressed on every one," complained an observer at the Columbian Fair, obviously a supporter of the Agricultural Myth, before listing typically Canadian subjects to be covered in future works of art: "She is noted for her handsome women, and for being a greater cattle producer (for her population) than any other country, while humor finds here a congenial home."[57] The conflict between cosmopolitanism and regionalism—one of the central issues of Canadian modernism in the 1920s—was clearly sharpened by Canada's participation in world fairs, and it was less a conflict between an original self-image and an imitative one than a choice between an urban and a rural identity.

As a member of Britain's imperial family, Canada naturally compared its showings to those of its sister colonies, particularly Australia. Irked by America's "self-glorification over her century's progress,"[58] at the Philadelphia Fair, James Douglas proudly sketched Australia's achievements, taking almost as much pride in its success as if it were Canada's own: "It would ill become us to estimate, even at its true value, the advance we have made within the same period—an advance, considering the drawbacks of climate and situation, not by any means inconsiderable; but modesty need not interfere with our appraising the attainments of our sister colonies at the antipodes."[59] Canada also measured itself gladly against northern European nations because geographical and economic situation seemed alike and Scandinavians were deemed racially equal. The matter was considerably more difficult when it came to appreciating radically different cultures, specimens of which were often displayed as anthropological curiosities.[60] Andrew Spedon, for instance, claimed to admire the 1867 Exposition for uniting "the sable sons of Africa; the tawny tribes of Asia, the intelligent European, and the ingenious American; diversified by their own peculiar costumes, customs and characteristics, yet all mingling together, under one roof, in one common brotherhood, as one great universal family of the world"[61] but his true feelings became abundantly clear when he was confronted with an "African orchestra" in an ethnic restaurant: "On a raised dais was a band of African minstrels of both sexes. The musical instruments were peculiarly singular and uncouth. . . . The [players] were blowing away vociferously, thumping terrifically, and sweating profusely. The music, or rather the discordant notes, were occasionally accompanied by the weird-like [*sic*], grinding voices of the performers. . . . On entering, a waiter came forward, conducted us to a seat and then gabbled out something in the *Black Language.*''[62] Similar abuse was heaped on China and Japan, whose exhibits were considered too incomprehensible to be civilized,[63] although Japan's showings, especially at Philadelphia and Chicago, spawned fashions in oriental architecture and interior decorating. A contributor to the *Canadian Methodist Magazine* argued that civilization was synonymous with Christianity and that world fairs provided important object lessons in juxtaposing the solid produce of the Christian nations with the effetely decorative works of cultures which did not subscribe to the Christian faith.[64] Most visitors to world fairs were confirmed in their ethnocentricity, especially as cultural diversity occasionally became an excuse for thinly veiled pornography. (Andrew Spedon demonstrated the most common response when he fled from a Paris dance-café, startled by can-can dancers ''leaping several feet high and throwing themselves into such fantastic positions that were sufficient to startle the eyes of a Canadian,'' who did not ''relish . . . such eccentric displays of gesture and revolution''),[65] whereas the cultural modesty expressed by one contributor to *Harper's* in 1867 was truly extraordinary:

> The vast extent to which the remoter countries are represented in Paris . . . may play havoc with some of the generalizations of our Western half culture. One of these is the idea, so common in Europe and America, that there is but a single type of what we term ''civilization,'' and that this type is represented by France, England, and America; that the variations of those far-off regions from ourselves denote variation from civilization itself, and that in whatever proportion they shall make progress that progress will inevitably be toward the manners and usages of the advanced societies of Western Europe and America.''[66]

The writer concluded that there were cultures subscribing to an entirely different kind of progress which could only be ruined by interference by others. Did colonial exhibitors, urged to select the categories of their initial displays to meet the expectations of the mother country, ever feel that they too had been forced into an inappropriate mold?

If some observers of world fairs praised them as heavenly cities of Christian brotherhood, others—true to the expositions' paradoxical nature—saw them as concentrations of all that was materialistic and sterile about nineteenth-century cities, indeed civilization. Aesthetes like Edmond Goncourt mourned the 1867 Fair as ''L'Exposition universelle, le dernier coup au passé: l'*américanisation* de la France, l'industrie primant l'art . . . en un mot la Fédération de la Matière.''[67] Moralists saw the

L. ''The Paris Exhibition—The Great Eiffel Tower Completed,'' *The Dominion Illustrated.*

exhibitions as evil Towers of Babel, representations of man's sinful confidence in his own resources. The 1887 Paris Fair especially attracted moral censure, particularly among conservative French Canadians, who considered it highly inappropriate that the French Revolution should be honoured with a Centennial. To one J. L. Gougeon, the Champ-de-Mars shortly after the closure of the exposition seemed like a desolate desert presided over by the Eiffel Tower as the tombstone of a vanished world: "ce n'est que ruines et débris informes, que briques et ferrailles dispersées, et pans de murs qui s'écroulent, retraçant l'image d'une sorte de Herculaneum et de Pompéi."[68] The buildings of the world were pitifully fragile compared to the solidity of faith, Gougeon believed, a view fervently shared by Tardivel, who recovered from the offensive sight of the Eiffel Tower—a monument, he thought, to the scientific spirit of Freemasonry—by visiting an ecclesiastical exhibition at Brussels, its determined archaism expressive of an integrity far more durable than the superficial glamour of materialist progress.[69]

And yet the reactionary idealism of a Jules-Paul Tardivel was counterpointed by progressive developments, which eventually contributed to significant adjustments in Canada's self-image. Women—long represented by intricate needlework, such as "a beautiful carpet, made by the ladies of Hamilton" and "a splendid carpet, wrought in Berlin wool, by the ladies of Toronto . . . for the benefit of the church,"[70] —became remarkably active in many other roles at world fairs toward the end of the century. Inspired by the success of the "Women's Building" at the Columbian Fair,[71] the National Council of Women in Canada asked for a section to be allotted to women at the 1900 Paris exposition, a request denied by the commissioners "because they felt that the separate classification of women's work was no compliment to women, but the reverse."[72] Instead, the council was encouraged to prepare a report entitled *Women of Canada: Their Life and Work*, compiling extensive information on such matters as women's legal and political status, their educational and professional options, their role in literature, the arts, the churches, social reform and immigration. Although it is doubtful that the Council really agreed with the commissioners as gladly as the introduction to the report indicates they did, *Women of Canada* remains an important document, enhanced by the presence of women journalists covering the fair, such as Robertine Barry of *La Patrie* and Agnes Scott of the *Ottawa Witness*. Born out of the paradoxically conservative *and* experimental spirit of world fairs and the equally paradoxical rivalry among nations, stimulating and potentially destructive at the same time, *Women of Canada* signals a significant phase in Canada's national development toward a fuller recognition of its pluralism. And this was perhaps the most important lesson to be learnt by Canadians on their travels.

Although the photographic album rapidly replaced the travel-book after the 1890s, Canadians' travel to Europe did of course not change abruptly as the new century began. By 1910, travellers dashed about the continent in "large Fiat Touring Car[s] painted in a very brilliant yellow striped with black,"[73] frequented the "kinema," admired airships, and were bemused by the British Museum's insistence on registering all women visitors for fear they might be troublesome suffragettes, but the attendant changes in attitude were as yet subtle. Travelling to George V's coronation in 1911, a prominent Vancouver businessman fully enjoyed his status as imperial citizen, especially as dignitaries from Australia also boarded the train on the west coast: Canada's motto "From Sea to Sea" designated an almost seamless integration into a fraternal world.[74]

That faith, however, was shattered only three years later as North-American tourists escaped by the skin of their teeth from a Europe that went up in flames practically overnight. Joseph Whitman Bailey, a lawyer from New Brunswick, was fortunate enough to gain passage on the Cunarder *Andania*, when his own reservations were cancelled by the military. Even as the liner crossed the Atlantic, it was painted "the steel gray coloring of a ship of war" and all lights were carefully dimmed "leaving as our only security against collision two inconspicuous red lights low down on the deck."[75] Relieved, Bailey reached Canada, still stunned by the sudden eruption of violence: only a few weeks earlier, he had seen the Archduke Ferdinand's body being taken down the Danube and had been assured by Austrian observers that all was calm.

As Canada joined the war, the only immediate reports about Europe considered worth reading by an anxious public were news from the front. Sketches about Paris or London now focused on relief organizations or analyzed the general morale; a former tourist's nostalgic recollections of Versailles might be sharply revised by a piece like "Our Portion of Versailles: The Story of How the Graves of Canadian Heroes are Tended by a Young French Girl."[76] To compensate for the loss of travel writing about Europe, one of periodical literature's mainstays, publications like the *Canadian Magazine* and *MacLean's* emphatically turned to Canada's own touristic resources, familiarizing their readers with all parts and aspects of the nation, especially with British Columbia and the prairie provinces. Sketches on Canada's more colourful immigrants and assessments of their contributions to the nation's cultural and economic life completed the efforts of a country forced into isolation and into a sudden recognition of its own resources. When travel-writing reacquired a certain *vogue* between the wars, Canada had changed forever and with it had its travellers. But that could be the subject of another book.

Notes

Notes to Chapter One

1. George Galt, "Canada First," *Books in Canada* 14.7 (Oct. 1985): 13.
2. See for example "Voyageurs canadiens-français en Italie au dix-neuvième siècle," *Vie française* 16.1/2 (1961): 15-24; "Voyageurs, pèlerins, et récits de voyages canadiens-français en Europe de 1850-1960," in *Mélanges de civilisation canadienne-française offerts au professeur Paul Wyczynski* (Ottawa: Ed. de l'Université d'Ottawa, 1977), 242-65; "L'Italia nella cultura franco-canadese," in Luca Codignola, ed., *Canadiana: problemi di storia canadese* (Venezia: Marsilio, 1983), 91-106.
3. Octave Crémazie, *Oeuvres 1: Poésies*, texte établi, annoté et présenté par Odette Condemine (Ottawa: Ed. de l'Université d'Ottawa, 1972).
4. See Journal of Elisha Budd de Mill, 3 vols. (1850-51), De Mille Manuscript Collection, Dalhousie U.
5. See Sybille Pantazzi, "Canadian Prize Books," *Canadian Collector* 5.3 (Mar. 1970): 24-27.
6. Paul Rutherford, *A Victorian Authority: The Daily Press in Late Nineteenth Century Canada* (Toronto: U of Toronto P, 1982), 130.
7. Louis Fréchette, *Mémoires intimes* (Montreal: Fides, 1961), 74.
8. G. de T. Glazebrook, Katharine B. Brett, Judith McErvel, *A Shopper's View of Canada's Past: Pages from Eaton's Catalogue* (Toronto: U of Toronto P, 1969), 143.
9. *Montreal Gazette* 10 Nov. 1841 and 18 Oct. 1842.
10. See Gilbert L. Gignac and Jeanne L. L'Espérance, "Thoughts of Peace and Joy: A Study of the Iconography of the Croscup Room," *Journal of Canadian Art History* 6.2 (1982): 137-78. According to this article, the artist may also have been a female member of the Croscup family.
11. See Denis Martin, "Les Collections de gravures du Séminaire de Québec: histoire et destins culturels" (MA thesis, Université Laval, Québec, 1980).
12. Ibid., 198.
13. See Pantazzi, "Canadian Prize Books."
14. Review of Sandford Fleming, *From Old to New Westminster, The Week* 1 (1883/84): 547.
15. Charles Roger, *Glimpses of London and Atlantic Experiences* (Ottawa: Robertson, Roger, 1873), 3. Also Eva-Marie Kröller, "Nineteenth Century Photography and the Canadian National Image," *Zeitschrift der Gesellschaft für Kanada-Studien*, 5.2 (1985): 83-91.
16. Bayard Taylor, ed., *Cyclopedia of Modern Travel: A Record of Adventure and Discovery, For the Past Fifty Years, Comprising Narratives of the Most Distinguished Travellers Since the Beginning of this Century* (Cincinnati: Moore, Wilstach, Keys, 1856), viii.
17. See Eveline Bossé, *La Capricieuse à*

Québec en 1855: les premières retrou-
vailles de la France et du Canada
(Montréal: La Presse, 1984).

18. W.L. Morton, "Victorian Canada," in
    W.L. Morton, ed., *The Shield of Achilles*
    (Toronto: McClelland and Stewart, 1968),
    314.

19. On Cimon, see Pierre Savard, "Voya-
    geurs canadiens-français dans l'Alle-
    magne de Bismarck et de Guillaume II,"
    *Zeitschrift der Gesellschaft für Kanada-
    Studien* 3.1 (1983): 57f.

20. Rutherford, *Victorian Authority*, 130.

21. Ashworth papers, Public Archives of
    Canada.

22. See Archambault papers, Public Ar-
    chives of Canada.

23. See Gertrude Fleming papers, Public

Archives of Canada.

24. Henry   Morgan,   "Adolphe-Basile
    Routhier," in *Canadian Men and Women
    of the Time* (Toronto: Briggs, 1898),
    893.

25. J.-M. Dandurand, "Le Sport versus
    l'esprit," *Nos Travers* (Montréal: Beau-
    chemin, 1901), 14.

26. On Robertine Barry, see Aurélien Boivin
    et Kenneth Landry, "Françoise et
    Madeleine: pionnières du journalisme
    féminin au Québec," *Voix et images* 4
    (1978/ 79): 233-43.

27. Reginald Martel, "Un Roman différ-
    ent," *La Presse*, 25 septembre 1971, C2.

28. "The Passing of the Book of Travel,"
    Scribner's 21 (1897): 785.

Notes to Chapter Two

1. Fred C. Martin papers, Public Archives
   of Canada.

2. Sylvia Pantazzi, "Baedeker's Canada of
   1894," *Canadian Collector* 4.9 (Sept.
   1969): 22.

3. Obituary, *Woodstock Sentinel Review*, 2
   Sept. 1908.

4. Ibid.

5. See Napoléon Legendre, "Les Etrangers
   à Québec," *Echos de Québec* (Québec:
   Côte, 1877), 173-80.

6. Nérée Gingras papers, Archives du
   Séminaire du Québec.

7. Jules-Paul Tardivel, *Notes de voyage en
   France, Italie, Espagne, Irlande, Angle-
   terre, Belgique et Hollande* (Montréal:
   Senécal, 1890), 330.

8. Benjamin Paquet papers, Archives du
   Séminaire de Québec.

9. Moses Harvey, "Notes of a Trip to the
   Old Land," *Stewart's Quarterly* 5
   (1871-72): 354.

10. Kathleen Coleman, *To London for the
    Jubilee* (Toronto: Morang, 1897), 106f.

11. Kathleen Coleman, "Woman's King-
    dom," *Toronto Mail*, 2 Jan. 1892, 5.

12. Jean-Baptiste Antoine Ferland, "Extraits

de lettres écrites à quelques'uns de ses
amis du Canada," *Le Foyer canadien* 3
(1865): xlv.

13. H.H. Langton, *James Douglas: A
    Memoir* (Toronto: U of Toronto P,
    1940), 32.

14. Sandford Fleming papers, Public Ar-
    chives of Canada.

15. See Pierre Savard, "Voyageurs, pèlerins
    et récits de voyages canadiens-français en
    Europe de 1850 à 1960," *Mélanges de
    civilisation canadienne-française offerts à
    Paul Wyczynski* (Ottawa: Editions de
    l'Université d'Ottawa, 1977), 242-65, for
    an overview. For Canadian travel in a
    country not extensively covered in this
    study, see Pierre Savard, "Voyageurs
    canadiens-français dans l'Allemagne de
    Bismarck et de Guillaume II," *Zeit-
    schrift der Gesellschaft für Kanada-
    Studien* 3.1 (1983): 54-64; Eva-Marie
    Kröller, "Nineteenth-Century Canadi-
    ans and the Rhine Valley," in *Gaining
    Ground: European Critics on Canadian
    Literature*, ed. Robert Kroetsch and
    Reingard Nischik (Edmonton: NeWest
    P, 1985), 234-46.

Notes to Chapter Three

1. See Thomas E. Appleton, *Ravenscrag: The Allan Royal Mail Line* (Montreal: McClelland and Stewart, 1974); Brian J. Young and Gerald J.J. Tulchinsky, "Sir Hugh Allan," *Dictionary of Canadian Biography* 11: 5-15.

2. Frank C. Bowen, *History of the Canadian Pacific Line* (London: Sampson, Marston, 1928).

3. Allan Line, *Illustrated Tourist's Guide to Canada* (Liverpool: Turner and Dunnett, 1879), 16.

4. Ibid., 9.

5. Ibid.

6. Ibid.

7. Allan Line, *Allan Line Royal Mail Steamers 1854-1900: St. Lawrence Route Montreal to Liverpool* (n.p., 1900?), 27.

8. Allan Line, *Illustrated Tourist's Guide*, 12.

9. Appleton, *Ravenscrag*, 140.

10. François-Xavier Garneau, *Voyage en Angleterre et en France dans les années 1831, 1832, et 1833*, ed. Paul Wyczynski (Ottawa: Ed. de l'Université d'Ottawa, 1968), 122.

11. Ibid., 123.

12. Joseph Howe, "The Novascotian Afloat," *The Novascotian* 28, 12 July 1838, 1. See also James A. Roy, *Joseph Howe: A Study in Achievement and Frustration* (Toronto: Macmillan, 1935), 62-87.

13. Ibid., 1.

14. Ibid.

15. See Phyllis R. Blakeley, "Sir Samuel Cunard," *Dictionary of Canadian Biography* 9: 172-86.

16. W.M. Cochrane, "Thomas C. Watkins," *The Canadian Album: Men of Canada; or, Success By Example, in Religion, Patriotism, Business, Law, Medicine, Education and Agriculture* 1 (Brantford, Ont.: Bradley, 1891): 265.

17. Thomas C. Watkins papers, Public Archives of Canada. (This is a large scrapbook containing clippings from newspapers Watkins wrote for, the names of which cannot always be determined.)

18. Ibid.

19. Ibid.

20. Ibid.

21. Ibid.

22. Henry Morgan, *The Tour of H.R.H. The Prince of Wales through British America and The United States, By a British Canadian* (Montreal: Lovell, 1860), 99.

23. *Murray's Handbook for Travellers in Northern Italy* (London: Murray, 1877), 19.

24. Gertrude Fleming papers, Public Archives of Canada.

25. See Edmund Allen Meredith papers, Public Archives of Canada.

26. See George Munro Grant papers, Public Archives of Canada.

27. See *Grand Hotel: The Golden Age of Palace Hotels, An Architectural and Social History* (London: Dent, 1984).

28. David Watkin, "The Grand Hotel Style," *Grand Hotel*, 17.

29. Thomas Langton papers, Public Archives of Canada.

30. Edmund Allen Meredith papers, Public Archives of Canada.

31. Conyngham Crawford Taylor, *The Queen's Jubilee and Toronto "Called Back" from 1887 to 1847* (Toronto: Briggs, 1887), 136.

32. See Goldwin Smith, *Reminiscences*, ed. Arnold Haultain (New York: Macmillan, 1911), 91f.

33. See Edmund Swinglehurst, *Cook's Tours: The Story of Popular Travel* (Poole: Blandford, 1982).

34. J.-C.-K. Laflamme papers, Archives du Séminaire de Québec.

35. See Léon Provancher, *De Québec à Jérusalem: journal d'un pèlerinage du Canada en Terre-Sainte* (Québec: Darveau, 1884), 27.

36. F.T., "From London to Antwerp," *Belford's Monthly Magazine* 2.6 (November 1877): 788.

37. Quoted in "Murray's Handbook Advertiser," *Murray's Handbook for Travellers in Central Italy, Including Florence, Lucca, Tuscany, Elba, etc., Umbria, The Marches, and Part of the Late Patrimony of St. Peter* (London: Murray, 1880), 73.

38. Karl Baedeker, *Paris and Environs with Routes from London to Paris: Handbook for Travellers* (Leipsic: Baedeker, 1900), 1.

39. *Murray's Handbook for Travellers in*

Central Italy, Part 2: Rome and its Environs (London: Murray, 1856), vii.

40. *Murray's Handbook for Travellers in Northern Italy, Part 1: Sardinia, Lombardy and Venice, Parma, Piacenza, and Modena, Part 2: Lucca, Pisa, Florence, and North Tuscany* (London: Murray, 1854), xv.

41. Ibid.

42. Emeline A. Rand, *In the National Gallery: Four Letters on the Development of Italian Art* (Toronto: Briggs, 1894), 64.

43. Alphonse Leclaire, "Le Beau et son expression par les arts," *Revue canadienne* 31 (1895) 10.

44. Ibid., 79.

45. Ibid., 78.

46. Eugène Aubert, "L''Ave Maria' à Venise par Carl Becker," *Revue canadienne* 31 (1895): 328; see Eva-Marie Kröller, "Nineteenth-Century Canadians and the Rhine Valley," in *Gaining Ground: European Critics on Canadian Literature*, ed. Robert Kroetsch and Reingard Nischik (Edmonton: NeWest, 1985), 234-46 for a more detailed discussion of these matters.

47. *Murray's Handbook for Travellers in Central Italy including Tuscany, The Tuscan Islands, Umbria, The Marches, And Part of the Late Patrimony of St. Peter* (London: Murray, 1900), 219. For a discussion of Browning's reception in Canada, see Claude Bissell, "Literary Taste in Central Canada during the later Nineteenth Century," in *Twentieth Century Essays on Confederation Literature*, ed. Lorraine McMullen (Ottawa: Tecumseh, 1976), 24-40.

48. Thomas Langton papers, Public Archives of Canada.

49. Constance Rudyard Boulton, "A Canadian Bicycle in Europe," *Canadian Magazine* 7 (1896): 330.

50. Sara Jeannette Duncan, *A Voyage of Consolation: Being in the Nature of a Sequel to Experiences of An American Girl in London* (New York: Appleton, 1898), 104; for critiques of modern tourism, see also Daniel Boorstin, "From Traveler to Tourist: The Lost Art of Travel," in *The Image: A Guide to Pseudo-Events in America* (New York: Harper, 1961), 77-117; Hans Magnus Enzensberger, "Eine Theorie des Tourismus," in *Einzelheiten* (Frankfurt: Suhrkamp, 1962), 146-68. For semiotic analyses of tourism, see Dean MacCannell, *The Tourist: A New Theory of the Leisure Class* (New York: Schocken, 1976) and Jonathan Culler, "Semiotics of Tourism," *American Journal of Semiotics* 1.1 (1981), 127-140.

51. Jules Fournier, "Un grand explorateur," in *Mon Encrier* (1922; Ottawa: Fides, 1965), 105.

52. Thomas Langton papers, Public Archives of Canada.

53. On Von Gloeden, see Carlo Bertelli, Giulio Bollati, *Storia d'Italia, Annali 2: L'Immagine fotografica, 1845-1945* (Torino: Einaudi, 1979), 84-86.

54. Grant Allen, *The European Tour* (New York: Dodd, 1899), 81.

55. Chester Glass, *The World: Around It and Over It. Being Letters Written By the Author from England, Ireland, Scotland, Belgium, Holland, Denmark, Germany, Switzerland, France, Spain, Monaco, Italy, Austria, Greece, Turkey, Turkey-in-Asia, The Holy Land, Egypt, India, Singapore, China, Japan, California, Nevada, Utah and New York* (Toronto: Rose-Belford, 1881), 4.

56. John Ashworth papers, Public Archives of Canada.

57. *Murray's Handbook for Travellers in Northern Italy* (1877), ix.

58. *Murray's Handbook for Travellers in Northern Italy* (1897), 20.

59. Ibid.

60. *Murray's Handbook for Travellers in Northern Italy* (1900), 48.

Notes to Chapter Four

1. Andrew Learmont Spedon, *Sketches of a Tour from Canada to Paris, By Way of the British Isles, During the Summer of 1867* (Montreal: Lovell, 1868), 10.

2. Grant Allen, *The European Tour* (New York: Dodd, 1899), 1.

3. Ibid., 12.

4. Ibid.

5. Ibid., 65.

6. J.H. Siddons, "The Canadian on His Travels," *The British American Magazine* 1 (1863): 125.

7. Ibid., 126.

8. Henry Morgan, *The Canadian Men and Women of the Time: A Hand-Book of Canadian Biography* (Toronto: Briggs, 1898), 502.

9. Thomas Stinson Jarvis, *Letters from East Longitudes; Sketches of Travel in Egypt, the Holy Land, Greece, and Cities of the Levant* (Toronto: Campbell, 1875) 107f.

10. Ibid., 128.

11. Ibid., 29.

12. Ibid., 104.

13. Ibid., 210.

14. Ibid., 29.

15. J.E. Costin, *Le Guide du Voyageur de Montréal à Paris via Liverpool et Londres* (Montréal: Imprimerie du "Samedi," 1899), 3.

16. William Henry Parker papers, Public Archives of Canada.

17. C.B. Sissons, ed., *My Dearest Sophie* (Toronto: Ryerson, 1955),114.

18. Ethel Davies papers, Public Archives of Canada.

19. Robert Bell papers, Public Archives of Canada.

20. Barbara Ehrenreich and Deirdre English, *For Her Own Good: 150 Years of the Experts' Advice to Women* (New York: Doubleday, 1978), 111.

21. John Ashworth papers, Public Archives of Canada.

22. H.H. Langton, *James Douglas: A Memoir* (Toronto: U of Toronto P, 1940), 6.

23. Urgel-Eugène Archambault papers, Public Archives of Canada.

24. W.C. Caldwell papers, Public Archives of Canada.

25. Robert Harris, *Some Pages from an Artist's Life* (n.p., 1910), 17.

26. *Abeille du Petit Séminaire de Québec* 12.38 (5 juin 1879): 152.

27. Jean-Jacques Lefebvre, "Les Canadiens aux universités étrangères, 1760-1850," *Royal Society of Canada, Proceedings and Transactions* 3rd ser. 55 (1961), sec. 1, 21-38. I am obliged to Marc Lebel for the information that Lefebvre's list is selective.

28. Thomas-Etienne Hamel papers, Archives du Séminaire de Québec.

29. J.-C.-K. Laflamme papers, Archives du Séminaire de Québec.

30. Ovide Brunet papers, Archives du Séminaire de Québec.

31. Egerton Ryerson, *Story of My Life* (Toronto: Briggs, 1884), 360.

32. J. George Hodgins, *Documentary History of Education in Upper Canada* 12 (Toronto: Cameron, 1905): 104.

33. Ibid., 103.

34. Ibid.

35. Ibid., 104.

36. Ibid.

37. Ibid., 126.

38. Ibid.; see Fern Bayer, *The Ontario Collection* (Markham: Fitzhenry and Whiteside, 1984).

39. See Laurier Lacroix, "Essai de définition des rapports entre la peinture française et la peinture canadienne au 19e siècle," in *Les Relations entre la France et le Canada au XIXe siècle: colloque 26 avril 1974*, Les Cahiers du Centre Culture Canadien 3 (Paris: Centre Culturel Canadien, 1974), 39-43; Art Gallery of Ontario, *Canadians in Paris, 1867-1914* (Toronto: AGO, 1979); Canadian women painters of the period are listed in National Council of Women of Canada, *Women of Canada: Their Life and Work* (n.p., 1900).

40. Gilbert Parker, "Canadian Art Students in Paris," *The Week* 9 (1891/92): 70-71.

41. See Ernest Thompson Seton, *Trail of an Artist-Naturalist* (New York: Scribners, 1941).

42. Napoléon Bourassa, "Le Carnaval à Rome: souvenirs de voyage," *Revue Canadienne* 1 (1864): 54.

43. See Eva-Marie Kröller, "Walter Scott in the United States, English Canada and in Quebec: A Comparison," *Canadian Review of Comparative Literature* (Winter 1980), 32-46.

44. Louis Fréchette, "Chez Victor Hugo," *Proceedings and Transactions of the Royal Society of Canada for 1890* (Montreal: Dawson, 1891), sec. 1., 67.

45. Walter B. Harte, "Canadian Journalists and Journalism," *New England Magazine* 5.4 (1891): 411 -41.

46. Hugh Johnston, *Shall We or Shall We Not? A Series of Five Discourses Preached*

in the Pavilion Music Hall (Toronto: Briggs, 1886), 36.

47. J.-B. Proulx, *Cinq mois en Europe, ou*

voyage du Curé Labelle en France en faveur de la colonisation (Montréal: Beauchemin, 1888), 123.

Notes to Chapter Five

1. Adolphe-Basile Routhier, *A travers l'Europe: impressions et paysages*, t. 1 (Québec: Delisle, 1881), 352.
2. Thomas Stinson Jarvis, *Letters from East Longitudes: Sketches of Travel to Egypt, The Holy Land, Greece, and Cities of the Levant* (Toronto: Campbell, 1875), 11.
3. *Murray's Handbook for Travellers in Northern Italy* (London: Murray, 1877), xvii.
4. Ibid., xxv.
5. See Jean Strouse, *Alice James: A Biography* (Boston: Houghton Mifflin, 1980).
6. Barbara Ehrenreich, Deirdre English, *For Her Own Good: 150 Years of Experts' Advice to Women* (New York: Doubleday, 1978), 93; See Sandra Gwyn, *The Private Capital: Ambition and Love in the Age of Macdonald and Laurier* (Toronto: McClelland and Stewart, 1984) and Peter Gay, *Education of the Senses, The Bourgeois Experience: Victoria to Freud*, vol. 1, (New York: Oxford UP, 1984).
7. Susan Sontag, *Illness as Metaphor* (New York: Vintage, 1977).
8. Gertrude Fleming papers, Public Archives of Canada.
9. Sandford Fleming papers, Public Archives of Canada.
10. Obituary, *Ottawa Citizen*, 22 Dec. 1931.
11. Ibid.
12. "Wedding in St. Alban's—Fleming-MacKintosh Nuptials," *Ottawa Citizen*, 9 Nov. 1891.
13. Unidentified clipping, Sandford Fleming papers, Public Archives of Canada.
14. Obituary, *Ottawa Citizen*, 26 Nov. 1946.
15. Kathleen Coleman, "Woman's Kingdom," *Toronto Mail*, Jan. 2, 1892: 5.
16. A.E.L., "Summer Days at Vichy," *Belford's Monthly Magazine* 3 (1878): 87.
17. C.R.W. Biggar, "Rome Revisited," *Canadian Magazine* 4 (1894-95): 583.
18. Ibid.
19. Grace E. Denison, *A Happy Holiday: A Tour through Europe* (Toronto: n.p., 1890).
20. Ibid.
21. Ibid.
22. Ibid.
23. Grace E. Denison, "The Evolution of the Lady Cyclist," *Massey's Magazine* 3 (1897): 284.
24. Denison, *Happy Holiday.*
25. Ibid.
26. Ibid.
27. Ibid.
28. Ibid.
29. Ibid.
30. Ibid.
31. Grace E. Denison, "The Useful Accomplishments," *Toronto Saturday Night*, 30 Dec. 1899: 8.
32. Constance Rudyard Boulton, "A Canadian Bicycle in Europe," *Canadian Magazine* 7 (1896): 111-20. According to Henry Morgan, a C.R. Boulton, daughter of Lt.-Col. Hon. Charles Arkoll Boulton, "displayed ability as a writer for the periodical press, and edits a newspaper in Man." (*Canadian Men and Women* [1898] 102). I was unable to confirm that C.R. Boulton is identical with Constance Rudyard Boulton, as other sources list Boulton's daughters' names as Ellen Mary, Heather and Susan.
33. Lily Dougall, *The Madonna of a Day* (London: Bentley, 1896), 3.
34. See Ted Ferguson, *Kit Coleman: Queen of Hearts* (Toronto: Doubleday, 1978).
35. Kathleen Coleman, "Woman's Kingdom," *Toronto Mail*, 30 Jan. 1892: 5.
36. Coleman, 16 Jan. 1892: 5.
37. Ibid.
38. Ibid.
39. Ibid.
40. Ibid.
41. Coleman, 6 Feb. 1892: 5.
42. Coleman, 30 Jan. 1892: 5.
43. Coleman, 27 Feb. 1892: 5.
44. Coleman, 6 Feb. 1892: 5.
45. Ibid. On the relationship between jour-

nalism and the city, see Michael Wolff and Celina Fox, "Pictures from the Magazines," in *The Victorian City: Images and Realities* 2, ed. H.J. Dyos and Michael Wolff (London: Routledge and Kegan Paul, 1973): 559-82.

46. Alice Jones, "A Day in Winchester," *The Week* 5 (1887-88): 702.

47. E.C. Cayley, "Walter Pater," *The Week* 11 (1893-94): 1041.

48. Alice Jones, "Florentine Vignettes," *The Week* 9 (1891-92): 153.

49. C.A.M., "An Artist Abroad," *The Week* 5 (1887-88): 480.

50. G., "Rome in January," *The Week* 1 (1883-84): 265.

51. L.L., "Letter from Italy," *The Week* 4 (1886-87): 300.

52. Goldwin Smith, *A Trip to England* (Toronto: Robinson, 1888), 38.

53. Alice Jones, "Florentine Vignettes," *The Week* 9 (1891-92): 152.

54. Ibid., 153; on the travel motif in Ruskin, see Richard L. Stein, *The Ritual of Interpretation: The Fine Arts as Literature in Ruskin, Rossetti, and Pater* (Cambridge, MA: Harvard UP, 1975).

55. Jones, "Stray Thoughts in Venice," *The Week* 8 (1890-91): 413.

56. Ibid., 414.

57. Ibid., 413.

58. Ibid.

59. L.L., "Letters from Italy," *The Week* 4 (1886-87): 152.

60. G., "Rome in January," *The Week* 1 (1883-84): 266.

61. Jones, " Florentine Vignettes," 153.

62. See John Talon-Lesperance, "Art in French Canada," *The Week* 5 (1887-88): 133-34.

Notes to Chapter Six

1. See Carl Berger, "The True North Strong and Free," *Nationalism in Canada*, ed. Peter Russell (Toronto: McGraw Hill, 1966), 17.

2. Ralph Connor, *Corporal Cameron of the North West Mounted Police* (Toronto: Westminster, 1912), 307-8.

3. See Mark Girouard, *Return to Camelot: Chivalry and the English Gentleman* (New Haven: Yale UP, 1981) for a discussion of the Victorian Cult of Knighthood.

4. Caniff Haight, *Here and There in the Home Land: England, Scotland, As Seen By a Canadian. Profusely Illustrated* (Toronto: Briggs, 1895), 139.

5. Moses Harvey, "Notes of a Trip to the Old Land," *Stewart's Quarterly* 5 (1871-72), 354.

6. Sylva Clapin, *Londres et Paris: souvenirs et impressions de voyages* (St. Hyacinthe: n.p., 1880), 15.

7. Edmond Lambert, *Voyage d'un Canadien-Français en France* (Paris: Alphonse Lemerre, 1893), 2.

8. Anon., "Notes bibliographiques," *Revue canadienne* 45 (1903): 335.

9. Brian Carey, "An Imperial Gift," *History of Photography* 10.2 (April-June, 1986): 147-49.

10. Harvey, "Notes of a Trip to the Old Land."

11. Haight, *Here and There in the Home Land*.

12. James Elgin Wetherell, *Over the Sea: A Summer Trip to Britain* (Strathroy, Ontario: Evans, 1892), 16.

13. Ibid.

14. J.-B. Proulx, *Cinq mois en Europe, ou Voyage du Curé Labelle en France en faveur de la colonisation* (Montréal: Beauchemin, 1888), 127.

15. Ibid.

16. Andrew Spedon, *Sketches of a Tour from Canada to Paris, By Way of the British Isles, During the Summer of 1867* (Montreal: Lovell, 1868), 196, 199.

17. See Célina Bardy, *Oeuvres littéraires* (Québec: La Libre Parole, 1908).

18. Benjamin Sulte, "Le Canada en Europe," *Revue canadienne* 10 (1873): 204.

19. Pamphile LeMay, "Impressions de voyage: à mon inséparable compagnon de voyage," *Revue canadienne* 31 (1895): 744.

20. Hector Fabre, "Voyage en Europe," *Chroniques* (Montréal: Guérin, 1980), 209f.

21. Gilbert L. Gignac and Jeanne L. l'Espérance, "Thoughts of Peace and

Joy: A Study of the Iconography of the Croscup Room," *Journal of Canadian Art History* 6.2 (1982): 151.

22. See Kathleen Coleman, *To London for the Jubilee* (Toronto: Morang, 1897); Adolphe-Basile Routhier, *La Reine Victoria et son jubilé* (Québec: Darveau, 1898).

23. See Routhier, *La Reine Victoria*, 99 and 126.

24. See Narcisse Henri Edouard Faucher de Saint-Maurice, *De Québec à Mexico: souvenirs de voyage, de garnison et de bivouac* (Montréal: Duvernay frères et Dansereau, 1874).

25. Joseph Marmette, "Souvenirs de Paris et de Londres," *Récits et souvenirs* (Québec: Darveau, 1891), 225.

26. See Faucher de Saint-Maurice, *Le Canada et les Canadiens pendant la guerre franco-prussienne* (Québec: Côté, 1879).

27. Adolphe-Basile Routhier, *A Travers l'Europe: impressions et paysages*, t.2 (Québec: Delisle, 1883), 14.

28. Richard D. Lancefield, *Victoria, Sixty Years a Queen: A Sketch of Her Life and Times* (Toronto: Ross, 1897), 493.

29. Thomas C. Watkins, "The Gallia: Life on the Ocean Wave," Watkins papers, Public Archives of Canada.

30. W.D. Howells, *Their Wedding Journey*, ed. John K. Reeves (Bloomington and London: Indiana UP, 1968), 135.

31. François Pelletier papers, Archives du Séminaire de Québec.

32. Northrop Frye, "Conclusion to the *Literary History of Canada,*" *The Bush Garden* (Toronto: Anansi, 1971), 221.

33. Moses Harvey, "Notes of a Trip to the Old Land," *Stewart's Quarterly* 5 (1871/72): 354.

34. Edmond Lambert, *Voyage d'un canadien français en France* (Paris: Alphonse Lemerre, 1893), 4.

35. Egerton Ryerson, *Story of My Life* (Toronto: Briggs, 1884), 357.

36. Maria Elise Lauder, *Evergreen Leaves; or "Toofie" in Europe* (Toronto: Rose, 1884), 18. For a discussion of the seafaring metaphor, see Hans Blumenberg, *Schiffbruch mit Zuschauer: Paradigma einer Daseinsmetapher* (Frankfurt: Suhrkamp, 1979).

37. Léon Provancher, *De Québec à Jérusalem: journal d'un pèlerinage du Canada en Terre-Sainte* (Québec: Darveau, 1884), 24.

38. J.-C.-K. Laflamme papers, Archives du Séminaire de Québec.

39. H.H. Langton, *James Douglas: A Memoir* (Toronto: U of Toronto P, 1940), 18.

40. Thomas Stinson Jarvis, *Letters from East Longitudes* (Toronto: Campbell, 1875), 241.

41. Ibid.

42. Martin Gilbert, *Jerusalem: Rebirth of a City* (London: Chatto and Windus, 1985), 88.

43. Henry Wentworth Monk, *The Great Modern Problem* (Ottawa: n.p., 1896), 1.

44. William Holman-Hunt, *Pre-Raphaelitism and the Pre-Raphaelite Brotherhood* (London: Chapman and Hall, 1913), 310f. For further details of Monk's life, see Richard S. Lambert, *For the Time Is at Hand* (London: Melrose, 1947).

45. M.D. Conway, "More of the Great Show at Paris," *Harper's* 35 (1867): 789.

46. Hugh Johnston, *Toward the Sunrise: Being Sketches of Travel in Europe and the East, To Which is Added a Memorial Sketch of the Rev. William Morley Punshon* (Toronto: Briggs, 1881), 195.

47. Ibid.

48. Ibid.

49. Ibid., 206.

50. On Provancher, see Victor-Alphonse Huard, *La Vie et l'oeuvre de l'abbé Provancher* (Québec: Garneau, 1926).

51. Journal du Séminaire de Québec, 3:311.

52. Journal du Séminaire de Québec, 4:373.

53. Provancher, *De Québec à Jérusalem*, 230.

54. Ibid., 240.

55. Jarvis, *Letters*, 62.

56. Langton, *James Douglas*, 19.

57. Jarvis, *Letters*, 16.

58. Ibid., 109.

59. Ibid., 176.

60. Johnston, *Toward the Sunrise*, 220.

61. Adolphe-Basile Routhier, *A Travers l'Europe* t.2 (Québec: Delisle, 1883), 275.

62. Jules-Paul Tardivel, *Notes de voyage* (Montréal: Sénécal, 1890), 354.

Notes to Chapter Seven

1. James Douglas, *The Reign of Peace, Commonly Called the Millenium: An Exposition of the Nineteenth and Twentieth Chapters of the Book of Revelation* (Toronto: Chewett, 1867), 1.
2. P. Colonnier, "Les grands travaux des modernes comparés à ceux des anciens," *Revue canadienne* 28 (1892): 88.
3. Moses Harvey, "Human Progress—Is it Real?" *Stewart's Quarterly* 5 (1871-72): 230.
4. "London the Great in Ruins," *Saturday Reader* 3 (1866-67): 406 and 405.
5. See Carl Berger, *Science, God, and Nature in Victorian Canada* (Toronto: U of Toronto P, 1983).
6. Harvey, "Human Progress," 235.
7. Moses Harvey, "Thoughts on Great Cities," *Maritime Monthly* 3 (1874): 432.
8. On the "flâneur," see Walter Benjamin, "Charles Baudelaire: Ein Lyriker im Zeitalter des Hochkapitalismus," in Walter Benjamin, *Gesammelte Schriften*, ed. Rolf Tiedemann and Hermann Schweppenhäuser (Frankfurt: Suhrkamp, 1974), 509-690.
9. See Carl E. Schorske, "The Idea of the City in European Thought: Voltaire to Spengler," in *The Historian and the City*, ed. Oscar Handlin and John Burchard (Cambridge, MA: MIT and Harvard UP, 1963). See also Marcel Trudel, *L'Influence de Voltaire au Canada* (Montreal: Fides, 1945), 2 vols.
10. See Leo Spitzer, "Anglo-French Etymologies," *Modern Language Notes* 59 (1944): 223-50.
11. Hector Fabre, "La Vieille Rue Notre-Dame," *Chroniques* (Montréal: Guérin, 1980), 72.
12. Napoléon Aubin, Preface of the *Fantasque*, quoted in Jean-Paul Tremblay, *A la recherche de Napoléon Aubin* (Québec: PUL, 1969), 28.
13. Arthur Buies, *Chroniques canadiennes, humeurs et caprices* (Montréal: Sénécal, 1873), 153.
14. Hector Fabre, "La Vielle Rue Notre-Dame," 72.
15. See Dana Brand, "The Spectator and the City: Fantasies of Urban Legibility in Nineteenth-Century England and America," (Ph.D. thesis, Yale U, 1981); Dana Brand, "Reconstructing the 'Flâneur': Poe's Invention of the Detective Story," *Genre* 18.1 (Spring 1985): 36-56.
16. Victor-Lévy Beaulieu, *Pour saluer Victor Hugo* (Montréal: Editions du Jour, 1971). On Sue's influence in Quebec, see Yves Dostaler, *Les Infortunes du roman dans le Québec du XIXe siècle* (Montréal: Hurtubise, 1977), 29.
17. Arthur Campbell, *The Mystery of Martha Warne: A Tale of Montreal* (Montreal: n.p., 1888).
18. J.J. Procter, "London in the Olden Time," *New Dominion Monthly* (1875), 15.
19. Ibid., 16.
20. Paul Rutherford, *A Victorian Authority: The Daily Press in Late Nineteenth-Century Canada* (Toronto: U of Toronto P, 1982), 130.
21. See E.B.B., "Biographical Introduction," in Caniff Haight, *A United Empire Loyalist in Great Britain*, (Toronto: Briggs, 1904), 4.
22. Caniff Haight, *Here and There in the Home Land: England, Scotland and Ireland, As Seen By a Canadian. Profusely Illustrated* (Toronto: Briggs, 1895), 139.
23. Ibid., 198.
24. Ibid., 213.
25. Ibid.
26. Ibid., 228.
27. Kit, *To London for the Jubilee* (Toronto: Morang, 1897), 9.
28. Ibid., 73.
29. Ibid., 54.
30. Ibid., 72.
31. Ibid., 76.
32. Emily P. Weaver, "Pioneer Canadian Women: 'Kit,' the Journalist," *Canadian Magazine* 49 (1917): 277.
33. Kit, *To London*, 84.
34. Ibid., 13.
35. Quoted in Ted Ferguson, *Kit Coleman: Queen of Hearts* (Toronto: Doubleday, 1978), 2f.
36. Kit, *To London*, 98.

37. Ibid., 102.
38. Adolphe-Basile Routhier, *La Reine Victoria et son jubilé* (Québec: Darveau, 1898), 99.
39. Ibid., 126.
40. Karl Baedeker, *Great Britain: Handbook for Travellers* (Leipsic: Baedeker, 1890), 466.
41. Andrew Spedon, *Sketches of a Tour from Canada to Paris, by Way of the British Isles, during the Summer of 1867* (Montreal: Lovell, 1868) 99f.
42. Ibid., 44.
43. Maria Elise Lauder, *Evergreen Leaves; or "Toofie" in Europe* (Toronto: Rose, 1884), 384.
44. Spedon, *Sketches of a Tour*, 100.
45. Charles Dickens, *Bleak House* (London: Chapman, 1901), 1.
46. Karl Baedeker, *London and Its Environs: Handbook for Travellers* (Leipsic: Baedeker, 1892), 72.
47. Ibid., 31.
48. Spedon, *Sketches of a Tour*, 105.
49. "The Lions of London: Extracts from the Private Letters of a Canadian," *New Dominion Monthly* (1869-70), 16.
50. Ibid.
51. Robert Harris, *Some Pages from an Artist's Life* (n.p., 1910), 8.
52. Ibid.
53. See Emily Carr, *Growing Pains* (Toronto: Clarke, Irwin, 1966).
54. Spedon, *Sketches of a Tour*, 130.
55. See Hugh Johnston, *Toward the Sunrise: Being Sketches of Travel in Europe and the East, To Which is Added a Memorial Sketch of the Rev. William Morley Punshon* (Toronto: Briggs, 1881), 94: "The Church of England has not a great number of preeminent preachers. I have listened to sermons in large and influential churches, and wondered to hear only average men speaking with no gracefulness of manner, no unction or tenderness, no pathos or power. How is this? Is it because the system of patronage has the rare facility of putting the wrong man in the wrong place? Is it because of the low rank assigned to the sermon in comparison with the liturgical offices; the litany, the creeds, the frequent repetitions of the Lord's Prayer, the chanting and intoning in which the sense is smothered in the harmony of sounds, occupying nearly three-fourths of the time of Sabbath services? . . . [The clergyman's] very connection with the State gives to him an arrogance, and loftiness, and affected superiority over other ministers to whom he may be immeasurably inferior in ability and culture and grace."
56. See Goldwin Smith, *A Trip to England* (Toronto: Brackett, 1888).
57. Jules-Paul Tardivel, *Notes de voyage en France, Italie, Espagne,Irlande, Angleterre, Belgique et Hollande* (Montreal: Sénécal, 1890), 70.
58. On Tardivel, see A.I. Silver, introduction to Tardivel's *For My Country*, trans. by Sheila Fischman (Toronto: U of Toronto P, 1975), vi-xl, and Pierre Savard, *Jules-Paul Tardivel, la France et les Etats-Unis* (Québec: PUL, 1967).
59. Tardivel, *Notes de voyage*, 70.
60. Edmond Paré, *Lettres et opuscules* (Québec: Dussault and Proulx, 1899), 50.
61. See Adolphe-Basile Routhier, *A Travers l'Europe: impressions et paysages* 1 (Québec: Delisle, 1881): 117.
62. Tardivel, *Notes de voyage*, 76.
63. See Richard D. Altick, *The Shows of London* (Cambridge: Belknap, 1978).
64. K. Baedeker, *London and its Environs* (1892), 312-19.
65. Kathleen Coleman, "Woman's Kingdom," *Toronto Mail*, 12 Mar. 1892: 6.
66. "The Lions of London," *New Dominion Monthly*.
67. Spedon, *Sketches of a Tour*, 146.
68. Lydia Leavitt, *Around the World* (Toronto: Murray, n.d.), 100. Lydia Leavitt, "an actress of some note," as her husband's obituary indicates (*Brockville Evening Recorder*, 22 June 1909) was married to Thaddeus W. H. Leavitt, a Canadian who spent his youth prospecting for gold in South Africa, Australia, and New Zealand. He was the author of several books (*The History of Victoria and Melbourne*, *The History of Tasmania*, *Australian Representative Men*, *Kattie, Kangaroo, Klondike: Tales of the Gold Fields*), as well as co-authoring a number of works with his wife, née Lydia Brown of Elgin, with whom he settled in Brockville, where he founded and edited the *Brockville Times*. The Leavitts' voyage around the world included a visit to Australia, where Mrs. Leavitt drew many interesting comparisons between

the two dominions.

69. John Godden, *Notes and Reminiscences of a Journey to England* (Montreal: Lovell, 1873), 38.

70. Kathleen Coleman, "Woman's Kingdom," *Toronto Mail*, 16 Apr. 1892: 5.

71. Coleman, 27 Feb. 1892: 6.

72. Coleman, 2 Apr. 1892: 5.

73. Coleman, 27 Feb. 1892: 5.

74. Ibid.

75. Coleman, 19 Mar. 1892.

76. Ibid.

77. John McKinnon, *Travels in Britain, France, Prussia, Switzerland, Italy, Belgium and Holland* (Summerside, P.E.I.: Schurman and Taylor, 189?), 185.

78. Hugh Johnston, *Toward the Sunrise: Being Sketches of Travel in Europe and the East. To Which is Added a Memorial Sketch of the Rev. William Morley Punshon* (Toronto: Briggs, 1881), 110.

79. Spedon, *Sketches of a Tour*, 104.

80. Ibid., 164.

81. L.H. Hubbard, "Paris by Gaslight," *Belford's Monthly Magazine* 3 (1878): 569.

82. Spedon, *Sketches of a Tour*, 171.

83. See David H. Pinkney, *Napoleon III and the Rebuilding of Paris* (Princeton: Princeton UP, 1958).

84. See Wilfrid Eggleston, *The Queen's Choice: A Story of Canada's Capital* (Ottawa: Queen's Printer, 1961).

85. C. Pelham Mulvaney, *Toronto Past and Present Until 1882* (rpt. Toronto: Caiger, 1970), 39.

86. Ibid., 48.

87. William H. Withrow, *A Canadian in Europe* (Toronto: Rose-Belford, 1881), 57.

88. Adolphe-Basile Routhier, *A Travers l'Europe: impressions et paysages* (Québec: Delisle, 1881), 226.

89. Ovide Brunet papers, Archives du Séminaire de Québec. The impact of the demolitions must have become even more poignant as Montreal and Quebec too underwent major changes in the second half of the nineteenth century; see, for example, Hector Fabre's elegiac 1862 sketch "La Vieille Rue Notre-Dame," in *Chroniques* (Montréal: Guérin, 1980), 67f. "L'historien futur de la rue Notre-Dame devra me faire causer. Je lui fournirai des renseignements précieux, des souvenirs piquants; je lui ferai connaître ce que c'est au juste qu'un flâneur convaincu. Il faut qu'il vienne bientôt cet historien! Car la rue Notre-Dame se dépouille de sa vieille physionomie, la rue Notre-Dame des anciens jours s'en va rapidement. Elle n'est plus étroite et resserrée sur tout son parcours; le chemin de fer urbain augmente le nombre des passants, trouble les conciliabules des flâneurs au coin des rues, et leur donne le scandale de la vitesse."

90. Arthur Buies, *Chroniques canadiennes: Humeurs et caprices*, t. 1 (Montréal: Sénécal, 1884): 284.

91. Ibid., 286.

92. Ibid., 289.

93. Alexander MacDonald, *Stray Leaves or Traces of Travel* (New York: Christian P, 1914), 30.

94. Johnston, *Toward the Sunrise*, 1.

95. Hugh Johnston, *Shall We Or Shall We Not? A Series of Five Discourses Preached in the Pavilion Music Hall* (Toronto: Briggs, 1886), 116. Johnson's invectives were too much even for the otherwise straightlaced *Saturday Night*. In April 1892, a contributor noted: "Rev. Hugh Johnston's recent attack upon the theatres and the people who frequent them is perhaps as striking an instance of that holy frenzy into which preachers can work themselves as any even afforded by a Toronto pulpiteer. How could any respectable theatre-goer, after sitting through Dr. Johnston's sermon and hearing his extravagant charges against actors and audiences, maintain any faith in his judgement on any matter? In his congregation are men who attend the theatre with a motive just as good as that which actuates their whole life-conduct, and they were never injured by it, and never saw anyone injured by it, save those whose inherent depravity is such that they go out in search of injury and infamy and who will find a bog to wallow in if they have to dig one in the sacred confines of the church itself. How can good men who are as familiar with the inside of the theatre as with the inside of the church, and who conscientiously go to the former for intellectual pleasure and to the latter for spiritual pleasure—how can such men repose unshaken confidence in the ministrations of a man who tells them the

theatre is the very antechamber of hell and that the devil himself is playwright, stage manager and star actor all in one? They will not believe it, knowing better."

96. Johnston, *Toward the Sunrise*, 120.

97. J.-B. Proulx, *Cinq Mois en Europe, ou voyage du Curé Labelle en France en faveur de la colonisation* (Montréal: Beauchemin, 1888), 134.

98. Ibid., 136. On the Curé Labelle, see Elie-J. Auclair, *Le Curé Labelle: sa vie et son oeuvre* (Montréal: Beauchemin, 1930); Robert Lévesque, Robert Migner, *Le Curé Labelle: Le colonisateur, le politicien, la légende* (Ottawa: La Presse, l979); Gabriel Dussault, *Le Curé Labelle: Messianisme, utopie et colonisation au Québec 1850-1900* (Montréal: Hurtubise, 1983).

99. See Geo. Maclean Rose, *A Cyclopedia of Canadian Biography* (Toronto: Rose, 1888), 755f.; Castell Hopkins, ed., *The Canadian Album: Men of Canada, or, Success By Example* (Brantford and Toronto: Bradley Garretson, 1896), 85; Henry Morgan, *Canadian Men and Women of Their Time* (Toronto: Briggs, 1898), 892; Morgan, *Canadian Men and Women*, 977.

100. Quoted in Maurice Lemire, ed., *Dictionnaire des oeuvres littéraires du Québec,* t. 1 (Montréal: Fides, 1978), 44.

101. Routhier, *La Reine Victoria*, 283.

102. See Stephan Oettermann, *Das Panorama: Die Geschichte eines Massenmediums* (Frankfurt: Syndikat, 1980).

103. Routhier, *La Reine Victoria*, 249.

104. Ibid., 254.

105. Ibid., 255.

106. Ibid., 256.

107. Ibid., 258f.

108. Ibid., 212f.

109. Ibid., 372.

110. Ibid., 221.

111. Moncrieff Williamson, *Robert Harris 1849-1919: An Unconventional Biography* (Toronto: McClelland and Stewart, 1910), 53.

112. Proulx, *Cinq Mois en Europe*, 118.

113. See Alfred Rambaud, "Québec et la guerre franco-allemande de 1870," *Revue d'histoire d'Amérique française* 6 (1952-53): 313-30.

114. Faucher de Saint-Maurice, *Le Canada et les Canadiens-Français pendant la guerre franco-prussienne* (Québec: Côté, 1888), 18.

115. On the impact of the Franco-Prussian War on French art, see Robert Rosenblum and H.W. Jansen, *Nineteenth-Century Art* (New York: Abrams, 1984).

116. Octave Crémazie, "Journal du siège de Paris et lettres écrites pendant la guerre franco-prussienne et la Commune, aôut 1870-mai 1871," in *Oeuvres II: prose* (Ottawa: Ed. de l'Université d'Ottawa, 1972), 241. On the Siege, see also Edmond Goncourt, *Journal*, t. 4 (Paris: Charpentier, 1911) and Alistair Horne, *The Terrible Year: The Paris Commune 1871* (New York: Viking, 1971).

117. Ibid., 241.

118. Ibid., 228.

119. Ibid., 264.

120. See for example, J.-F. Dubrueil, "La France et les châtiments de Dieu," *Revue canadienne* 10 (1873): 508-19.

121. Adolphe-Basile Routhier, quoted in Rambaud, "Québec et al guerre," 324.

122. Hector Fabre, quoted in Rambaud, "Québec et la guerre," 326.

123. See Withrow, *A Canadian in Europe*, 270.

124. Johnston, *Toward the Sunrise*, 117.

125. Harvey Frith, "Paris at the Outbreak of the Commune," *Maritime Monthly* 2 (1873): 72.

126. McKinnon, "Travels in Britain," 194.

127. See Oettermann, 274; also *Cyclorama of the Battle of Sedan, Corner Front and York Streets* (Toronto: McKay, n.d.).

128. James De Mille, *A Comedy of Terrors* (Boston: Osgood, 1872), 64.

129. Ibid.

130. Karl Baedeker, *Paris and Environs with Routes from London to Paris: Handbook for Travellers* (Leipsic: Baedeker, 1900), v.

131. Williamson, *Robert Harris 1849-1919*, 84.

132. Jules-Paul Tardivel, *Notes de voyage en France, Italie, Espagne, Irlande, Angleterre, Belgique, et Hollande* (Montréal: Sènécal, 1890), 333.

133. J.-B. Proulx, *Cinq Mois en Europe*, 63.

134. See Journal of Elisha Budd de Mill, 3 vols. (1850-51), De Mille Manuscript Collection, Dalhousie U.

135. Adolphe-Basile Routhier, *A travers l'Europe: impressions et paysages* t. 2

(Québec: Delisle, 1883): 386.

136. J.S. Raymond, "Entretien sur les études classiques," *Revue canadienne* 9 (1872): 605.

137. Léon Provancher, *De Québec à Jérusalem: Journal d'un pélerinage du Canada en Terre-Sainte* (Québec: Darveau, 1884), 623.

138. Geo. Maclean Rose, *A Cyclopedia of Canadian Biography: Being Chiefly Men of the Time* (Toronto: Ross, 1886), 135.

139. See William Hay, "The Late Mr. Pugin and the Revival of Christian Architecture," *Anglo-American Magazine* 2 (1853): 70-73. Also, "Architecture for the Meridian of Canada," *Anglo-American Magazine* 2 (1853): 253-55.

140. See *Canadian Magazine* 8 (1896/97): 193; "The success of W. H. Withrow's *Valeria, the Martyr of the Catacombs; a Tale of Early Christian Life in Rome*, is indicated by the fact that a fifth Canadian edition of three thousand copies has just been printed. It has also been republished in London and New York. It is neatly bound and well illustrated, and throws much light on the early Roman Church to which St. Paul ministered, abounding in elements of heroism, pathos and tragedy."

141. See Ludwig Hertling and Engelbert Kirschbaum, *The Roman Catacombs and Their Martyrs* (London: Darton, Longman and Todd, 1960).

142. William H. Withrow, *The Catacombs of Rome, and Their Testimony Relative to Primitive Christianity* (New York: Nelson and Philips, 1877), 552.

143. See Johnston, *Toward the Sunrise*, 410.

144. Lorne Pierce, ed., *The Chronicle of a Century (1829-1929): The Record of One Hundred Years of Progress in the Publishing Concerns of the Methodist, Presbyterian, and Congregational Churches in Canada* (Toronto: Ryerson, n.d.), 107.

145. Pierre Savard, "Les Noms de paroisse au Québec pendant trois siècles," *Aspects du catholicisme canadien-français au dix-neuvième siècle* (Montréal: Fides, 1980).

146. Tardivel, *Notes de voyage*, 334.

147. See E.E.Y. Hales, *Pio Nono: A Study in European Politics and Religion in the Nineteenth Century* (London: Eyre and Spottiswoode, 1956).

148. See Christopher Hibbert, *Rome: Biography of a City* (New York: Viking, 1985); Jean Neuvecelle, ed., *A History of Rome and the Romans* (New York: Crown, 1962).

149. See Angelo Principe, "Il Risorgimento visto dai Protestanti dell'Alto Canada 1846-1860," *Rassegna storica del Risorgimento* 66 (1979): 151-63.

150. See, for instance, "Garibaldi at Caprera," *The Canadian Spectator* 1 (1878): 314-15; "Death of Victor Emmanuel," *The Canadian Spectator* 1 (1878): 14; C. Pelham Mulvaney, "Garibaldi-Died at Caprera, June 2nd, 1882," *Rose-Belford's Canadian Monthly and National Review* 8 (1887): 627.

151. Alice Jones, "The Italian Royal Family," *The Week* 10 (1892-93): 199.

152. Arthur Campbell, *A Ride in Morocco and Other Sketches* (Toronto: Briggs, 1897), 107.

153. Chester Glass, *The World: Round It and Over It* (Toronto: Rose-Belford, 1881), 205.

154. Moncrieff Williamson, *Robert Harris 1849-1919: An Unconventional Biography* (Toronto: McClelland and Stewart, 1970), 84.

155. Charles R.W. Biggar, "Rome Revisited," *Canadian Magazine* 4 (1894-95): 572.

156. W. Cheetham, "Canadian Nationality," *The Canadian Spectator* 1 (1878): 64; see also Alfred J. Bray, "Roman Catholic Church in Canada: Viewed in its Civil Aspects," *The Canadian Spectator* 1 (1878): 9-10.

157. Alice Jones, "Letter from Rome," *The Week* 8 (1890-91): 220.

158. See Sybille Pantazzi, "Canadian Prize Books," *Canadian Collector* 5.3 (Mar. 1970): 24-27.

159. Withrow, *A Canadian in Europe*, 141.

160. B.P., "Funérailles de Victor-Emmanuel," *L'Abeille du Petit Séminaire de Québec* 11.15 (14 février 1878): 60.

161. Routhier, *A travers l'Europe*, t. 1: 306.

162. Henri Cimon, *Aux Vieux Pays: impressions et souvenirs*, nouvelle édition (Chicoutimi: Deslisle, 1907), 152.

163. Mgr. Gerbet, *Esquisse de Rome chrétienne*, quoted in J. S. Raymond, "Destinée providentielle de Rome,"

Revue canadienne 1 (1864): 108.

164. Provancher, *De Québec à Jérusalem*, 599.

165. Routhier, *A travers l'Europe*, t. 1: 267.

166. Ibid., 268.

167. See Adolphe-Basile Routhier, "Une Page d'histoire: La sentinelle du Vatican," *Causeries du Dimanche* (Montréal: Beauchemin et Valois, 1871): 273-92.

168. Routhier, *A travers l'Europe*, t. 2: 352.

169. Tardivel, *Notes de voyage*, 343.

170. Campbell, *A Ride in Morocco*, 141.

171. See Henry James, *Italian Hours* (London: Heinemann, 1909).

172. Campbell, *A Ride in Morocco*, 119.

173. Ibid., 143f.

174. Sara Jeannette Duncan, *A Voyage of Consolation: Being in the Nature of a Sequel to Experiences of An American Girl in London* (New York: Appleton, 1898), 170.

175. G., "Rome in January," *The Week* 1 (1883/84): 266. See also Chester Glass 159: "These people [that is to say, the models on the Scala di Spagna], probably the laziest in the world, . . . hire themselves to the School of Art and

the large number of painters and sculptors at Rome, to be painted or chiselled as Madonnas, saints, heroes, or any other character required. One little boy can make a very respectable living in the double capacity of an imp of darkness and a cherub; an old man with snowy locks will sit alternately as a Roman Senator and a Christian martyr; a handsome young woman may one day represent Venus, or Cleopatra, the voluptuous queen of the East, and the next day sit for a stern vestal virgin of the Pagan days of Rome. There are many ways of making a living, but that of being a model is probably the easiest."

176. See Provancher, *Du Québec à Jérusalem*, 704f.

177. See Angelo Principe, *The Concept of Italy in the Italian Canadian Publications: 1900-1940*, (Ph.D. Diss., U of Toronto, 1987); Roberto Perin, "I rapporti tra Italia e Canada nell'Ottocento," *Le Relazioni tra l'Italia e il Canada*, special issue of *Il Veltro: Rivista della civiltà italiana* 29, 1-2 (Gennaio-Aprile 1985): 73-90.

Notes to Chapter Eight

1. Luella Creighton, *The Elegant Canadians* (Toronto: McClelland and Stewart, 1967), 102.

2. Ibid.

3. John King, "The American Centennial Exhibition," *Canadian Monthly and National Review* 8 (1875): 311.

4. M.D. Conway, "The Great Show at Paris," *Harper's* 35 (1867): 248.

5. Andrew Spedon, *Sketches of a Tour from Canada to Paris, By Way of the British Isles, During the Summer of 1867* (Montreal: Lovell, 1868), 199.

6. Ibid.

7. On world expositions, see especially, Richard D. Mandell, *Paris 1900: The Great World's Fair* (Toronto: U of Toronto P, 1967); Utz Haltern, *Die Londoner Weltausstellung von 1851: Ein Beitrag zur Geschichte der bürgerlich-industriellen Gesellschaft im 19. Jahrhundert* (Münster: Aschendorff, 1971);

Werner Plum, *World Exhibitions in the Nineteenth Century: Pageants of Social and Cultural Change* (Bonn: Friedrich Ebert-Stiftung, 1977).

8. See "Germany and the Paris Exposition," *Massey's Magazine* 2 (1896): 221.

9. M.D. Conway, "More of the Great Show at Paris," *Harper's* 35 (1867): 777.

10. "The Recent Exhibition, and True Rivalry with the United States," *The Anglo-American Magazine* 1 (1852): 387.

11. W.R. Stewart, "Canada at the Paris Exposition," *Canadian Magazine* 15 (1900): 387-88.

12. William M. Withrow, "Education at the Centennial Exhibition," *Canadian Methodist Magazine* 6 (1877): 195.

13. D. H. Hitchcock, "The Cafés of the Paris Exhibition," *Harper's* 35 (1867): 161.

14. Ibid.

15. Spedon, *Sketches of a Tour*, 164.
16. See J.C. Taché, *Descriptive Catalogue of the Productions of Canada Exhibited in Paris in 1855* (Paris: Pinard-Denton, 1855) 237. On Taché, see Eveline Bossé, *Joseph-Charles Taché (1820-1894): un grand représentant de l'élite canadienne-française* (Québec: Garneau, 1971).
17. M. D. Conway, "The Great Show at Paris," 248.
18. Withrow, "Education," 208.
19. Eugene Rimmel, *Recollections of the Paris Exhibition of 1867* (London: Chapman, n.d.), 179.
20. W. Hamilton Gibson, "Foreground and Vista at the Fair," *Scribner's* 14 (1893): 29.
21. Hitchcock, "The Cafés," 155.
22. Joseph Marmette, *Récits et souvenirs* (Québec: Dorveau, 1891), 245.
23. M.D. Conway, "The Great Show at Paris," 239.
24. See Eugene Rimmel, *Recollections . . . 1867* 2: "Without undertaking long and perilous journeys, without running the risk of being frozen in the North, or melted in the South; we have seen the Russian drive his *troïka* drawn by Tartar steeds, the Arab smoke the *narghilé* or play the *darbouka* under his gilt cupolas, the fair daughters of the Celestial Empire sip their tea in their quaint painted houses; we have walked in a few minutes from the Temple of the Caciques to the Bardo of Tunis, from the American log-hut to the Kirghiz tent."
25. See "Promenade au palais de cristal," *L'Abeille du Petit Séminaire de Québec* 4.3 (8 juillet 1852).
26. Dianne Newell, "Canada at World's Fairs, 1851-1876," *Canadian Collector* (July-Aug. 1976): 11. The *Illustrated London News* commented on the Canadian exhibit on 31 May 1851, using the typical metaphors of imperialism: "Civilisation has begun its useful work in the far west; European industry has planted the spade there, and some of the fruits are now before us—speaking much and creditably for the past, but speaking still more cheeringly of what is yet to come. The Canadian division is situated to the south side of the Western Nave, next beyond the East Indian division. Its products are not so showy, but are yet more valuable as evidences of social wealth and social advancement. They are the spoils of peace, not of war, and industrial beginnings of a junior branch of the great civilising family of the universe, not the gaudy remains of an effete barbarism, which has been demolished, but not yet replaced by anything better."
27. See *Hunt's Hand-Book for the Official Catalogues: An Exploratory Guide to the Natural Productions and Manufactures of the Great Exhibition of the Industry of All Nations* (London: Spicer and Clowes, 1851) for a floorplan.
28. Marmette, *Récits et souvenirs*, 241.
29. Quoted in Morris Zaslow, *Reading the Rocks: The Story of the Geological Survey of Canada 1842-1972* (Toronto: Macmillan, 1975), 58. The *Montreal Gazette* sharply condemned Taché for exhibiting "throughout, the most deplorable want of activity, of business habits and knowledge, and of urbanity, even while he has displayed an excess of vanity, and a determination that, while he does nothing for himself, nobody else shall get the credit of doing anything."
30. Taché, *Descriptive Catalogue*, 203.
31. Thomas Langton papers, Public Archives of Canada.
32. Spedon, *Sketches of a Tour*, 197f. Spedon's objections to Canada's self-image as a wild territory are somewhat surprising, considering his own publications which included sketches entitled *The Woodland Warbler* (1857) and *Tales of the Canadian Forest* (1861).
33. Ibid., 196.
34. Rimmel, *Recollections*, 325.
35. See Charles Greenberg, "Canadian Pavilions," *Royal Architectural Institute of Canada Journal* 35.8 (1958): 288-89.
36. William H. Withrow, "Notes of a Visit to the Centennial Exhibition," *Canadian Methodist Magazine* 4 (1876): 530.
37. Ludovic Nadeau, "The British Empire at Wembley," *The Living Age* 322 (1924): 32.
38. Taché, *Descriptive Catalogue*, 292.
39. See Merle Curti, "America at the World Fairs," *American Historical Review* 55 (1950): 833-56.
40. Moncrieff Williamson, *Robert Harris 1849-1919: An Unconventional Biography* (Toronto: McClelland and Stewart, 1970), 53.

41. Ibid., 57.
42. Thomas C. Watkins papers, Public Archives of Canada.
43. See W.R. Stewart, "Canada at the Paris Exposition," *Canadian Magazine* 15 (1900): 391.
44. See Arthur Buies, *Chroniques canadiennes: humeurs et caprices* (Montréal: Sénécal, 1884), 284. See also, Edouard Montpetit, "Les Expositions canadiennes à l'étranger," *Revue économique canadienne* (1912), 331-45.
45. Withrow, "Education," 195.
46. Ibid., 198.
47. James Douglas, "The Centennial Exhibition," *Canadian Monthly* 9 (1876): 536. On Douglas, see H. H. Langton, *James Douglas: A Memoir* (Toronto: U of Toronto P, 1940).
48. See, for instance, Gustave Drolet, *Zouaviana* (Montréal: Sénécal, 1898), 345, and Thomas C. Keefer, *Paris Universal Exhibition, 1878* (Ottawa: MacLean, Roger, 1881), 19.
49. Keefer, *Paris Universal Exhibition, 1878*, 12.
50. Taché, *Descriptive Catalogue*, 295.
51. Quoted in J. Russell Harper and Stanley Triggs, *Portrait of a Period: A Collection of Notman Photographs 1856-1915* (Montreal: McGill, 1967).
52. Lists provided by the Notman collection, McCord Museum, Montreal; the first quotation is from *The Photographic News*, 18 Oct. 1867: 504; the origin of the second cannot be verified.
53. See Sandra Gwyn, *The Private Capital: Ambition and Love in the Age of Macdonald and Laurier* (Toronto: McClelland and Stewart, 1984).
54. See Dennis Reid, *Our Own Country Canada: Being an Account of the National Aspirations of the Principal Landscape Artists 1860-1890* (Ottawa: National Gallery of Canada, 1979).
55. Taché, *Descriptive Catalogue*, 212.
56. See John George Bourinot, "Our Intellectual Strength and Weakness," in *Criticism* (Literature of Canada, Gen. ed., Douglas Lochhead) (Toronto: U of Toronto P, 1973), 1-9.
57. J.A. Radford, "Art at the World's Fair," *Canadian Magazine* 2 (1893/94): 130.
58. James Douglas, "The Philadelphia Exhibition: The Australian Colonies,"

Canadian Monthly 10 (1876): 239.
59. Ibid.
60. A key-text for the appreciation of the often virulent racism at the fairs is J.W. Buel, *The Magic City: A Massive Portfolio of Original Photographic Views of the Great World's Fair and its Treasures of Art, Including a Vivid Representation of the Famous Midway Plaisance* (St. Louis: Historical Publishing, 1894). See the comments on "Three Dancing Girls from Egypt" (n.pag.): "While their exhibitions were sensationally, if not sensually, amusing, the girls were not otherwise calculated to attract attention save it be by their immodest costumes. Writers of Oriental stories have created the impression among the uninformed that houris of the East are sylph-like and beautiful; but close contact reveals them as we behold them here, destitute of animation, formless as badly-stuffed animals, as homely as owls, and graceless as stall-fed bovines. But truth compels us to add that the dancing girls in the Midway were not the best types of their race in either form or in character, and that their abdominal muscles were the only portions of anatomy or mind which showed any cultivation, while these, to their shame, were displayed to serve the basest uses."
61. Spedon, *Sketches of a Tour*, 192.
62. Ibid.
63. See Radford, "Art at the World's Fair," 129. "The works of the Japanese none but themselves attempt to understand; they are excruciatingly humorous and amusing to a foreigner, and are out in drawing and color."
64. See William Williams, "Religious Aspects of the Centennial," *Canadian Methodist Magazine* 5 (1877): 49-56.
65. Spedon, *Sketches of a Tour*, 184.
66. Conway, "The Great Show at Paris," 243.
67. Edmond et Jules Goncourt, *Journal*, t. 3: 1866-70 (Paris: Charpentier, 1911): 102.
68. J.L. Gougeon, *Souvenirs: impressions et réflexions* (Montréal: Beauchemin, 1904), 158. To many tourists, however, miniature versions of the Eiffel Tower became a coveted souvenir. In *A Happy Holiday* (1890), Grace Denison describes an American tourist preparing herself for

the New York customs officer: "She had invested in a mammoth inkstand in imitation of the everlasting Eiffel Tower. It was heavy and vulgar and ugly, and good for nothing but to chuck overboard, and disgust the small fish of the harbor, but she did it up in a box, and tied a rope around it and anchored it under her skirts, and went limping uneasily about with it for hours before we landed, its great undisguisable bulk thumping her unmercifully and bulging out in unexpected angles all over her."

69. Tardivel, *Notes de voyage*, 157. See also Pierre Savard, *Jules-Paul Tardivel, la France et les Etats-Unis, 1851-1905* (Québec: PML, 1967), 58.

70. William C. Richards, *A Day in the New York Crystal Palace and How to Make the Most of It* (New York: Putnam, 1853), 105.

71. See Jeanne Madeline Weimann, *The Fair Women* (Chicago: Academy, 1981).

72. National Council of Women of Canada, *Women of Canada: Their Life and Work* (n.p., 1900?).

73. Mabel Cameron papers, Public Archives of Canada.

74. J. J. Miller, *Vancouver to the Coronation: A Four Months' Holiday Trip* (London: Watt, 1912).

75. J.W. Bailey papers, Harriet Irving Library, University of New Brunswick.

76. E. Montizambert, "Our Portion of Versailles: The Story of How the Graves of Canadian Heroes are Tended by a Young French Girl," *Canadian Magazine* 46 (1915/16): 317-20.

Note on Sources

Gathering the primary sources for this study became in itself an illuminating exploration of cultural differences and could well serve as the basis for a comparative analysis of literary canons and institutions in English Canada. For travel reports in French, I was largely able to rely on John Hare's *Les Canadiens-français aux quatre coins du monde: une bibliographie commentée des récits de voyage, 1670-1914* (1964), which contained almost eighty pertinent references to books and periodical material. The *Dictionnaire des oeuvres littéraires du Québec*, edited by Maurice Lemire (1978-), supplied summaries and analyses of, and bibliographies on, the major *récits de voyage*. Useful angles of approach were outlined in Pierre Savard's pioneering essays ("Voyageurs canadiens-français en Italie au dix-neuvième siècle," *Vie française* 16, 1/2 [1961]: 15-24; "Voyageurs, pèlerins, et récits de voyages canadiens-français en Europe de 1850-1960," in *Mélanges de civilisation canadienne-française offerts au professeur Paul Wyczynski*: [1977]; "Voyageurs canadiens-français dans l'Allemagne de Bismarck et de Guillaume II, *"Zeitschrift der Gesellschaft für Kanada-Studien* 3:1 [1983]:54-64; and others) and in Serge Jaumain, "Paris devant l'opinion canadienne-française: les récits de voyages entre 1820 et 1914," *Revue d'Histoire de l'Amérique française* 38:4 (printemps, 1985): 549-67. Critical editions of Octave Crémazie's work (1972, 1976) and Paul Wyczynski's edition of François-Xavier Garneau's *Voyage en Angleterre et en France, dans les années 1831, 1832 et 1833* (1968) supplied textual, historical, and cultural information, which I supplemented with readings in selected nineteenth-century periodicals, particularly the *Revue canadienne*, one of conservative French Canada's longest-lived and most influential periodicals.

No specific research tools exist as yet for English-Canadian travel outside of Canada, although a few titles do appear in Reginald Watters, *A Checklist of Canadian Literature and Background Materials 1628-1960* (2d ed., 1972). Thus, book reviews and serialized travel reports in Victorian periodicals became a main source, and publications like *The Week*, *Stewart's Literary Quarterly Magazine*, the *Saturday Reader*, the *Canadian Monthly and National Review*, *Belford's Monthly Magazine* (the latter two later merged in *Rose-Belford's Canadian Monthly and National Review*), the *New Dominion Monthly*, *Massey's Magazine*, the *Maritime Monthly*, the *Dominion Illustrated*, the *Canadian Methodist Magazine*, *Canadian Magazine*, *Canadian Illustrated News*, the *British American Magazine*, and the *Anglo-American Magazine* had to be searched. Few periodical indexes have as yet been compiled; a welcome exception was Marilyn Flitton's "The *Canadian Monthly* 1872-1882" (Master's thesis, Simon Fraser University, 1973). As William Briggs was frequently listed as the publisher of travel books, W. Stewart Wallace's *The Ryerson Imprint* (1954), which lists the main publications of the Methodist publishing house, could be consulted for supplementary titles. Fruitful sources were also contemporary American periodicals like *Scribner's* and *Harper's*, where Canadian authors published their works. A most useful repository for the titles collected, both in English and in French, were the Canadian Historical Imprints on Microfilm (CHIM), also a valuable source for related matters such as travel agencies, insurances, and guidebooks.

Unpublished primary materials were gathered with the help of the *Union List of Manuscripts* and with indexes and finding aids prepared by the librarians at the Public Archives of Canada and the Archives du Petit Séminaire de Québec.

In sketching the biographical backgrounds and genealogical connections of individual travellers, contemporary handbooks provided information, among them Cyprien Tanguay, *Répertoire général du clergé canadien* (1893), J.-E.-A. Allaire, *Dictionnaire biographique du clergé canadien-français* (1910), R.P.L. Le Jeune, *Dictionnaire général du Canada* (1931), Henry Morgan, *Sketches of Celebrated Canadians* (1862), *The Canadian Men and Women of the Time: A Handbook of Canadian Biography* (1898), George Maclean Rose, *A Cyclopedia of Canadian Biography: Being Chiefly Men of the Time* (1886), William Cochrane, *The Canadian Album: Men of Canada* (1891), the *Canadian Parliamentary Companion* and the *Canadian Parliamentary Guide*, E.M. Chadwick, *Ontarian Families* (1894). Biographies, like V.-A. Huard, *La Vie et les oeuvres de l'abbé Provancher* (1926), Elie-F. Auclair, *Le Curé Labelle: sa vie et son oeuvre* (1930), Eveline Bossé, *Joseph-Charles Taché (1820-1894): un grand représentant de l'élite canadienne-française* (1971), and James A.

Roy, *Joseph Howe: A Study in Achievement and Frustration* (1935), helped round the picture of individuals and time period, as did autobiographies and memoirs, among them Egerton Ryerson, *Story of My Life* (1884) and H.H. Langton, *James Douglas: A Memoir* (1940). Biographical information on Victorian women can be difficult to find unless they were truly well-known, but Henry Morgan's *Types of Canadian Woman* (1903) and *Women of Canada: Their Life and Work*, published by the Canadian National Council of Women in both English and French for the 1900 Paris Exhibition, were helpful. Ted Ferguson, *Kit Coleman: Queen of Hearts* (1978) and the chapters on Agnes Scott and Florence Randal in Sandra Gwyn, *The Private Capital: Ambition and Love in the Age of MacDonald and Laurier* (1984) are pioneering works in retracing the lives of Victorian women in Canada.

In filling in the historical and cultural background of this book, I have made use of more general studies like Walter Houghton, *The Victorian Frame of Mind, 1830-1870* (1957), Theodore Zeldin, *France, 1848-1945: Politics and Anger* (1979), and Peter Gay, *Education of the Senses*, vol. 1 of *The Bourgeois Experience: Victoria to Freud* (1984), and more specific works. Useful information on ideology in Victorian Canada came especially from Carl Berger, *A Sense of Power* (1970) and *Science, God, and Nature in Victorian Canada* (1983), W.L. Morton, *The Shield of Achilles* (1968), Ramsay Cook, *The Regenerators: Social Criticism in Late Victorian English Canada* (1985), Linda Kealy, ed., *A Not Unreasonable Claim: Women and Reform in Canada* (1979), Fernand Dumont et al., *Idéologies au Canada français* (1971), Jean-Paul Bernard, *Les Rouges: libéralisme, nationalisme et anticléricalisme au milieu du XIXe siècle* (1971), René Hardy, *Les Zouaves: une stratégie du clergé québécois au XIX siècle* (1980), Pierre Savard, *Jules-Paul Tardivel, la France et les Etats-Unis, 1851-1905* (1967) and *Aspects du catholicisme canadien-français au XIXe siècle* (1980).

Materials on the history of travel and travel literature in general were gathered from Percy G. Adams, *Travel Literature and the Evolution of the Novel* (1983), William Mead, *The Grand Tour in the Eighteenth Century* (1914), Paul F. Kirby, *The Grand Tour in Italy (1700-1800)* (1952), Edmund Swinglehurst, *Cook's Tours: The Story of Popular Travel* (1982), Wolfgang Schivelbusch, *The Railway Journey: Trains and Travel in the Nineteenth Century* (1979), Thomas E. Appleton, *Ravenscrag: The Allan Royal Mail Line* (1974), Christopher Mulvey, *Anglo-American Landscapes: A Study of Nineteenth-Century Anglo-American Travel Literature* (1983), and Paul Fussell, *Abroad: British Literary Traveling Between the Wars* (1980). Daniel Boorstin, *The Image: A Guide to Pseudo-Events in America* (1961), Dean MacCannell, *The Tourist: A New Theory of the*

Leisure Class (1976), Hans Magnus Enzensberger, "Eine Theorie des Tourismus," in *Einzelheiten* (1962), and Jonathan Culler, "Semiotics of Tourism," *American Journal of Semiotics* (1981/82) helped me understand anthropological and semiotic aspects of tourism. Information on nineteenth-century European cities and their problems is abundantly available. Particularly useful were H.F. Dyos and Michael Wolff, *The Victorian City: Images and Realities* (1973), Dana Brand, "The Spectator and the City: Fantasies of Urban Legibility in Nineteenth-Century England and America" (Ph.D. diss., Yale University, 1981), Francis Sheppard, *London 1808-1870: The Infernal Wen* (1971), David H. Pinkney, *Napoleon III and the Rebuilding of Paris* (1958), and Christopher Hibbert, *Rome: Biography of a City* (1985). Nineteenth-century art forms and public entertainment were described in Robert Rosenblum and H.W. Jansen, *Nineteenth-Century Art* (1984), Fern Bayer, *The Ontario Collection* (1984), Dennis Reid, *Our Own Country Canada: Being an Account of the National Aspirations of the Principal Landscape Artists in Montreal and Toronto, 1860-1890* (1979), Friedrich Geist, *Passagen: Ein Bautyp des 19. Jahrhunderts* (1969), Richard D. Altick, *The Shows of London* (1978), and Stephan Oettermann, *Das Panorama: Die Geschichte eines Massenmediums* (1980). For the chapter on world expositions, Utz Haltern, *Die Londoner Weltausstellung von 1851: Ein Beitrag zur Geschichte der bürgerlich-industriellen Gesellschaft im 19. Jahrhundert* (1971) was particularly informative.

Index

DATE DUE
